The Orange Woods

The Orange Woods

Seasons in the Country Artfully Lived

Marilyn Woods

E. L. Marker
Salt Lake City

E. L. Marker, an imprint of WiDo Publishing
Salt Lake City, Utah
widopublishing.com

Cover art by Linda Pickering
Cover photography by Carly Coberly
Cover design by Steven Novak
Book design by Marny K. Parkin

ISBN 978-1-947966-32-1

To Jack

"We write to taste life twice,
in the moment, and in retrospection."
—Anaïs Nin

Prologue

I had been told that at some point in your writing, your book will speak to you. Mine did. This is not a story about grief or art or making wine or Mother Nature, although all figure prominently throughout. This is a story of a peaceful pastoral paradise where I lived for twenty years. In these recollections of the place and its unending enchantment, there are stories of our love affair, adorable children, extraordinary friends, a loyal dog, special occasions, triumphs and failures, oranges and grapes and games, and my cherished family.

Chapter 1
Pauma Valley by Chance?

Being a city girl, I resisted for a long time, but my charismatic and persuasive husband eventually charmed me into country living.

I lived the first year of my life in Bartlesville, Oklahoma, population 13,000. Small, but certainly not insignificant, the town headquartered Phillips Petroleum, one of America's most important oil companies. My dad, a petroleum engineering graduate of Colorado School of Mines in Golden, Colorado—the home of Coors Beer—began his career in that same unpretentious Oklahoma town as a roughneck in the oil fields. His meteoric rise in the oil business moved our family swiftly to Oklahoma City first, and soon after to Dallas, Texas, where I grew up.

Peyton Place, the 1960s-era television series set in rural Massachusetts, which marked the birth of the primetime American soap opera, rocked my world as a new mother, serving as a fantasy getaway from diapers and formula. The fictional rural Minnesota saga *Mayberry RFD* was a family favorite in the late 1960s. Jack sat patiently next to our daughter, Jamie, through every episode of *Little House on the Prairie* in the mid-1970s. Small towns on the big screen provided escape for us all until JR, the legendary cowboy we loved to hate, brought the big-city television tale *Dallas* into our lives. With that, our folksy fascinations were overshadowed by the big, splashy family drama of good and evil set in the big state of Texas.

The draw of small-town charm returned for us in the 1980s. Working at PBS in Washington DC—the most rewarding job of my career in broadcast—Garrison Keillor's folksy tales of Lake Woebegone's happenings in Minnesota enthralled me.

Small-town sagas and their multifaceted cast of characters have long fascinated me, even more so when I actually lived in one and amongst them.

෨

We first visited idyllic Pauma Valley, California, on a brisk New Year's Day, the first day of 1997. My husband, Jack, and I cruised Highway 76 north of San Diego, headed for a getaway in Palm Springs. After a rollicking weekend babysitting grandbabies, Maddie and Sophie, while our oldest son, Brent, and his wife, Laurie, escaped to celebrate their fourth wedding anniversary, we were craving R&R, good food, a spa, and quiet.

My business, a small group of radio stations, had recently sold, leaving me with a modest equity share. Coincidentally, a legendary radio station in San Diego had around the same time presented an attractive position as a talk show host to Jack. We were entertaining the idea of leaving LA and heading back to San Diego, where we had lived a blissfully happy decade and a half as our children grew up in the 1970s and 1980s.

Songs from *High Lonesome Sound*, our current favorite Vince Gill CD, serenaded us as we headed east through lush rolling hills and citrus groves, reminiscent of the California of the fifties that had captivated us both. Well aware of what he had in mind, Jack playfully squeezed my knee and asked, "How would you feel about getting a country place with some property?"

He had been trying to talk me into this for thirty-five years. I had managed to resist until this point, but now, with my career in broadcasting coming to an end, I blithely said, "I don't care how far out we live. I'm no longer a working girl, I can easily drive to visit my family and friends and the art museum. Maybe something with a gym nearby? How about you?"

"I'd like a golf course—"

"Interesting," I said, interrupting with building enthusiasm. "In retirement, I've always pictured us in a pristine rural community full of agriculture and animals, a little church, and . . ."

At that very moment, we rounded a curve and came upon the most breathtaking sunlit vista I'd ever laid my eyes on—the lavender foothills of Palomar Mountain ahead, the emerald green of a world-class golf course on the right, and a storybook, steepled white church atop a hill, surrounded by endless orange groves, on the left. This, plus a jagged little row of country shops—a post office, a quaint beauty shop, and a colorful and inviting Mexican food spot—made up the not-so-hustling-or-bustling metropolis of Pauma Valley, California, population 989.

What I didn't realize at the time was that Jack knew Pauma Valley from his years piloting small planes. Flying out of Brown Field in San Diego, heading northeast, his flight instructor had pointed out the Pauma Valley Country Club's private airstrip early on, in the event an emergency landing was ever necessary. Jack had never forgotten the lure of the club's phenomenal golf course.

Spotting an Open sign, he recklessly made a sharp turn into the unpaved parking lot in front of a funky deserted looking building.

"Let's go in," he said.

"Honey, what for?" I asked, bewildered. "We've just begun to talk about where we want to retire and what kind of life we plan for our future."

"Babe, look at the incredible citrus groves around here. We've always said we might enjoy living in the country," he pressed gently. "Plus, we do want to be near San Diego. Let's check out what's happening in Pauma Valley."

I acquiesced, a bit reluctant but also somewhat curious.

We parked in the worn-down asphalt parking lot next to Serrato's Auto Shop. Inside Pauma Properties, we met the unfortunate realtor on duty that New Year's Day as Ohio State defeated Arizona State in the Rose Bowl. Mike Fitzpatrick missed the Big Ten win but emerged a bit of a winner himself when he agreed to show us available properties.

Our realtor saved the best for last. After showing us a few places, he drove slowly to a country lane with a hand-painted sign that read Mesa Drive. I squeezed Jack's hand as Mike navigated the long, curved driveway lined with an emerald-city-like expanse of magnificent trees on either side. They welcomed us with the pageantry of a Mother Nature receiving line. Each resplendent tree was decked out in glistening shades of green and festooned with what looked like limes, perfectly shaped yellow-green fruits. Later, we learned the plentiful citrus were soon-to-be juicy oranges, ready for harvest in March or April.

Stepping out of the realtor's car, the smell of the country air, unbelievably sweet, fresh, and earthy at the same time, made me dizzy.

Ahead, the house screamed 1970s, which momentarily disappointed. But stepping inside, we were overcome with the most sublime, expansive view from every angle. I squeezed Jack's hand. Looking out the windows, the property stretched as far as we could see—lush green valleys and hills surrounded by lavender-grey, irregular mountains. Much to the realtor's chagrin, the foggy day compromised the unparalleled view to the west. But the lack of visibility did not deter us.

Both given to impulse throughout our lives, Jack and I were wild about this last property. A modest home set in the middle of an orange grove, surrounded by grand mountains and an unending valley—this possible paradise loomed both scary and thrilling at the same time. Having lived in major cities for decades, we found the appeal of country living irresistible. All the way to Palm Springs, we played house in the country in Pauma Valley in our minds.

By the time we arrived at our hotel in Palm Springs, we had made a verbal offer to the owner, a professor of organizational management at San Diego State University who had spent occasional weekends writing textbooks from the single leather chair in the octagonal-shaped living room of our future home. He accepted our offer the next day. We closed in April, just as the last orange blossom fell to the ground and the next season's—our season's—oranges began to ripen on our trees.

Chapter 2

The Name

Rapidly, Jack and I fell in love with our new home, a warm ochre stucco—the color of creamed corn—with a Spanish-style tile roof perched on a hill in the center of verdant agriculture with transcendent views.

I read once, "If you love your home, name it." I really like my car. Her name is Pearl. But neither Jack nor I named The Orange Woods. Brent did.

"He'll be the first member of the family to be a millionaire," my proud father prophesized about his first grandson, thirteen-year-old Brent, long before the dot-com boom made millionaires out of everybody's neighbor. Dad's prediction came true. Not only did Brent become the first, he's the only so far.

My oldest son is charismatic, extremely well educated, and has an unparalleled work ethic. All this, plus a smattering of luck, occasional good guidance, and his marriage to an extraordinary woman he met in college on the East Coast, coalesced to make him outrageously successful. So, it didn't surprise when he mustered up all his intuition, wit, and creativity on this unforgettable April morning when the family first visited our new venture to offer three definitive comments.

The first: "Mom and Dad, you two are real risk takers. I can't believe your guts and your vision. I hope your purse strings match."

Then, later, as we strolled the acreage of Valencia orange grove: "This is incredible. All these oranges belong to you guys—and you're the Woods? You ought to call it The Orange Woods."

And lastly, in an aside to his brother and sister: "I'm taking bets on how long Mom will last as a country girl."

We did name it The Orange Woods.

I lasted twenty years.

Chapter 3

All the Orange Juice You Can Drink

My husband, a Cary Grant lookalike, reigned as the consummate story-teller of our family, captivating people wherever and whenever he spoke. His gift entertained and informed a multitude of listeners over the radio waves in major cities for decades; made him the popular center of gatherings at cocktail parties; and, later in life, enthralled little grandchildren eagerly awaiting their next Papa story.

For years, I begged him to write his story, chock full of the kinds of experiences a pure whitebread girl from the bubble in Dallas could never imagine. How his great-grandfather was shot and killed driving a wagon through eastern Kentucky, and his three-year-old daughter left screaming as the horses ran for safety. How that same great-grandfather's woven shirt with three gunshot holes hung over the fireplace until Jack's grandmother, the little girl in the back of the wagon, left Kentucky to migrate to the steel mill mecca, Gary, Indiana. Or how that same grandmother, at age eighty-three, singlehandedly replaced the entire roof on her home. How, in a jealous rage, his dad pulled his mom out of a car and dragged her half a block by the hair on her head. Or how Jack's teenage heart shattered when his serious junior high crush ran away with the Australian Bullwhip Artist when the circus came and left town. My husband's life, full of offbeat, thrilling, and often unbelievable stories, enraptured me and my ordinary upbringing. He told me his stories flawlessly, repeatedly, as if performing onstage.

There is one tale, my favorite, which I'll retell in my own words here. With it, Jack charmed me with the magic of the Golden State, which he discovered first as a ten-year-old. It became a big part of our enduring fascination with Southern California.

ᘓ

Jack referred to his father as a force. My father-in-law, a tough son-of-a-bitch, sometimes violent, terrified me early on but I eventually understood his gruffness and played to the miniscule soft spot in his heart. I found it exceedingly difficult to like him, much less love him, when he had abused my husband badly for years before the Marines took over. I did love, however, that he had introduced his young son to California.

Jack's father had a penchant for foul language and skanky women. He drove transport trucks and trailers cross-country from Gary, Indiana to the Gold Coast when he wasn't sweeping out boxcars for the EJ&E Railroad, which served the steel industry around Chicago. A chronic bellyacher, many times he got even for the low pay and long backbreaking hours by helping himself to a boxcar's cargo under cover of night.

Jack's dad grew from a spoiled little boy into a startlingly handsome, crafty, and intelligent guy. However, he never got over being a spoiled brat. He went bald early, and vanity kept him in a baseball hat turned backward, covering the top of his high forehead, for the rest of his life. Physically fit, with broad shoulders on a compact frame, he signaled, "Don't mess with me." Rarely did I catch him out of his uniform: Montgomery Ward's steel grey twill Dickies, with a Lucky Strike hanging out of the left side of his mouth.

Jack's sweet face, with freckles scattered over his snub nose, lay beneath jet-black hair parted precariously down the middle of his also high forehead. His father stormed in and out of his life like a vicious hurricane, raging, cussing, exploding, busting up furniture, or busting up his son in unexplained rampages. In spite of it all, Jack hungered for his attention. He worshipped his absentee father, no matter how often he abandoned him or how hard he hit him.

Without warning, very early on a summer day of Jack's tenth year, his dad burst in, shook him awake, shoved him out of the house, and man-handled him into the big cab of an 18-wheeler—the "Windy City Warrior," a 1944 heavy-duty Mack Truck designed for long-distance hauling of big payloads. When he became a rabid football fan years later, Jack recalled the giant silver trailer fronted by a shiny blue cab, describing it as "Dallas Cowboy" blue. In his ten-year-old mind, the rig loomed gigantic, filling the entire block, big as a building. His father had contracted to deliver the vehicle plus the empty trailer behind it to Los Angeles.

While gawking at the truck, Jack, who had never been out of Gary, caught sight of the impressive hood ornament—the company's trademark, a pugnacious, blunt-nosed bulldog, which would remain a powerful symbol of American trucking. At the first stop for diesel, when his dad walked into the station, Jack stood on his tiptoes to touch the smooth backside of the bulldog, whose stature and strength reminded him of his father: strong, vigorous and forceful. *I could never be that powerful*, Jack lamented to himself as he straightened up in the big leatherette seat, but he grinned as he imagined himself as his dad's copilot, heading west across two-lane America of the mid-1940s.

"California, here we come, Jackie."

Off they went, heading west. The young boy kept his mouth shut, hardly able to believe his good fortune—all this time alone with his dad.

The ride proved unbelievably hot in the sweltering, deafening cab. In July, the temperature in the southwestern part of the United States regularly soars to three sizzling digits—110, 111, even 115 degrees are standard fare.

Blythe is located near the California/Arizona border in the Sonoran Desert, at the junction of Interstate 10 and US 95—a bit of a detour from the straight-line route—but it was the home of Wilbur's Roadside Fruit Stand and Market. Jack's dad, a regular, stopped there on every cross-country trip to dabble in Indian jewelry trades, Mexican cigarettes, and/or local women, and to load up with giant blocks of ice, which served to air-condition the un-air-conditioned trucks he transported.

Pulling up in the deserted, steaming asphalt parking lot of Wilbur's Market, Dad punched his sleepy little passenger, whose hand-me-down striped T-shirt from his cousin Jess was soaked with sweat. "Wake up, you're gonna like this place, Jackie. Time to pee."

Jack rubbed his eyes, squinting at the blasting high noon sunshine. On his right, he caught sight of a large broken-down sign atop two rotted four-by-fours. The little guy read, "Wilbur's Roadside Fruit Stand and Market—All the Orange Juice You Can Drink for 25 Cents." Jack couldn't believe his eyes! How he loved orange juice, a rare treat in the little boy's life. From Wise Way Market, where his mom checked groceries, she would bring home "Sunkist Orange Juice from California Oranges" once a month on payday.

Not sure where his dad had gone, after unsticking his sweaty little legs from the seat, Jack cautiously jumped down from the cab and sauntered toward the sign. Once more, he blinked and again, in living color: "Wilbur's Roadside Fruit Stand and Market—All the Orange Juice You Can Drink for 25 Cents." Mirages in the desert—could this be one? He blinked his eyes again; still there. "Fresh squeezed," painted diagonally across one corner, even had little orange stars scattered around it. Deep in his pocket his hand searched, and by some stroke of random luck, he found a lone quarter.

Rubbing the back of his sweaty neck, he slowly neared Wilbur's market. A hand-painted Open sign hung crookedly in the window of the ramshackle white store. His dad, a man on a mission, barreled out of the store carrying a huge block of ice with giant metal tongs, startling Jack. With a grunt and a thud, he plopped the ice down on the floor of Jack's side of the cab, much like he had plopped Jack down in the seat a day and a half earlier. Back his dad went into the market and back out he came again, staggering a bit from the second fifty-pound weight and the excruciating heat, to drop another block of ice on the floor, filling the space.

"At least this'll keep our peckers cool, Jackie," he bellowed.

Jack wondered where he would put his feet. More important, however, he wondered how to get in line for the cold, sweet orange juice.

Careful to stay out of his father's way, Jack peeked through the door, then pushed it open slowly. A little bell announced his presence. Not daring to speak up, he moved toward the counter and realized he was the only taker on that scorching hot July afternoon. His dry mouth watered as Wilbur set a glass of the cold orange juice right before him on the counter. Ice crystals formed on the top of the clear six-ounce glass with a small blue cornflower on the side. Jack hesitated at first, but then he made eye contact with Wilbur, who nodded his head up and down and smiled. Jack quickly gulped the entire glass of the refreshing magic of citrus.

As he guzzled his second fill-up, Jack contemplated Wilbur—so different from his combative father, from whom he endured sudden, unpredictable outbursts, rough treatment, and orders barked loudly. Here stood a gentle man, soft-spoken and seemingly kind. Unshaven, wearing oversized denim coveralls with a tire gauge in one of the front pockets and a collection of keys and a whistle hanging from a belt loop, Wilbur stood much taller than his dad. But, Jack thought, he looked softer, too, even a little squishy, and he sure smiled a lot. *How did these two get to be friends?* he wondered.

Later, Jack would learn their friendship stemmed from Tolleston Junior High back in Gary. After dropping out of high school, Wilbur and his teenage wife, with savings from double shifts in the steel mills, bought a mobile home and a plot of land in Mesa Grande, Arizona, and headed west, leaving snow shovels and the mill's onerous night shifts behind.

When Jack emptied the third glass, his father's pal approached with another. "Here, Jackie, have some more. Full of vitamin C. It will make you strong," Wilbur offered.

The little guy drank another and another—all the orange juice he could possibly drink. Finally, taking a breather, he reached into his pocket for his quarter.

"On the house, squirt," Wilbur insisted.

Even Dad, with his gruff façade, smiled at being reunited once more in this desolate spot on the highway with his scruffy old friend. "Good to see you, Wilbur—a real kick in the pants," he said before once again plopping Jack up in the big truck and heading west on the lone highway.

Jack and his father delivered the truck and immediately hopped a Greyhound bus in downtown LA for the interminable and boring trip back to Gary and the safety of Mom.

His dad disappeared once more.

⅓

Jack, with his crystal-clear memory, told the story of the delectable and plentiful ice-cold California orange juice—25 cents for all he could drink—hundreds of times. A grown man reliving a rare moment of joy as a young boy with the father he seldom saw and always feared.

In 1997, fifty-three years later, in the tiny office of the Pauma Valley Real Estate Company on Highway 76 in picturesque North County San Diego, California, as we signed the contract purchasing our new hilltop villa home—eight acres and two hundred and fifty Valencia orange trees—Jack slowly put the pen down on the desk, turned to me, flashed his signature broad grin and mused, "I've got it again, babe. All the orange juice I can drink . . . for just $350,000."

Chapter 4

Danke Schoen

My very first trip to California came a quarter of a century after Jack's.

I was so giddy, I barely made it to the car—our new car—a sleek white 1970 Oldsmobile. Jack channeling his inner Sir Galahad, opened my door, closed it behind me, and then tossed our lunch basket, stocked with peanut butter and jelly sandwiches, Fritos, two Dr Peppers, and road maps, into the back seat. He hopscotched in a flash around the back of the car and leaped over the side of the open convertible into the driver's seat—without opening the door. Obviously, he was as excited as me. I laughed at his acrobatic antics all the way to the city limits—at which point an arresting sensation hit me. I already missed my kids a lot.

We had just said good-bye—kissed three pudgy little faces, mouths full of Captain Crunch and powdered sugar mini-donuts. Sensing my change in demeanor, Jack pinched my cheek, winked at me and smiled, turned up Joe Cocker on the radio, and amped up the speed. I got over my mothering pangs quickly. I was riding next to my damn sexy husband, and we were leaving Houston—heading for Vegas, baby!

Jack had been married before and had a nine-year-old daughter, Jackie, who lived with her mom. My sons from my first marriage, Brent and Bo, lived with us. Jamie belonged to us both. This was our first adults-only vacation in the few years we had been married. We'd never managed a getaway from the three little ones—Brent, nine; Bo, five; and Jamie, just over three. Time, money, and runny noses had conspired to that end. But the stars had aligned this hot August morning in Houston, and my Wonder Woman of a mother had waved and blown kisses from her kitchen window before returning to sticky fingers in time to save the ivory damask upholstery of the dining room chairs.

On stage at the landmark Desert Inn Hotel the night we arrived in Vegas, everything sparkled. I stumbled along through the crowd, following Jack and the maître d' to our front-row seats, stupefied in Wonderland.

Our host—none other than superstar Wayne Newton, whose hit "Red Roses for a Blue Lady" was at that time jockeying for position on Billboard's Top 100 with the recent boy wonder groups The Beatles and Jackson 5, as well as proven hit makers Simon & Garfunkel and B.J. Thomas—opened the show with his previous hit, "Danke Schoen."

Not yet an aging pop star but rather The Midnight Idol, Mr. Las Vegas, Newton reigned supreme as the highest-paid act in Vegas at the time. Jack's position as music director at an important radio station at the end of the payola days afforded us opening-night and front-row tickets often, but this was grander than that: travel expenses, gourmet food and drink, five-star hotel accommodations, and VIP seating to this star attraction on the strip.

Newton's appearance was flashy—tight-fitting, shiny gold pants, lots of spangles, a large eagle belt buckle, and a pencil-thin moustache—not my style, but the show, with its extraordinary musicians, dancers, costumes, and lights, electrified the room.

Newton and this trip eventually led us to a life in California. Even today, when I hear "Danke Schoen," I am grateful.

Quickly, Vegas bored us both. The next morning, over eggs Benedict, Jack, given to spontaneity, eagerly shook things up. "Let's go to California—you've always wanted to go. And we're so close—we've gotta do this."

"Really? Now?" I replied in astonishment. I couldn't believe it. Jack continually blew me away like this with surprises, which I loved. "Sure, we can be there in time for dinner. Let's go!"

After Jack's first California visit as a ten-year-old, he had returned eight years later as a Marine Corps recruit for boot camp at MCRD in San Diego and basic infantry training at Camp Pendleton, the era in his life he credited with making him a man. After the Marines, he and three buddies, also enamored of everything California had to offer, hitchhiked there from their home in Gary, Indiana, and spent a few months shoveling cow manure in Riverside County, east of Los Angeles, far removed from Hollywood and the glamour of show biz.

Jack never faltered in his overwhelming ardor for the legendary Golden State—the movie studios, Gene Autry, Santa Anita Racetrack, Disneyland, the Dodgers—and especially the never-ending orange groves that lined the streets of quaint towns like Garden Grove, Westminster, and Orange. Over and over, he had conveyed the magic to me in his inimitable storytelling style.

Deciding not to waste our precious dollars in the penny slot machines, we packed our bags and were on the road before lunchtime. Six hours later, we pulled into San Diego.

ର

My first exposure to the fabled state of California played out in a magical, dreamlike manner. Jack insisted we hug the coast on the legendary coast highway 101 so I could take in the wonder of the Pacific Ocean.

On Carlsbad State Beach, our first stop, I stood in awe of the breathtaking expanse of the ocean—its heaven-sent palette of the deepest ultramarine, cerulean blues, and vibrant turquoises, and the slow, steady motion of the white-capped waves. In my first-time stupor, I welcomed a soft sea spray on my face as we drifted hand in hand. The smell of the ocean wafted my way—a clean, bracing combination of salt and oil, earth and musk, and a brine sort of incense unlike anything I had ever smelled before. We walked silently together on the sand amid the shells and the seagulls.

Magical stops along the way—Dana Point, San Juan Capistrano, Ventura and Santa Barbara. San Luis Obispo, Pismo Beach, and Carmel by the Sea. We stopped last at Pebble Beach, the apex of our whirlwind tour of the long, narrow state that borders the largest and deepest ocean on earth.

Central California had a completely different appeal, but I was spellbound nonetheless. At a romantic dinner on a budget our last night before our long trip back to Texas, I summoned up my courage and blurted out, "Honey, let's move here. We need to live in California. Can you get a job here? I'll check groceries, if necessary. Whatever it takes, let's live here."

ର

It took Jack over a year to connect with a radio station in San Diego, but before the end of the second year, we were Californians.

Driving into the southern part of the state with those same three little rambunctious, freckle-faced kids, we drove straight to Mickey and Disneyland. They were sold immediately, too, but it was It's a Small World's fantasyland, not the orange groves, that convinced them.

The same magic that had stayed with Jack all those years since his very first trip to California as a little guy had hypnotized me immediately and convinced me to uproot our family and move to this paradise. The exhilarating culture of orange blossoms, warm beaches, Snow White, and sunshine had compelled us westward. *Danke Schoen.*

Jack wrote a little ditty soon after we returned to our kids and routine:

> *She was born in Oklahoma*
> *But raised up a Texas Girl*
> *I took her out to California*
> *She took me round the world.*

Chapter 5

Gypsies

Marilyn and her family are quite the gypsies . . ."

In his 1966 Christmas letter, three years before we became Californians, my often-pompous uncle Tom revealed our upcoming relocation to his friends and family with this comment. My father's blood boiled at his older brother's cavalier statement, as he was over-the-moon proud of his son-in-law and our new opportunity.

Jack and I were moving again, this time to New York City. He had accepted a position at WNBC in Rockefeller Center. We would stay there for three years.

Before satellite changed everything, the radio business had two tracks to success for on-air talent: stay the course in a city and dominate the ratings, or, like Jack, move from market to larger market and finally to the number one market in the country. Jack pursued the latter option, in part because salaries most often are commensurate with the size of a market, as is the prestige. Plus, we both did have a bit of wanderlust and desire for adventure.

His path began in Rockford and Davenport, Illinois. After that he was tempted into Texas radio by the iconic, flamboyant broadcast pioneer Gordon McClendon for an on-air position on his legendary flagship station, KLIF, in Dallas—my hometown, and the place where we met.

Jack's career took us from Dallas to Houston, then Indianapolis, Denver, Cleveland, and New York before we made the decision to move to California and let our children settle into junior high and high school and college in one place, vagabonds no more. Over these years, we left California twice: once to return to Dallas, the second after the kids were in college to go to Washington DC, where, along with a group of investors, we raised financial backing to buy radio stations back in California once more.

In a way, I guess we *were* gypsies, migrating across our country from city to city, our young children, assorted pets, and growing accumulation of furniture and household goods in tow. Jack joked, "You can tell how successful a radio guy is by the size of his U-Haul."

We rarely stayed longer than two or three years in a place. So, it both surprised and fulfilled us in a multitude of ways when we ended up spending twenty years living at The Orange Woods.

Chapter 6

Henri Matisse

Very early in The Orange Woods days I began the two-year Docent Training Program in Art and Art History at the San Diego Museum of Art in Balboa Park. The program is longer than those at many art museums and exceedingly rigorous. Along with the steep learning curve of becoming a farmer, my studies of art and art history consumed my life as my retirement years began.

At the end of the two-year training at the museum, Jack, in his inimitable, over-the-top style, surprised me with a graduation present.

He teased me a bit when I sat down on the sunset deck to the lovely dinner for two he had prepared. "I have a little present to commemorate your accomplishment, but you can't open it until you dine on my crab legs in lemon butter," he said, gesturing to the butter warmer on a little stand over a lit votive in the center of the table. Luis Miguel's "No Me Platiques Más" played softly in the background.

At the end of our leisurely meal, as the setting sun washed the crayon sky, Jack held up a flat gift box about the size of the crusty baguette left on the table. "Guess what's in here," he said, grinning.

"I have no idea," I said with a pout.

He relented quickly and handed me the present. On top were a paste-on bow and a ticket that read *Musée d'Orsay*.

"What's this?" I asked, afraid to believe.

"Want to go to Paris with me? I need a good guide for the art museums there and I understand you're an expert now," Jack said, leaning his sturdy, protective frame back in his chair and clasping his hands together tent-style in front of his smiling face. I hurriedly unwrapped the gift and found a pair of airline tickets—San Diego to Paris—inside.

Good thing we lived in the country, because I let out an unbelievable scream of unabashed elation, followed by an unending flood of frantic, excited questions, shattering the twilight tranquility.

"When, honey?"

"For how long?"

"Where are we staying?"

I continued to pummel him with inquiries, and when I could stand it no longer, a magnetic force thrust me onto his lap and I peppered his face with kisses.

଼

At the entrance to the Musée d'Orsay the next April—yes, *April in Paris*—I clutched our tickets in one hand and dragged Jack by the other.

"Honey, hurry, it's opening now!"

A visit to this museum for me packed more punch than the Super Bowl Halftime Show, Academy Awards, and Opening Night Ceremonies of the Olympics combined. I bounded toward the entrance.

"Marilyn, slow down," Jack cautioned. "Don't forget Oaxaca."

In the same kind of hurry, trying to get to the Rufino Tamayo Pre-Hispanic Museum in Oaxaca before it closed three years before, I had fallen and broken my arm.

I slowed down.

The Musée d'Orsay in Paris, the former Gare d'Orsay Beaux-Arts railway station, located in the center of the city on the bank of the Seine opposite the Tuileries Gardens, loomed large—a stunning structure. The magnificent building itself was a work of art.

We enjoyed smaller museums like this. Jack and I had been overwhelmed by the size of the Louvre and underwhelmed by the size of the *Mona Lisa* there the day before.

I behaved like the proverbial kid in the candy store in the Musée d'Orsay with its Impressionist and Post-Impressionist paintings, gushing over one masterpiece after another. Manet's scandalous *Olympia*, Van Gogh's iconic *Starry Night*, Monet's dreamy, peaceful landscape of *Poppy Fields Near Argenteuil* . . .

"Is that where the Cowardly Lion, Toto, and Dorothy fell asleep?" Jack whispered, referencing our first delightful Halloween at The Orange Woods: three little granddaughters, captivated by the Land of Oz, dressed in blue-and-white gingham dresses and glistening red shoes. I elbowed him playfully in the gut.

Jack and I spent the entire day in the museum, stopping only for a fluffy croissant and salad at noon. We were spellbound and anxious to get back to the art. I became frantic as closing time approached. So much more art; so little time.

My levelheaded husband suggested, "Let's get a cappuccino and make a plan."

Quickly, I prioritized: I absolutely needed to see Henri Matisse's *Luxe, Calme et Volupté!* I adored Matisse for his bold, expressive, and decorative use of color and patterns. His monumental paintings revolutionized Modern Art. In my training at the San Diego Museum of Art, I had spent countless hours researching his painting *Bouquet*, the large floral splash of vibrant colors so popular with museum visitors. I couldn't wait to share my newly acquired knowledge about Matisse with guests on my tours, which would start when I returned home in a week.

When Jack and I rounded the corner and came upon *Luxe, Calme et Volupté*, I staggered a bit before racing to the painting. Discrete strokes of bold colors covered the painted surface, creating an image of a fantasy getaway to a seaside on the French Riviera. Matisse's imaginative portrayal of happy bathers exuded beauty, happiness, relaxation, and escape. The figures sunning at the water's edge in Saint-Tropez captivated me. A sense of peace and pleasure emanated from the canvas. Dreamy. I longed to be on that beach and feel that feeling. As I absorbed the *oeuvre* of the great French master, my appreciation of his work grew. This piece drew me in magnetically; Matisse's imagery of a tranquil refuge would haunt and inspire me for all our days at The Orange Woods.

I purchased a book in the museum bookstore before we left and learned that Matisse's painting takes its title, which means "richness, calm, and pleasure," from a line by one of the most compelling poets of the nineteenth century, Charles Baudelaire. Back at our hotel, a pleasant young girl offered an English translation of the poem "L'Invitation au Voyage," phrases, such as patina of time, the rarest flowers, and amber's uncertain redolence, we came to cherish.

That evening, over a Grand Marnier dessert soufflé at Le Soufflé, our little hideaway on a quiet street near our hotel, Jack and I continued to discuss the painting and its symbolism.

"That's what I imagine The Orange Woods to be, honey," I said. "It is a peaceful and beautiful place of pleasure where, like Baudelaire wrote, "all the world would whisper." I think Matisse might have wanted to paint our "luxe, calme et volupté."

Chapter 7
The First Season

Our seasons at The Orange Woods began slowly. We savored it first as a weekend getaway as we wound down our obligations and stressful lifestyle in Los Angeles. So did our friends and family, who came regularly and endured the camplike atmosphere, often sleeping on futons or the floor. Sometimes Jack and I snuck away to our little paradise without telling a soul. We relished the peace and quiet without a project or people. Times like this were restorative—filled with good books, leisurely naps, and simple meals. With each visit, our devotion to the place grew. We knew we had made the right decision.

In 1997, our first summer at The Orange Woods, the temperature soared.

Jamie and my daughter-in-law, Laurie, lounged in the shade between the house and the guesthouse on my multicolored Hawaiian quilt, surrounded by three active and adorable little girls: Maddie and Bayley, both three, romped happily in the gardens nearby; one-year-old, tow-headed Sophie struggled to keep up.

Bo, who now enjoyed his dream job at KRTH in LA and lived in Burbank, and Jack collaborated on trimming the overgrown hedges to open up the view from what we had christened The Sunset Deck. On the upper terrace, Jamie's husband, Bud, planted three cherry trees—a Brooks, a Tulare, and a Rainier—from his family's farms in Bakersfield. Brent, along with Jack's oldest friend, Gary, and Wally, his new friend who had become our grape-growing mentor, spent the day with an ominous-looking posthole digger—a two-man auger. The neatly drilled holes would soon receive our Sangiovese grapevines.

As the workers, our family and friends, labored on our property on this scorching hot day, I prepared a feast of ribeye steaks, sweet white corn, fresh vegetable kabobs, and Mom's brown sugar–laced baked beans for the farmhands and the sleep-deprived mommies—a man-sized reward meal with lots of trimmings. I planned to serve it on vintage floral linens in the warm amber glow of evening as the summer sun set over the mountains.

Ice-cold Lone Star beers, our Texas favorite, ended the workday. Thanks and good-byes were offered profusely to our friends, and the gathering dwindled to just the family. In the funky bright orange 1970s kitchen, I focused seriously on preparing the special occasion gratitude feast for my family, who had toiled in unison throughout the day in the blistering, relentless sunshine.

The evening turned out even more perfect than I could have imagined. At twilight time, everyone arrived at the table freshly showered and smelling like spring rain. The hot foods were searing hot; the sizzling steaks, cooked to perfection, were served direct from our brand-new grill. The colds, meanwhile—chardonnay, more beers, lemonade, and sparkling water—were the chilliest. A fresh blueberry, nectarine, and whipped cream compote stood by for dessert.

Everyone helped themself to heaping portions of the celebratory feast as the setting sun turned the sky to a glowing blaze of colors. A round of seconds, piled high on plates, confirmed my inner Barefoot Contessa. The sweet sounds of Patsy Cline—"I Fall to Pieces," "Leavin' on Your Mind," and my favorite, "Crazy"—filled the air. The lights of the houses scattered in the valley below twinkled, signaling the coming of night. The full moon, rising in the oncoming nighttime sky, sneaked up behind us. I had staged our dinner al fresco under the July full moon—also called the Buck moon, because it marks the time of year when the male deer starts to grow new antlers. To myself, I mused about us growing our new antlers there at The Orange Woods. Silently, I counted my blessings.

Relaxed, with full tummies, we lifted our glasses to toast the incredibly productive work weekend, happy family togetherness time, and our new adventure—and at the exact moment we did, my Martha Stewart fantasy shattered when three-year-old Maddie, perched in her booster chair at the end of the table, banged her sippy cup down loudly and, with a pint-size, exaggerated huff, said loudly, "Daddy, can I get down? This is so boring."

Chapter 8

The Mural

What the . . . what . . . ?" Jack stammered several months later. "What the fuck is this?"

Seldom, if ever, at a loss for words, he stormed to my side of our bedroom, wildly waving the envelope he had found under his pillow as we got ready to climb into bed.

"Honey, what does it look like? It's a greeting card—a Halloween card."

"But, but—there's a naked pumpkin on it! I mean there's a woman—at least I think it's a woman. Yeah, it *is* a woman! And she's got a jack-o'-lantern head! Look at this. She's sitting *on* a pumpkin in a pumpkin patch. What the hell?"

"It's our painter friend, honey, the artist."

"What painter? Who are you talking about?"

It took a while to calm him down. I had to assure him that nobody had sent us pornography through the US mail and remind him of the thrill we had experienced two months earlier in August with this woman sporting a pumpkin on her head. Soon my husband and I, both clad in our pajamas, were laughing and marveling at the shock value, creativity, and humor in this surprise bit of mail from our friend, painter, sculptor, performance artist, and muralist MB Hanrahan. Her Halloween card depicted a woman wearing nothing save stilettos and the pumpkin on her head, exquisitely carved to look a little friendly yet a little bit evil.

We would go on to discover over the next decade and a half that in addition to being an artist, MB was also a Buddhist, a hippie, twenty years sober, a photographer's model, a dedicated volunteer and neighborhood activist, and the daughter of a model and an award-winning television script writer. And, most important to us, she created an important part of The Orange Woods's magic.

A few years before the Orange Woods days, at a Boys and Girls Club Auction in Santa Barbara, I had successfully bid on "eight hours of in-home mural painting." Sometime later, I contacted MB, who had donated her service.

I'm sure she envisioned ivy and hummingbirds on a bathroom wall, and I could tell that my request pleasantly surprised her. "Wow, this place is very cool," she offered as she firmly shook my hand.

Forever a devotee of preeminent modernist Marc Chagall's art, I was delighted in the way he portrayed his lovers floating above a village, their feet scarcely touching the ground, in *The Birthday*, a print of which Brent had given us early in his college years. In the piece, the infatuated admirer sweeps down like a comet, or an angel, and gracefully bends over backwards to kiss his demure sweetheart. Chagall epitomized whimsy, and we wanted whimsy!

I fancied a larger-than-life rooster, much like the signature fanciful bird that pervades the Russian artist's somewhat reverie/somewhat surreal work. Rooster, indeed! MB out-Chagalled Marc, creating a ten-foot creature— poetic and playful at the same time—on our patio wall that we instantly adored. It was a big bird with a lot of heart.

We were so pleased with our MB mini-masterpiece that sometime later, we commissioned her to do a second project. A relatively new art form— the floor canvas—intrigued me, especially Suzani patterns, Persian embroideries first encountered along the legendary Silk Road. Never one to be daunted, MB researched the ancient art form and designed an elaborate canvas for our entry hall featuring pomegranates, which symbolize fertility. We would find it both thrilling and interesting that within the next six years, five little grandbabies would crawl, jump, dance, and spit up on that same floor canvas.

Several years later, after we purchased The Orange Woods, we imported MB and her Volkswagen bus, circa 1982, crammed with dented, half-full gallons of every color of house paint imaginable. A few months into our two-decade love affair with The Orange Woods, we had made an outlandish decision: the thirty-five-foot-long, ten-foot-high stucco wall that ran the length of our guesthouse begged for a mural. MB was the perfect person to create it, our first art installation at The Orange Woods.

Together, we planned a mural that would tell the story of our flight from Los Angeles, our stressful jobs, and the mind-boggling traffic to the serenity of the valleys surrounding Palomar Mountain. At the museum, I had studied murals and learned they were one of the most popular types of art in all classical civilizations, dating back to the earliest paintings in the Chauvet Caves of France (ca. 30,000 BC).

Wearing paint-spattered cargo pants and a ragged plaid shirt, MB arrived ready to work on a hot August morning. She covered her spiky, short, platinum hair with a black-and-white bandana and topped it with a crumpled painter's hat. Then, together, we mapped out the story and she sketched her plan, Chagall style.

The project took her five dedicated days—drawing the design lightly on the wall with charcoal, mixing paint colors, loading brushes, climbing up and down a ladder to paint, cleaning brushes, and diligently working all day long. Each day, when it got too dark to paint, she ate a simple, healthy meal, had a shower and a meditation, then collapsed on the bed in the guesthouse.

In our mural, rich with uplifting colors, MB incorporated the little white church on the hill; a book symbolizing our new "simple" life in retirement; both the sun and the moon—our new timetables; our Valencia orange grove; a bluebird; a large heart; and our soon-to-be-planted grape-vines, which eventually made our lives anything but simple. Over the years, that damn bluebird and his friends ate more than their share of our grapes.

On the fourth day of our artist-in-residence's presence, our captivated four-year-old granddaughter Bayley, still in her Princess Belle pajamas, sat nearby sucking orange slices, gazing intently. MB, taking a break, smiled at the little one, strolled over, and sat down next to her. "I bet you are an artist, huh? Come help me paint?"

Bayley's eyes lit up; she smiled shyly. Gently, MB led her to the paint and handed her a kid-sized brush. "Why don't you paint the dots on Miss Ladybug?"

Prudently, Bayley grasped the brush with her sticky little hand and stuck it into the black paint. Taking her own sweet time, she painted six round black dots on the back of the tiny red ladybug, which MB had placed low on the mural so the children would glimpse it easily. Bay finished with a big flourish, a bigger smile, and a blob of black paint on her sweet little face.

MB continued her work, depicting the coyote whose howling we lis-tened to at night; red roses in bloom; winged angels; the cityscape we had fled; the provincial village we now lived in; and, finally, a Chagall-style giant rooster. Our mural exploded with Chagall-like whimsy!

On day five, the dreamlike, pastoral mural was complete. MB had told our story—big city folks morphing into farmers—in living color. She signed the work, "With Love, MB Hanrahan." She departed on a blistering hot August afternoon, two months before Jack's shocking Halloween card arrived.

CB

Over the ensuing years of our life at The Orange Woods, we received regular holiday cards from MB, each of which I took out of Box 1140 at the post office and surreptitiously put under Jack's pillow. They never ceased to surprise, shock, and delight him. Each one was unique and innovative—a startling photograph of the same woman in some kind of nude: MB stretched sexily on a crimson velvet throw à la Marilyn Monroe for Valentine's Day; MB with a plucked turkey in the most precarious of places for Thanksgiving; a red, white, and blue MB with Roman Candles in new and original sites for the Fourth of July; MB seductively tinseled and lit up as a Christmas tree, leaving far too little to the imagination. Another favorite of mine, a Halloween card—"MBWitched"—featured MB suggestively riding a broom and wearing a witch's hat, high-heeled black boots, and lace gloves, with miniature witch hats *almost* covering her boobs. Jack particularly liked "Ducky for Daddy," a Father's Day piece where she languished nude in a bathtub full of water, surrounded by dozens of bright yellow rubber duckies.

The cards eventually began to come less frequently. I bound mine in a book, which I placed on the coffee table when the grandbabies weren't around; needless to say, it was a great conversation starter.

Chapter 9

Texas-sized Rock

One day, as MB painted our mural, I drove home from the art museum in Balboa Park. As I approached the turn onto our country lane and the neighboring nursery, I slowed. Curious, I wondered if I could buy plants there or if it was a wholesale grower, like many in our area.

Slightly off to my left, a massive rock among the plants caught my eye—a huge sandstone boulder, the color of cinnamon. The rock was shaped much like the very distinctive land of Texas, my home state. As a little girl, I had delighted in drawing the irregular shape of my state, the largest in our country at the time.

We had been trying to decide how to display our house numbers at the entrance to The Orange Woods. Now I had found a perfect solution. I could picture large brass numbers, displayed right across the organic face of this fabulous rock map of Texas, stretching from El Paso, through Midland/Odessa, and past Waco. I had to have this rock; it perfectly symbolized the bold, brash, big Texanness of life I'd grown up loving.

CB

I called the moment I got home.

"Hi. I'm calling from Pauma Valley. Our property is very close to your growing grounds there." Deep breath. I continued, "There is a large rock there I'd really like to have. Would you sell it to me?"

"Lady," he said, "if you can get that boulder to your house, you're welcome to take it—no charge."

I needed that boulder badly. The next morning, I walked to the nursery, a multi-acre field of palms, evergreens, small citrus and olive trees with several tented areas scattered around. I walked up and down the paths between the plants and in no time, a roughened sort approached. He said nothing, but his body language and questioning expression spurred me to speak my very best Baja Spanish.

"*¿Cómo te llamas?*" I asked. "*Me llamo Marilyn. Tu Jefe en Riverside me dijo . . .*" I struggled to make the guy understand I wanted the rock and the *jefe* had said I could take it. Jose, Napoleon short and oxen strong, grunted, but his disposition changed markedly when I asked, "*¿Puedes trabajar para mí un día?*"

On the spot, Jose, a bull in faded jeans, and I negotiated what I hoped would be delivery of the giant rock for thirty dollars. I left the money and returned to The Orange Woods, not sure when or if the rock would show.

Within the hour, a large earthmover with what I later learned in my farming education was a front-end loader bucket snaked toward the entrance to our driveway. Balanced in the bucket was my Texas rock, at least seven feet wide and four feet high.

Jose placed the rock exactly where I directed.

Late afternoon, Jack and I walked to the end of the driveway. "Where on earth do you come up with such wild, hairbrained ideas?" he asked in protest, too late.

My handyman of a husband spent a great deal of time the next day drilling the holes and placing the eight-inch numbers perfectly measured and straight. Regularly, Jack lamented the fact that he married an engineer's daughter. For me, everything had to be straight, even, and level. He, despite his intense Marine Corps training, operated less rigidly than me. If it measured one-sixteenth of an inch off, it drove me crazy. Him, not so much. He eventually subscribed to the "measure twice, cut once" philosophy and saved himself a great deal of rework.

Our house numbers on the ever-recognizable outline of my Texas-shaped rock marked a unique and perfect entry for The Orange Woods.

Chapter 10

Conversation Pit

In the beginning, I could tell the house was a seventies mashup with zero character. I did not realize it housed a conversation pit. The listing omitted that but did say it was an "oak-studded property," which turned out to mean it had one giant Engelmann oak and a collection of scrub oaks down in the canyon.

During our initial and only visit before our purchase, when we rounded the corner toward the large, octagon-shaped living room, Jack grabbed my arm—fortunately, or I would have tumbled headfirst into the eighty-foot-square, tri-level, rectangular conversation pit facing the fireplace.

A bachelor who built the home we eventually turned into our castle probably installed the pit. Over time, we heard riotous tales of both him and the second owner, also a bachelor and a photographer who cavorted on the hills and canyons, taking pictures of nude models.

Our future home's 1,800 square feet offered one bedroom and two and a half bathrooms; the master bath was as large as the bedroom. A sunken tub with a twenty-inch drop—no handrail for entry—overlooked a garden of weeds. The dated kitchen exploded with garish orange Formica. The living room ceiling called to mind a rundown ski lodge.

The step down onto the rickety wooden deck off the kitchen was another two-foot drop—no rails, no step. Jack grasped the sliding glass door for balance and safety, then offered his hand to me. "Careful where you step, M," he cautioned. "Some boards are missing."

The ramshackle garage, which housed not only "a raggedy-ass assortment of tools," according to Jack, but also the washer and dryer, was detached, with a perilous path between it and the house. The landscaping consisted of several dozen box hedge trees trimmed in perfect round balls that resembled Tootsie Pops.

We were undaunted, thankfully—due in large part to the extraordinary orange grove and unparalleled views—and plunged headfirst into the purchase, not the conversation pit. Not only were we naive to apparent obstacles, we were young—Jack sixty, me five years younger—eager, and, luckily, strong and energetic.

○3

In the beginning, we were part-timers at The Orange Woods, with a house to sell and work to complete in the LA area. Weekend escapes to the country—idyllic. No television, no computers, serene quiet.

On our first weekend getaway in our new home, we walked the groves together hand in hand, exploring. We listened to birds, observed the clouds overhead, smelled the blossoms, pondered the awesomeness of nature, and reveled in the isolation, peace, and quiet. We sensed our ever-present Day-Timers (daily planners that were our constant companions in our corporate existence, which would end soon) being replaced by the movement of the sun in the expansive sky to our west. Retirement loomed large and luxurious, and we longed to steal away to this secluded paradise, which would be weekends only until we both stopped working.

At the end of the day the first weekend, we enjoyed our first sunset together on that same wobbly, broken-down deck, sitting in lawn chairs. Jack left for a minute or two and returned with a big black marker. On the warped railing which extended the length of the deck, he carefully made one vertical black mark.

"Number one in what's going to be a long line of sunsets we share on this very deck, M," he said.

My heart skipped a beat.

Over the next months, my romantic husband added black marks neatly in a row on the railing each time we sat there to watch the sun go down. We later learned the kids speculated the marks were the number of times we had sex in our little getaway in the country. We let them think so.

Our early conversations about the house and property overflowed with endless wild ideas and plans for what would become our retirement life. Over and over we took deep breaths, inhaling the magnificent outdoors around us—the leaves, fields of wild grasses, smells of wood and bark, and patches of wild blossoms covering the hillsides from our perch on the Sunset Deck. Coyotes would bay in the canyon nearby. I would close my eyes, letting it sink in. Hard to fathom.

Our first evening after moving in, as the sun slipped beneath the horizon beyond, Jack got up, walked to me, and put his vintage Don Imus denim jacket with the flag on the back around my shoulders. He said, "Hey, I've got an idea," as we both shivered a bit from the evening air. "Let's make a fire and eat in the conversation pit."

I laughed. "You're kidding, right?"

Not a chance—and we did enjoy our first meal in our new house in the conversation pit, that exceptionally large divot in our living room, two steps down, covered in beige shag carpet.

Before the pit's swan song at The Orange Woods, I read a short article in a 1963 *Time* magazine, titled "Fall of the Pit." It outlined its numerous faults and awkward perils: "At cocktail parties, late-staying guests tended to fall in. Those in the pit found themselves bombarded with bits of hors d'oeuvres from up above, looked out on a field of trouser cuffs, ankles and shoes. Ladies shied away from the edges, fearing up-skirt exposure. Bars or fencing of sorts had to be constructed to keep dogs and children from daily concussions."

Jack didn't falter when I suggested dinner on the table instead, referring to the pit as a tripping hazard and a dirt magnet. He insisted we cook our first dinner over the fire in our most unordinary fireplace.

Neither one of us had heard before of the Heatilator, an old-style fireplace, basically a black box in the wall with a glass door, that used a special venting system that drew in cool room air and released it as warmer air. No firewood needed.

We enjoyed a memorable dinner our first night. We roasted veggie dogs (we were longtime vegetarians) to perfection on a coat hanger over the "fire" from our perch in the sunken seating. As Jack poured us glasses of celebratory wine, he proposed, "Someday, I picture us growing grapes here—making our own wine."

ᏄᏰ

Over the next few years, before our major remodel, the five grandkids, ages two to six, played together endlessly in the conversation pit, crawling in and out of it, performing their little plays on the steps, often snuggling up with a blanket on the shag carpet with some ragged stuffed animal for a nap. Sometimes the pit became their secret hideaway from the not-so-scary Pauma witch Jack had created for them in bedtime stories.

One spring day, dressed in matching cousin dresses—pastel polka dots— the four girls, Maddie, Bayley, Sophie, and Carly, staged a collective protest when workers hauled a huge concrete mixer into the house and set it smack dab in the middle of the living room floor, which had been stripped of its deplorable carpet.

"No, Neeny—it's our playhouse," Maddie, their leader, whined, pointing to the conversation pit, as the others chimed agreement.

Their protest was unsuccessful. The pit had to go.

Calvin, the lone grandson at the time, almost three, never left the construction site; he was fascinated by both the machine and the concrete it spit out. Wearing the yellow plastic hardhat Jack had given him on his little tow head, he watched all day as, little by little, the mixer churned and spewed tons of fresh cement, filling in the giant playpen where the kids had played games and hosted tea parties—events to which Jack and I were often invited.

That evening, as the wet concrete began to dry, both Jack and I grew a bit nostalgic at the disappearance of the conversation pit. "Lot of good times there," he mused as he carved the date and our names into the hardening cement with a screwdriver.

CB

The kids weren't the only ones to have fun in the cavity before it disappeared. Jack and I frolicked there, too. And the only person to have an accident? Happened to be me, and it occurred when TTT first came to The Orange Woods—two years before the concrete mixer made the conversation pit vanish.

Chapter 11
TTT

Family came first to enjoy our new home, but the second group to descend on The Orange Woods was TTT, my group of best girlfriends from Ventura.

The beginning of the Third Thursday Therapy Group remains a matter of debate, but it is agreed it started in the 1980s with regular get-togethers on Thursdays, after work, for happy hour and conversation. There were six of us, each connected in some way to my group of radio stations.

Faye organized special events for the city, for which the radio stations were frequently sponsors. Sue's role as a large bank's vice-president made her our most important advertising client. Alice and Steve's company did the majority of our print work. Teri and her husband owned the advertising agency our stations employed. And Nancy, our biggest competitor for advertising dollars, held court as the owner of the weekly newspaper in town. For a few years, we interacted only in a professional manner. The formation of TTT made it personal.

Away from the workplace, Faye, widowed as a thirty-year-old, had a series of love affairs over the years, including Fireman Ken; Chuck, the cruise ship gigolo; and dwarfishly short Mr. Green, the mysterious Texan. We enjoyed these relationships vicariously.

If you looked up "Rubenesque" in the dictionary, Faye's picture would be there. Soft, gentle, cushy, very beautiful, and always flowing. A gifted hostess, she entertained regularly. The night before her hysterectomy, she hosted a "coming out" party.

၆၃

"How in the heck did you two find this place?" asked my spunky friend Sue—dressed in lavender, as always.

Alice, my steamroller friend, barreled through the door in her plaid Patagonia shirt and with her long mane of copper-colored hair flopped in a messy pile on top of her head, professing at the top of her lungs, "Woodsie, this place is unbelievable. I love it!"

Teri, exhibiting more evidence of the Parkinson's diagnosis we had learned about two years before, approached slowly, smiling broadly, her speech softened, "This is paradise, Marilyn."

Nancy, with her signature shoulder-length platinum hair and fabulous silver and turquoise necklaces we lusted after, murmured agreement, patiently waiting her turn for hugs.

Faye, flowingly dressed for a party, interrupted, "What do I smell, Marilyn? It's heavenly."

"It's orange blossom time, girls," I replied excitedly.

Exuding her own special brand of magic, Faye had emailed us ahead of their housewarming visit: "Here are important items to consider. Does The Orange Woods have martini glasses? I will bring my vintage cocktail books, fondue, apron, petticoat, saddle shoes, bathing suit, cap, caftan, etc. Bring it on girls! F"

Immediately making herself at home in my down-home kitchen, Faye reached for cocktail glasses in the cupboard and lined up six on a wooden tray on the carrot-colored counter. With great precision, she began her own brand of mixology entertainment.

When the ice-cold drinks were ready, we reached eagerly for our glasses, but Faye held her hand up—mudra-style, in stop motion—and proclaimed, "I'll be right back."

With great aplomb, Faye tangoed toward the Valencia orange trees outside the dining room door and plucked six paperwhite blossoms. Carrying them like precious cargo, she returned to the tray of martinis and floated one unbelievably aromatic flower on each drink.

"Ladies, may I offer you the Orange Woods Orange Blossom Martini."

On its own, the floral scent of the budding orange is perfume. Mixed with vodka and vermouth, it is a sensory overload—radically dangerous!

One or the other of us returned to the nearest orange tree for more blossoms throughout the course of the evening. Faye continued to mix the martinis.

"What are you two planning here? I'd hate for you to change anything—everything is so cool," Alice mused over her second serving, which came with a fresh blossom.

I went into some detail explaining Jack's and my vision of expansion and remodel. Sitting together at the table in the sparse dining room, I told them, "We're going to knock out this wall, double the size of the dining room, and add a huge kitchen. Everything will get changed—new floor plan, carpet, paint," I said, sweeping my hand in a circular motion.

"Well, if it's coming down, let's write on this," Alice boldly suggested as she jumped up and patted the sickly yellow wall at her end of the dining room.

Already into my third Orange Blossom martini, I proclaimed loudly, "We're taking the damn wall down soon. Write whatever you want!"

They did, and then we danced. We danced our brains out—inside, outside, all around the house and property. The aphrodisiacal scent of orange blossoms filled the nighttime air. The music—blues, boogie, country, and rock—blasted through the open windows and doors and out over the hillsides. Didn't matter. Not a soul could hear. Jack, who loved my girl gang as much as I did, had opted to give us privacy for the night. Often, if Willie or Janis Joplin or The Beach Boys came up on the playlist, the dancing would cease, and the harmonies would ring out. We loved singing together. "Amazing Grace" was our favorite. Nancy's clear soprano and Sue's melodic alto blended beautifully and covered up the less-than-pitch-perfect voices among the rest of us.

More martinis.

TTT had a theme song, "Ooh Pooh Pah Pah Doo," a bluesy and gutsy rock song by Tom Hook and the Black Dogs, a group whose CD Faye had purchased after seeing them perform. As the recognizable intro started rocking with its strong bass beat, Sue, the best dancer among us, yelled, "Get the broom. Let's limbo."

We did, and Alice won the prize, easily clearing the broom at twenty-nine inches. At forty-six, she was the youngest. (In a contest of physicality, age matters.)

Nancy, the eldest and our own earth mother, had brought an oversized sunflower ornament for my new garden. At some point, the music moved me to dance holding the lone sunflower on a metal stem horizontally, high above my head. Alice, brandishing her limbo victory, twirled the broom over her head and we danced like lively children at parallel play, not paying attention to the others scattered around the room performing their individual dance moves in a collective orange blossom stupor. Someone pushed the repeat button and "The Most" came up for the eighth time.

At this point in my dance, I lost my balance, and my long legs sent me stumbling over Teri, who had plopped herself, exhausted, into one side of the pit. I tumbled most ungracefully into the abyss. As if we were some kind of human domino chain, one by one, the rest of the girls stumbled around the pit and fell, one by one, on top and over, leaving us looking somewhat like a litter of fuzzy, wrinkled puppies nestled against one another in their box.

Fortunately, the Orange Blossom Martinis had made me quite loose. We lay in a jumbled heap—bangles, beads, and potential bruises—for what must have been a ridiculous length of time. We laughed and laughed and laughed.

Up bright and early the next morning, we drank strong black coffee, nursed our hangovers, and continued writing and drawing on the walls—self-portraits, dogs, hearts and flowers and re-enactments of the limbo, our dancing and the recumbent bodies in the conversation pit—a collective 800-plus pounds and more than 300 years of woman. We signed our work.

The writing remained there for the two years until the wall eventually came down in the remodel. In season, the Orange Blossom Martini became the house drink.

CB

Over the twenty years of The Orange Woods magic, TTT cursed Ralph when he unexplainably left Sue; savored catered meals by Alice's chef daughter; furtively orchestrated Nancy's marriage to Jack's wine-making friend, Wally; endured heart conditions, cancer, and replacement joints; staged elaborate birthday gatherings; honored our moms and dads at our Parents Weekend gala; lost our moms and dads; celebrated grandchildren's births; and came to terms with grandchildren's homosexuality. Steve, Alice's husband, taught us to bonsai boxwoods. From the new technology of the

Internet, Sue's son she'd given up for adoption thirty years earlier found her—and us. We elected Barack; Steve Jobs died; Google, online banking, Twitter, the iPhone, and Airbnb became part of our daily lives. We suffered from the 2008 recession, the deepest since 1929. We mourned Teri's move to assisted living, welcomed Ralph back into our fold when he and Sue eventually reunited. We cheered Kelly Clarkson as the first American Idol.

The friendship of these women was a gift of endless love and support. Women connect in such a deep, meaningful way, rising to the needs of one another instinctively. Over the years and throughout the experiences, our TTT friendship deepened and widened. And, of course, the Orange Blossom Martini remained The Orange Woods's signature cocktail.

Chapter 12
Jo Malone Orange Blossom

Jack's gift to me our first Christmas we owned The Orange Woods surprised me. His entire face beamed as he handed me a tiny, festively wrapped package with a discreet Nordstrom label. If Jamie, our daughter, wasn't available to help him shop, he often put himself in the expert hands of a personal shopper there.

As I unwrapped the present, he squirmed a bit impatiently. "You don't have to save the paper. Open it!"

I pulled off the ribbons and slipped my finger under the tape to open the package. Inside, I found an elegant ivory box with a tiny black rectangle on front, the words Jo Malone London printed on it.

At the time, I seldom wore perfume—and when I did, just one fragrance: Robert Piquet's Fracas Eau de Parfum, which the sales lady at Saks Fifth Avenue described as a mix of "tuberose, seductive and lush, mingles with jasmine, jonquil, gardenia, Bulgarian rose and orange flower revealing a sensual base of sandalwood." Her carefully rehearsed sales pitch worked perfectly: I had paid more than one hundred dollars in 1971 for a bottle of this very French perfume so my unsophisticated self might smell sophisticated like Jack's boss's wife.

This Christmas morning, our first at The Orange Woods, my body flushed with warmth and affection for my personal Santa Claus—filled to overflowing with personality, so animated this happy holiday season.

"It's Orange Blossom," Jack boasted, grinning big like a little kid. "And it won't be long till we have our own blossoms on the trees." He took the bottle from my hands. "Here, smell it. It's exactly the same scent," he chirped as he sprayed me, the air above us, and the surroundings.

Touting the scent of perfume seemed so out of character for Jack, who regularly joked, especially as several of our now-teenage granddaughters pierced their noses, about how we women love to stick jeweled objects in every available hole in our heads and put flowers, fruits, and animal secretions all over our bodies.

Joyful happiness filled my soul as my beloved husband hoisted the atomizer above his shoulders, sprayed behind my ears once again, and nuzzled me. I kissed him softly on the cheek and whispered, "Merry Christmas."

Chapter 13

The First Vineyard

The pull of a vineyard tugged relentlessly for both Jack and me early on. Plenty of acreage spilled forth below us in what appeared to be a gentle slope.

We plotted, planned, and fantasized for weeks after settling into almost full-time retirement life at The Orange Woods. At year two, Jack continued to do his radio talk show in San Diego—until rage and anger began to dominate the airwaves. At this point, he opted out and spent another three years hosting a Saturday morning show, *Golfing Around,* with Charlie Jones, the deep-voiced sports broadcaster, and Tom Addis, CEO of Southern California PGA.

This gig proved the perfect pinnacle to Jack's five-decade broadcast career. He could hardly wait for Saturdays. In addition to being with the boys, he got a break from farming. For years, he delighted in talking about his job—a four-hour on-air broadcast gig. Opening both hands, palms up, mischievously he would joke, "Look, no calluses." At The Orange Woods, away from radio and into full-time farming, he got plenty of calluses.

ᏮᎦ

One leisurely Sunday afternoon, we decided to lay out our vineyard, which we had determined would be 1,200 vines of Sangiovese grapes—the defining grape of Italy, with the majority of vines concentrated in Tuscany. When the grape excelled, it produced the most distinguished, complex, and age-worthy wines; like Jack's special-occasion choice, Brunello di Montalcino, for example, or the top-shelf Chianti he paired with a heaping plate of spaghetti, marinara sauce, and a crusty loaf of bread.

Jack had spent countless weeks researching what grapes would grow best in our remote corner of San Diego County. Turns out, North County San Diego's climate perfectly mimics Tuscany's Montalcino, which rivaled Oaxaca in Mexico as our favorite romantic vacation destination. We loved central Italy's wide, low hills and long, sweeping views. The region alternates wonderfully between woods, vineyards, wheat fields, and olive groves. Jewel-like hamlets and villages dot the landscape. Plus, the wine is unequalled. We particularly savored the Sangiovese there, which is why we selected it for our vineyard.

Our cuttings would be ready to plant in the bare-root season—February, which was coming up. As soon as we laid out the vineyard, the remaining postholes would be dug, grape stakes placed, wires installed, and vines planted.

CB

Today was the day. All systems ready. Hiking boots, check. Sunscreen, check. Water bottles, check. Into the garage we went and armed ourselves with rebar, stakes, posts, hammers, mallets, and bundles of twine. Jack had figured we would lay out rows four feet wide with vines planted on each side on four-foot centers. He had methodically sketched a diagram and placed it neatly on a clipboard he carried.

We turned our boom box up as loud as it would go—Delbert McClinton, Hank Williams and Merle Haggard classics, perfect music for farming—and headed into the brush below.

By this time in our lives, Jack and I seldom fought. However, when we did, we staged a doozy. What followed on this afternoon would be remembered as the loudest, most untamed confrontation we would have in all our years at The Orange Woods.

It never occurred to me Jack intended to orient the rows north to south, horizontally, across the land below our home. Aesthetically, in my mind, our vineyards begged to run east to west—a vertical orientation. I could picture the rolling ribbons of leafy vines streaming from the top of our land and ending far below, toward the west and the sunset.

It started as a mild disagreement as we stood on the hillside.

"The rows need to be north to south, babe," Jack insisted. "You can't plant, prune, or harvest vines hanging on a slope."

I pouted and pontificated a bit about the artistic aspect of our venture. "Honey, this is essentially going to be our front yard, our landscaping. It needs to be pleasing visually. I can just see the undulating vibrant green streamers of lush grapevines snaking down the hillside."

The disagreement escalated, with Jack's shotgun, tongue-lashing style echoing loudly through the canyons. He stomped away from me repeatedly, yelling "Hell no" over his shoulder.

Occasionally he stopped, exhaled, turned, and reasoned, "Think about it, Marilyn," or insisted, "The ground has to be flat," or fired back, "Stop acting so stupid."

"But honey—"

"East-west is a fucking lamebrain idea," Jack shouted in a final burst of exasperation, and he threw the big roll of twine at me. The agitated volume exploded across the undeveloped valley. I grinned inwardly as it missed me and rolled halfway down the canyon.

I got a few licks of my own in but came up far short of Jack, the motor-mouth master of street language. I do think we both were exhilarated by this opportunity to scream, yelp, holler, and lock horns in the middle of nowhere with no one to hear. Sort of Tarzan-like.

The hostile, foul-mouthed spew of anger and petulance continued until, realizing I could never out-yell or out-argue a volatile Jack, I finally threw down my mallet and stomped back up to the house.

Thirty minutes later, I returned, sheepish, and joined back in as he plotted twenty-two rows of vines, north to south, across the land. We terraced the land the next month, and in late winter of 1999, we planted our vineyard.

For many harvests after, as I stood on flat ground on the east-west axis and picked plump, ripened grapes, I admitted, but only to myself, my husband had been right.

Chapter 14

Visitors

Jack, Jack did you hear that noise?" I panicked, bolting upright in bed. It was the middle of the night, and a terrible commotion clamored on the patio outside our bedroom.

"Damn, where's my pistol?" Jack barked as he jumped out of bed and surged toward the closet. I followed close behind. By the time he'd turned on the lights, searched the shelves, and found his Colt 45 in its leather holster, the noise had subsided. The reliable stillness of darkness in the country returned.

"I'll take a look around," my courageous protector said.

"Wait for me," I yelled. I grabbed the thirty-inch rebar my son-in-law Bud had put under my bed the first time Jack had gone out of town after our move to the country. I'd asked Bud to show me how to use the gun. Instead, without a word, he'd left the room and returned from the garage with the steel rod.

"You could kill yourself with a gun," Bud said. "Put it away and place this under your bed. Use it with a vengeance if the need arises."

Now, armed with my rebar weapon, I followed Jack into the night, which was lit by the nearly full moon. Cautiously, we circled around the back of the house with our flashlights.

Our patio was a train wreck. Every piece of furniture was overturned; plants and dirt were strewn everywhere; pots were broken. Interspersed between the destruction and debris were multiple piles of poop.

Puzzled for a moment, we solved the mystery as a band of coyotes howled loud and clear in the canyon, affirming exactly what they thought about us upending their two-acre playground to plant our vineyard in the canyon.

After a midnight snack of peanut butter and banana sandwiches, we settled back into our cozy bed. Jack remarked, "Damn, those coyotes were sure boisterous"—he looked at me—"but not nearly as loud as you when we laid out the vineyard."

The coyotes and Jack and I established our territories and coexisted peacefully going forward. We received a housewarming gift, an informative book about the coyote, from a farmer friend. In reading, I learned to love the creatures. They are socially monogamous; can appear in urban environments; and both male and female feed and care for their litters of up to twelve pups. Most importantly for us, they are famous for a wide repertoire of sounds, yips and barks, most often at night, which regularly echoed through our canyons.

CB

We filled the vineyard with tender young grapevines. As we sank them into the rich earth, plant by plant, the dirt on my hands regularly transferred to my sweaty face and clothes. It felt good. As we placed each vine, we encircled it with a temporary cage to protect it from our friends, the coyotes, and their prey, the bunny rabbits.

Waking each morning to our panoramic view of the pristine Pauma Valley and our now-thriving vineyard, framed by courtly, slate grey mountains, became routine. As I read my paper and sipped a close-to-scorching-hot cup of black coffee, the morning fog often encompassed the mountaintops to the west, calling to mind islands in Hawaii.

On one refreshingly cool August morning, the French doors were open wide, and the birds warbled their morning serenade. It was a lush green and extraordinarily beautiful scene. A feeling of Matisse's *Luxe, Calme et Volupté* prevailed.

Suddenly on this peaceful morning, I became aware of movement beyond our sunset deck above the vineyard, which was now four weeks short of harvest. An image jarred my quietness—a figure marching through the top row of grapes, stealthily moving rapidly north to south. I caught a glimpse of what appeared to be a large male in a camouflage outfit.

Nobody ever simply "dropped in" to The Orange Woods, a remote eight acres at 1,900 feet elevation in the foothills of Palomar Mountain. But the figure passed and I went back to the local section of the newspaper. Had to be a worker from a nearby grove, I reasoned.

Five minutes later, now on my second cup of coffee and on to the editorials, I saw another sizeable guy, also dressed in camouflage, with a backpack and some sort of headgear on, pass in front of me through the nearest row of grapes. He carried a substantial bundle of greenery, over his shoulder. Again, I rationalized the guy must be part of a neighbor's crew working their grove, passing through ours.

When the third figure, also quite fit and large, passed just beyond the Sunset Deck no more than twenty-five yards from the chair where I spent my peaceful, private mornings, I yelled for Jack.

He was on a long-distance phone call in the back of the house. When he didn't answer my plea for manly help, I raced down the long hall to his office, only to have him wave me off and continue his conference call.

My heart pumped wildly in my chest. The men had disappeared, and I had no idea whether they were surrounding the house for a break-in, planting bombs, or playing soldier.

As I reentered the hall, I caught sight of another burly figure, loaded with multiple massive heaps of whatever, barreling across our property. This time, I charged myself up to ready, raced out the door to the edge of the deck, and demanded, "Hey, what are you doing on my property?" Trying to move along with him, I stubbed my toe on the wrought iron railing. "Damn, that hurt," I growled under my breath.

"I'm getting off right now, lady," he replied as he continued his trek.

"What's that?" I motioned to the unwieldy bundle he carried over his shoulder.

"Dope," he replied succinctly.

"Who are you? Who gave you permission to trespass?"

"My boss, lady. Talk to him."

"Who the hell is your boss?" I demanded.

"Sheriff's Department," the guy yelled back as he moved on, down the row and out of my sight.

Trembling, I raced back to my husband's office. Still on the phone, still inaccessible. I turned to run back to the front of the house, but as I reached the glass entry door, I sensed action in our motor court to the east. Momentarily paralyzed, I couldn't think what to do.

Coming at me, also in camouflage, with black grease marks, NFL style, under both eyes and holding up a gleaming silver sheriff's badge, was yet another guy. Behind him, a giant army-green Suburban-type vehicle sat in the drive, engine running, the four trespassers inside.

My mind spun wildly. *Dope, sheriff, camouflage—what's going on?*

Holding his hand up in a no-fear gesture, the boss—a formidable figure covered with mud and sopping wet from the fog and morning dew—approached at our front door and introduced himself. His heavy-duty work boots reached his knees; his bleached-blond hair, wavy, even a bit kinky, was tied back in a ponytail. Around his head, he wore a black bandana; around his neck, I noticed what turned out to be night-vision goggles. Along with flashing his silver badge, he flashed an even wider smile.

As I opened the door and calmed down a little, he explained they were special agents from the Sheriff's Department and introduced himself as head of the San Diego County Narcotics Task Force. Under his direction, 100,000 cannabis plants had been removed from the south face of Palomar Mountain in the past two months.

Greatly relieved to meet this warrior who, along with his team, had apparently spent multiple nights on my property without our knowledge, I listened intently as he explained how, after weeks of surveillance via helicopter, they had confiscated a field of marijuana growing at the bottom of our property line below the vineyard the previous night.

Nervously, wanting to dispel any thought we might be the growers, I asked, "Is it growing wild?"

"Oh no," he said, "this is a major operation. All plants were enclosed in chicken wire cages and they were tapped into your water lines."

"How on earth is that possible?" I challenged.

"Come look at the plants," he said.

I did. Actually, it was my first up-close look at marijuana. A huge stash—more than two hundred mature plants—lay withering in the vehicle's long trailer. As if sensing my concern, my new friend made the charming gesture of taking one large leaf from a bag in the pile, smiling, leaning in, and handing it to me. "Souvenir?" he said.

We said our good-byes and off they went. As I stood there alone, holding the single, jagged, grey-green-leafed plant—which sort of resembled a bridesmaid bouquet—I found comfort in these protectors.

As I entered the house again Jack yelled, "Honey, sorry, I'm really late. No time for breakfast. Got to get ready to go!"

A bit dazed by the onslaught of the morning's action, I walked slowly down the long hall toward our bedroom, studying the marijuana in my hand, and heard the sounds of Jack's shower. I calmed myself, mischievously crept close to the shower curtain, and thrust the lone plant leaf into the stall.

"Where the hell you get that?" he yelled. My street-wise, ironworker, Marine husband knew the plant well.

As he hurriedly dressed, I recounted the scenario. Rushing off to his ten o'clock air shift, he grabbed the leaf, kissed me, and, with a big smile, said, "Thanks for the show material, babe!"

ᑕᎦ

"Wow folks, you're never going to believe what went on at my house overnight," Jack said an hour later as the newscast ended and he opened his mike to begin his show.

The moment his story ended, the receptionist buzzed the studio. "Urgent call for you, Jack."

The sheriff's office staff regularly listened to Jack's talk show, it turned out—they were loyal fans. They said the lone leaf was evidence and shouldn't have been given to me; and the situation as a whole certainly shouldn't have been broadcast. Assuring Jack we were definitely not at fault, they instantly sent a courier to the station and picked up the evidence.

At The Orange Woods, back in my chair, I returned to the newspaper, cold coffee and the peaceful solitude of country living.

Chapter 15

The Wine Label

MB Hanrahan, the mural artist, had painted a fiery round red sun in the sky over the grapevines in the upper corner of our mural at the end of her stay. In the center, a surprise for us: a whimsical couple, arms around one another. "I painted you two surveying your world from above," she said with a proud ear-to-ear smile. We adored her final, Chagall-esque touch.

That autumn, after we recovered from our first harvest, Jack came to me and said, "How about a lunch date?"

We dined on a big slice of pizza; afterwards he led me to the wine department.

"We need to think about our label," he said. "We'll bottle soon. Take a look at some of these."

Together, we wandered up and down the aisles looking at a sea of perfectly placed labels on various vintages. (I would learn later to appreciate the label-applying machines we didn't have. Each year, I applied between five and six thousand labels by hand, some straighter than others.) It didn't take us long to realize we were a few steps ahead of ourselves. Bottles came in different shapes, and so did labels. We needed to decide on bottles first.

Jack had successfully completed the Winemaking Certificate Program at UC Davis, but we still had a great deal of research to do about varietals and their appropriate bottles. We learned Bordeaux Bottles, with their pronounced high shoulders and deep punts, are used most for red wines. We recoiled a bit at the price of bottles, so we purchased a limited amount and recycled the rest from our regular consumption, our friends, and our friend Manny, who happened to be a bartender.

More research followed, this time on labels. During a return visit to Costco, looking at hundreds of labels, we considered options. Black and gold; reserved and sophisticated; cheeky and irreverent. Photo image? Text? Both?

"We need a label that jumps off the shelf at people," Jack said. "Something with sizzle!" I reminded him we were a family winery; but as time passed, it became clear he had his eye on a bigger prize.

After our second expedition to the wine aisles of Costco, we came home, unloaded bounteous quantities of unneeded goods, and relaxed over a glass of wine. It was too sunny on the west side of the house, so we settled in the shady area in front of our mural, near the fountain. With seven different patio spaces surrounding The Orange Woods, we could find a perfect spot for the weather at any given time of the day.

Halfway into the first glass, a big aha Oprah moment occurred. I'm not sure which one of us had the idea first—it may have been a simultaneous happening. I sat up straight, looked at the duo in the upper corner of the mural and pronounced, "They need to be our label." At exactly the same time, Jack pointed at the same corner. "Those two embracing it all—they need to be our label!"

It was quick. MB okayed us using the art; Alice digitally photographed the image; Jack produced the official writing of the verbiage, much of which the State of California dictated; and Steve managed the printing process. The Orange Woods's first varietal, Sangiovese, had a label. We were official.

♋

We had three wonderful years of our first vintage during which time we shared it with friends and family often. Then the sharpshooter bombarded our vines, devastating every single one.

The glassy-winged sharpshooter, Homalodisca vitripennis, is an insect inadvertently introduced into Southern California in the early 1990s and which subsequently wreaked havoc on many wine grape–growing areas of California, including our eight-acre paradise. Outbreaks of Pierce's disease took its gigantic toll before the State of California took control of the insect and the disease.

It took us a while to recover from this huge setback—physically, emotionally and financially—but within a year, we had replanted. This time it was 1,500 Cabernet vines and several hundred Viogniers. Jack rapidly committed to building a winery and a commercial vendor.

And a black dog would soon appear on the next label . . . and in our lives.

Chapter 16

Hague Bridge

Our middle child, Bo; Jennifer, a bright young teacher from Mahway, New Jersey; and their two dogs, Diddley and Murphy, began their lives together within months of Jack and I beginning our life in the country.

In 1994, three years before we purchased The Orange Woods, Bo, at thirty, was hopelessly alone. Both his siblings were married and had recently welcomed their first babies: two little girls. That year, Santa brought Bo a bouncing baby Golden Retriever, hoping a dog would take his mind off the bleak fact he had no wife, no babies, and no prospects at the time.

He was about to make a big career move, to host a morning news and music radio show across the country from his home in idyllic Southern California. On New Year's Day, 1995, he and his new puppy left the sunshine of the Golden State for the East Coast. A mad love affair ignited instantaneously between the two, each of them larger than life, full of personality. Diddley, the archetypical Golden, sported a lustrous double-layered copper-colored coat that provided him ample warmth in his new home in Norfolk, Virginia. Blond-headed Bo, legendary for wearing baggy shorts and flip-flops year-round, personified the California beach boy. He soon discovered he needed more. Wintertime in the East—no joke.

Getting up early to be on the air at five, relentless winter weather conditions, unending "early to bed" nights alone, plus a lack of female companionship, eventually took a toll on Bo, and Diddley in turn. Late-afternoon walks highlighted their day together. Bo ambled; Diddley galloped playfully ahead of him on the nearby Hague Footbridge, originally a wooden structure connecting Norfolk with the plantations on the other side of the river several hundred years ago. Padlocks meant to symbolize everlasting love lined the railings of the scenic wooden bridge.

On one particularly bleak winter afternoon, after checking the temperature, Bo was reluctant to tackle the ice on the sidewalk, but Diddley prevailed.

A crunch, crunch sound echoed in the still afternoon air as Bo's feet, clad in brown waterproof Timberland boots, plodded along in the snow. He cursed the damned cold air. Diddley, unfazed, romped happily as the two began their trek through Ghent Historic District, a pleasant residential area anchored by The Chrysler Museum of Art.

A short time later, a young woman walking a large dog appeared at the other end of the bridge. A flash of long, blonde hair topped by a bright red beanie jolted Bo at his end of the bridge. Thinking for a moment he might have frostbite vision, he blinked. But sure enough, there it was—a tall, slender figure bundled up in a puffy down jacket, magically approaching from the far end of the expansive walking bridge. A giant white Labrador pulled the beautiful creature on the other end of his leash with force.

Bo's heart raced as he realized the apparition coming toward him was drop-dead gorgeous; his brain froze as he took note of her athletic stride and model-like grace. He panicked—what to do, how to behave, what the heck to say? His hands began to sweat inside his leather gloves; he found it difficult to breathe.

Jennifer, trying her best to play it cool, found herself wondering if these two strangers were new to the neighborhood. She hadn't noticed them before; she would definitely have made a mental note of the playful dog and his master, this handsome hunk.

The four continued their flight paths, heading toward the center point. Features became clearer. Taking it all in, Bo thought, *Yikes, what's Diddley gonna' do? More importantly, what the heck am I gonna' do?*

"Diddley, slow down," Bo instructed, realizing they were close to the middle of the bridge. His heart thundered out of control and his mouth refused to move.

For her part, Jennifer struggled for a look at his ring finger and inwardly cussed the leather gloves he wore.

One last-ditch effort on Bo's part—*Say something, anything!*—fizzled. He chastised his radio self, who made his living with words, for falling monumentally short now of all times.

The critical moment approached, and as it did, both Bo and Jennifer quickened their step and nervously looked down at their booted feet, afraid of an awkward encounter in the middle of the bridge. In a bone-jarring instant, it ended; she passed by, and on her way to the far side of the bridge, pegged him a jerk who hadn't even returned her smile. Sick to his stomach over the missed opportunity, Bo headed for his far end of the bridge, the opposite way.

Jen and Murphy now picked up speed on a fast track to her cozy apartment, where warmth and lesson plans waited; Bo and his canine pal slogged along in the other direction toward solitude, Bo's shoulders slumped in dejection.

And then it happened.

As the sun began its trek westward toward the horizon, casting long, deep blue shadows not only of the tall evergreens nearby but also of the two duos as they separated, Bo experienced a rush of adrenaline—an undeniable call to action unlike anything he'd experienced in his life before. Feeling as if he would explode on the spot, he yanked on Diddley's leash, ordered him to stop, whirled around 180 degrees, and in his best announcer voice, yelled, "Hey, can our dogs meet?"

Jennifer turned, corralled Murphy with his leash, smiled, and started back toward Bo's end of the bridge. Murphy, ready for a warm bed, reluctantly followed.

The four met once again in the middle of the historic bridge, and this time the two strangers faced each other in nervousness. The two dogs licked one another playfully, zero nerves.

They had their first date the following Saturday.

Eight months later, Bo got down on his knee on the same bridge and asked Jennifer and Murphy to marry him and Diddley.

And on an extremely hot July afternoon (103 degrees) eighteen months later, the two were married in the rotunda of The Chrysler Museum of Art, overlooking the picturesque Hague Footbridge where they almost didn't meet.

Chapter 17

Mark

My dad was the first great loss of these years. We lost him in 2000, one short year after Bo and Jen were married.

More than anything, as a young girl, I yearned for my daddy's approval and attention. Less than affectionate, he had difficulty communicating one-on-one with me, his only daughter and eldest child. It pains me to look back and remember how I wished I were a boy so Dad would pay more attention to me. But I realized early on that getting good grades and doing my chores in a timely manner was my best chance of getting a modicum of approval.

From Dad, I also learned table manners the hard way. "Keep your elbows off the table, Slim," he often reprimanded. If my brother, Mark, or I didn't obey him, Dad reacted immediately. With lightning fast trajectory, he would flick his middle finger off his thumb at the offending elbow. Unbelievable sting. Didn't take us long to learn the house rules.

Regally tall and handsome, Dad was smart, glib, and charismatic. And entertaining. More than once, I witnessed my father jump from a flat-footed standing position over a dining room chair. He excelled as an unrelenting and competitive game player—bridge, poker, gin rummy, cribbage, and golf.

Dad loved turning most anything into a game of some sort. When he turned seventy, he devised "The Gardner Gift-giving Guide"—basically a graph for Christmas present exchange with two axes. The A axis, divided into five-year segments, represented age. The B axis, the monetary factor, began with five dollars and soared to a thousand. His theory, which delighted us all and became legend in the family, postulated, "the older you are, the more expensive your gift needs to be." He lorded his position, high in age and high in expected value of gift received, over his three wailing grandchildren, who landed low on the scale.

Tall and slender, my father wore his clothes well and was a real clothes horse. One of the family's favorite photographs is nineteen-year-old Mark

Gardner, tight end for the Colorado School of Mines football team, wearing his team sweater—navy with a large white block letter M on the front that covered most of Dad's thin chest. The only family member who fits into that sweater today is nine-year-old Cash.

Dad adored long-distance car trips. When we traveled, he wore dress slacks, a white shirt, and a conservative tie. In his professional life, he dressed in well-tailored business suits and wore garters to keep his conservative socks up. Classic business colors: black, navy, grey. No argyles for my dad. He reluctantly relinquished the garters sometime in the 1980s.

In his seventies, Dad took a liking to a one-piece jumpsuit, Dickie's brand Big and Tall, that almost ruined his fashion reputation.

"Nobody ever sees me in it," he would proclaim when we groaned disapproval. "It's my early morning wear."

Dad, the engaging bartender host, poured a generous cocktail. His specialty on both Thanksgiving and Christmas neighborhood brunches, Milk Punch, had been perfected by Brennan's in New Orleans. I can still smell the brandy—pretty darned stinky to me at the time. To the brandy, he added half and half and powdered sugar and fresh grated nutmeg. I continue to revive his crowd-pleasing recipe and serve it in the same vessel he did—the silver Apollo Cocktail Shaker, a going-away gift engraved with his name and 10-31-49, the date he left Phillips 66 in Oklahoma and moved us to Texas.

In Dallas, we lived two miles from Love Field, the only airport until Dallas Fort Worth International Airport arose on a prairie in 1974. How many times my dad flew in and out both domestically and internationally is hard to say, but he claimed frequent flyer status long before that program existed. He regularly flew Braniff, best known in those days for "the end of the plain plane" campaign, which introduced candy-colored planes and Emilio Pucci designed outfits for the stewardesses. Dad traveled with his Haliburton suitcase, an iconic aluminum industrial design conceptualized by a globe-trotting oil-field engineer. He owned four. The smallest one was a briefcase; I use it today for my sewing things—scissors, needles and thread.

As much as my dad, a most collegial sort, hated to fly and be away from home, he relished the camaraderie of air travel. Many times he would come home with a stranger in tow—most likely someone who had shared First Class cocktails with him. My persuasive and charming father would insist, "Come on home for dinner with me. We've got plenty of room, and my wife loves company. I'll take you wherever you need to go in the morning."

I remember Mom getting "miffed" (her term) when he showed up with unannounced weary travelers. I also recall her quick recovery as she turned into her beautiful and charming hostess self.

At seventeen, I left for college. My dad continued to charm, while his drinking increased.

ℭ

Many years after I lost my father, I wrote about him when I lived in San Diego and close to the airport.

> Living alone, an occasional visitor is nice.
> To be safe, I station myself early
> Waiting in the garden, looking south.
>
> Soon a generous hum drowns out the birds' songs
> The hum becomes a lumbering roar
> A silvery-white giant floats above the eucalyptus trees
>
> Majestic, powerful, beautiful. Like a building
> At the terrace's edge, my spirit lifts, my heart soars
> And then it's gone.
>
> BA273 Heathrow to San Diego glides through my life daily.
> Sometimes I scurry upstairs to the balcony
> Or to the arched window in the living room.
>
> I see it from the canyon, garden, or kitchen
> Occasionally with a grandchild, a friend, or gardener
> Mostly, I see it alone.
>
> Its momentary presence—commanding, comforting, dependable
> Like Dad, a giant of a man, also an international flier
> Silver-haired, silver-tongued, silver suitcase.
>
> His vast wingspan of love encompassed me
> Commanding, comforting, dependable
> Like BA273, in my flight path every day.

Chapter 18

Charline

A lithe slip of a girl, my mom came of age between the two wars. She belonged to the "greatest generation," and epitomized so much of the good about it. Demure, with an air of innocence about her, to me she personified the majesty of the Statue of Liberty and the pioneer spirit of Susan B. Anthony. More glamorous than Rita Hayworth, Mom embraced family and friends much like Jo, everybody's favorite sister in Little Women, the treasured book of my girlhood. I desperately wanted sisters.

I would have had one if Mom's appendix hadn't burst in childbirth in an understaffed, spartan hospital in Muskogee, Oklahoma, seven-hundred and fifty miles away from her home and family in Denver.

Married a little over a year to my father, a young roustabout in the oil fields, she'd been convinced to leave their family and friends in Colorado so Dad could begin what would prove to be a long and successful career in the oil industry. Alone, they buried the little baby they had named Marlene—a combination of their given names, Mark and Charline. My name, Marilyn, is both a tribute to the little girl who would have been my older sister and a second combination of my parents' names. The loss of that baby was the first of a series of unbearable heartbreaks my mother would endure in her lifetime.

My brother and I followed that first pregnancy at breakneck speed, me in May, him eighteen months later. Soon after, World War II began.

My father became a staunch soldier in the United States Army. As a petroleum engineer, he served laying pipeline throughout Europe as the United States entered those foreign soils, and later defending US territory in Manila in the Philippines. Mom returned to Colorado and bravely did her part in the war effort by keeping the home front safe for four long years.

After the war, Mom, the personification of grace and elegance with her long legs, willowy figure, and captivating smile, became one of Dad's greatest assets as he swiftly climbed the corporate ladder. My parents—a glamorous, young power couple—were much in demand in the Texas world of oil. Entertaining, travel, the country club, society, and an accelerated rise to the top of my father's field made our lives full of privilege and happiness. Mom's eternal joy, undying support, and positivity was responsible for much of our happiness, especially on holidays.

ଔ

When Bo visited one year at Christmas, he came into the dining room, hugged me, and said, "Mom, you always make holidays so wonderfully special." Did I say that to my mom? I should have.

Mom did something memorable for each occasion: bunny footprints leading to our baskets on Easter morning; green milk on our cereal St. Patrick's Day; homemade ice cream on the Fourth of July. Valentine's Day saw the dining room table covered with cinnamon Red Hots and heart-shaped conversation candies printed with messages—Be Mine, Kiss Me, and Too Cute—along with bright red carnations, Mom's favorite flower (perhaps because Denver, her home as a girl, reigned as the Carnation Capital of the world).

My merry mother radiated the magic of Christmas, the spookiness of Halloween, the patriotism of the Fourth of July, the romance of Valentine's, and the warmth of Thanksgiving, which has always been my favorite holiday.

Mom and her sister, my favorite aunt, spent countless hours chattering together in the kitchen as they prepared our feast each Thanksgiving. Their hilarious song-and-dance routines entertained us. In their ruffled little aprons with turkeys appliquéd on the pockets, and with hot pads or spatulas in their hands, the two sisters—my short, stocky aunt and my slender, graceful mother—giggled endlessly as they tap danced to "Doodly Do," a silly song from the Vaudeville era.

As the tempting, savory scents of home-baked pies—apple, pecan, and mincemeat—filled the house, they harmonized and we clapped wildly, begging for more. After a few soft-shoe moves and a curtsy, the happy pair turned their attention back to peeling the potatoes and basting the turkey.

Thanksgiving was a formal affair in our dining room, with my portly uncle seated at the end of the table, which glistened with our finest serving dishes, crystal candleholders, and autumn flower bouquets. Norman Rockwell's iconic 1943 *Saturday Evening Post* cover, "Freedom from Want," perfectly illustrated our family's holiday production.

When the mantle was passed to me, I abandoned the pomp and circumstance of the Thanksgiving repast I had grown up with, opting instead for buffet. My parents believed I had gone to the dark side.

∽

Dread came over me the moment I opened my eyes on that bleak spring morning in Dallas, the week before Palm Sunday.

Lifting my head off the pillow, I shuddered. Across the rose-colored room, my teenage sanctuary, the new midnight blue silk shirtwaist, complete with crisp, crinoline petticoat, that was to be my Easter dress hung like a billowing Blue Norther storm cloud.

Today, my mother planned to take me shopping for the perfect shoes to complete my Easter outfit.

In tenth grade now, I was an ungainly five feet ten inches tall, weighed 110 pounds, and wore a size ten—that's shoes, not my dress size. I could slump in my chair or hunker down when standing to disguise my full height but hiding my bigger-than-anybody-else's-feet—impossible.

When I voiced my angst to Mom about both my height and my large feet, she regularly replied, "Oh honey, think how tall you'd be if so much wasn't turned under for feet . . ."

If I didn't have enough hang ups already, upon entering North Dallas High School, my best friend, Judy, immediately hooked up with the tall, handsome basketball center and abruptly dribbled me off the court. Two other longtime friends left school every day in some upper-classman's jazzed up car. Through the grapevine, I learned about a party that I wasn't invited to, and I wallowed in self-pity. I wanted so much to be part of the "in crowd." But I would never be cute, sexy, or flirtatious—certainly not a "most popular" or Homecoming Queen candidate. Instead, I was tall, gawky, and unsure of myself—and my feet were two or three sizes bigger than all of my friends'. Sigh.

On this cloudy springtime Saturday morning, I slouched behind my smartly dressed mother on our shopping mission. She carried my Easter dress in a garment bag. Together, we crossed the vast expanse of the lavishly furnished first floor of the original Neiman Marcus store in downtown Dallas.

In the center of the main floor, a blast of competing aromatic scents hit me as we navigated through the perfume counters. I sniffed madly: Chanel Number Five, Shalimar, Tabu. Behind each gilded station refined saleswomen beamed, many dressed more elegantly than the sophisticated, oil-rich Neiman Marcus customers of the late 1950s.

I fell behind at the Evening in Paris counter when I caught a whiff of the familiar scent. The glamorous lady with platinum hair and deep red lipstick behind the sparkling glass counter smelled like a delicate floral bouquet of lilac and roses. I surreptitiously touched the glistening silver label on the bottle, which read "Soir de Paris." As I picked up the bottle, I pictured my grandmother's cobalt blue perfume bottle with the tassel that sat on her dresser, along with her silver-handled mirror. As I dallied, Mom reversed her course to hurry me along.

Beyond the perfume counters, through the accessories department brimming with the finest silk scarves and expensive leather purses, lay the shoe salon, which was full of women shoving their feet into pointy-toed shoes and a complement of elitist salespeople.

A middle-aged gentleman sporting a burgundy paisley cravat approached my mother. "How can I be of service today?"

My stomach churned.

"We're looking for Easter shoes," Mom said brightly, a stark contrast to my pouting teenage scowl.

We sat on the undulating upholstered bench nearby. The salesman turned to retrieve a sleek instrument I would later learn is The Brannock Device, the standard foot measuring tool for the world's footwear industry in those days. I furtively glanced side to side before removing my shoe.

When the gentleman sneered a bit at my bare foot, Mom handed me the peds, a skin-colored footie of sorts, she carried in her purse. Mom continually reminded me not to wear shoes without socks—"Your feet will smell, Marilyn." She also made me wear saddle oxfords, which were cute in size seven but resembled a boat in my size.

Reluctantly, I removed the second shoe and stretched the socklets over each foot. The shoe guy took my ankle and plopped my right foot's heel onto the ledge of the slanted projection of the low stool where he had placed the metal measuring device—startlingly cold on my bony foot. The man was flustered for an instant as I jerked my foot up, but quickly centered himself and, with authority, replaced my foot on the device and lined it up with the widest part, then moved the sliding width bar inward to secure my foot.

Leaning forward, I attempted to crouch down over my foot and the measuring device, hoping to hide the result. But there it screeched for the world to witness—size ten. I was mortified; my face flushed, and my eyes darted rapidly around the salon. I ached to run.

Mom smiled graciously as she handed the salesman a delicate Pappagallo kitten heel in soft ivory leather, which, she said, would "perfectly match the lace collar on my dress and my kid gloves."

After reading my size, the gentleman explained in a bit of a snit, "Shoes at the upper end of the curve are not in our regular stock. I'll have to go through the stockroom to the second floor. It will take some time."

Feeling some temporary relief at his departure, I sank back on the leather bench and let my guard down a bit. Mom patted my knee. I glanced around the salon. A heavyset grandmotherly type across from us tried on a pair of brown reptile skin pumps. The box said Andrew Geller. Two younger, pretty women nearby paraded in front of the floor mirror, the blonde in black silk embroidered pumps, her friend, the brunette, in a pair of Lucite and rhinestone peep-toe slingback heels, like Mom's fancy pair. Shoe boxes were scattered all over the floor in front of their chairs. I read another box label: Herbert Levine. Size 6.5B. Argh.

After about seven or eight agonizing minutes, the salesman returned. He positioned himself in the doorway leading to the stockroom, clear across the crowded floor, and loudly proclaimed, "We don't have a size ten."

If only the Creature from the Black Lagoon could have swept me up and whisked me away. I sensed hundreds of pairs of eyes throughout the store zero in on me as I fought back the tears. Thankfully, Mom realized it, and we scurried out.

I wore last year's gently used, black Capezio flats on Easter Sunday.

Cঅৈঅৈঅ

Five years later, I came home from college on spring break. Mom had put the current issue of my favorite fashion magazine on my bed. She knew President Kennedy and his beautiful young wife, Jacqueline Lee Bouvier, who appeared on the cover, fascinated me.

I began to devour the details of the fashionable and somewhat mysterious wife of the President. Her majestic, strong silhouette and her Francophile elegance fascinated me. Barefoot in bright white Capri pants, yachting at Cape Cod, glamorous in Oscar de la Renta jewel-toned gowns at White House galas, or hiding from the paparazzi behind her giant designer sunglasses—so beguiling. I lapped it up.

As I turned pages of the profile, at the bottom of the third page, I read, "Cont'd. on page 134." Halfway down the column there was a description of shoes Jackie had worn recently to a White House affair: a pair of emerald green *poie-de-soie*, French court–inspired, low kitten heels with a feminine ruffle at the toe, size ten.

Joy filled my youthful soul. I leapt off my bed, magazine clutched firmly in hand, and twirled around the room, ecstatic. Jackie and me, both size ten shoes. Me and the First Lady!

⅓

I would grow into a tall, somewhat geeky, woman. Several of my short friends would become somewhat squatty. Two granddaughters would be blessed with feet larger than mine. In fact, the average size of a woman's shoe, which in the fifties was size six, today is between size eight and a half and nine.

After that day, the size of my feet ceased to matter to me. Comfort took the upper hand. Thankfully, the selection of comfort shoes available has become extensive, and size ten women's shoes are now in the main inventory—even at Neiman Marcus.

Chapter 19
My Parents' Struggles

As a preteen, I didn't understand the severity of my brother's temper tantrums or my dad's constant glasses of scotch. I did, however, grasp something ominous and frightening when our parents called my younger brother and me into their bedroom one evening in the middle of May.

"Why won't Mom be at my birthday party?" I whined.

In a grave tone, Dad said, "Mommy is sick and she's going back to the hospital. The doctors are going to make her well. She'll be home very soon."

Mom, sitting between us, said nothing but hugged us both.

"Cecile is going to stay with you two while Mom's in the hospital," Dad said.

I liked my dad's longtime private secretary and Goren bridge master but feared the whole situation.

I turned thirteen nine days later, and Cecile invited my friends in the neighborhood to a birthday party in the triple-digit heat of late May. Mom had purchased my dress for the occasion, which rarely happened. Most of the time, she sewed my clothes. Not this time. Looking back, I am certain the worry over her illness and surgery had taken every bit of creativity out of her. My store-bought party dress: a pink pinafore, the color of a ballerina's satin toe shoes, trimmed with wide white eyelet lace. It gaped at least three inches under my arm on either side of my skinny frame. For a fleeting moment, I thought it curious that Mark wore a long-sleeve shirt when us girls wore summery party dresses. I certainly didn't recognize it as a sign of impending mental illness.

I hated that Mom had missed my party. She always made things special and happy.

In the early evening about two weeks after a disappointing birthday void of Mom's magical flourishes, from my upstairs bedroom I heard the doorbell ring. Curious, I went to the landing of the staircase and lay down on the carpet with my nose pushed through the uprights of the wooden banister, straining to hear. Dad's usual jovial manner sounded strangely subdued as he greeted Mom's two tall, handsome doctors; they were brothers who made house calls regularly after Mom's first surgery.

Over a period of almost a year, her thirty-ninth, Mom endured a myriad of doctor appointments, procedures, surgeries, and experimental treatments. Although it made me nervous when they came this evening, I liked her brother doctors who carried black leather bags full of instruments, like my aunt Mariana, a pediatrician in Denver. They made my mom smile sometimes.

There were no smiles this evening.

"Mark, we have to do another surgery," Dr. #1 said in a hushed tone. "There are complications. We plan a skin graft from her inner thighs to replace the infected areas on her chest."

As they continued solemnly, I caught the words "cancer" and "mastectomy," and my dad's solemn, questioning replies: "How long? Odds?"

The conversation got quieter. I could no longer hear.

As soon as the doctors left the house, I barreled down the stairs to my father, pounded my fists on his chest, sobbed, and screamed, "Daddy—what's going on? Tell me the truth."

No longer able to hide the brutal facts, he wrapped his long arms around me and held me close for a moment. "Let's sit down, honey."

He led me to the couch, pulled his ever-present soft white cotton handkerchief out of his pocket, and wiped the tears from my face.

I continued to weep as he told me that my beautiful, compassionate, fun-loving mother had breast cancer. Surgeries, to this point, had not healed her.

In bed that night, I cried myself to sleep, terrified that my mother might die.

Three weeks later, I rushed home from school. Today, Mom would be home once again from the hospital and yet another surgery. I took the stairs two at a time and anxiously rounded the corner. Slowly, I approached the door to her bedroom. My hand trembled as I gently turned the knob and pushed the door open, frightened, unsure what to expect.

A deathly silence prevailed. The bright and cheery room full of windows where my elegant, fashionable mother had always enchanted me as she dressed was darkened and silent. How many times I had stood, spellbound, as my beautiful mother pulled her nylon stockings on over her long graceful legs, stepped into her elegant slingback high heels, slipped into her fancy dress, donned her glittering costume jewelry, and applied her lipstick—Revlon's Fire & Ice—and perfume in this space that now reeked of a foreign, medicinal, unpleasant odor?

Across the room, on her side of the bed, I saw her—naked, with raw skin over much of her frail, anemic body. She lay under a long, open, metal-framed tubing covered lightly with a gauze fabric. A tabletop electric fan blew gently over her wounds. She slept.

cB

Fifty-three years later, in San Diego, I received a telephone call one October morning: "Can you please bring her to the event on Saturday?"

After eleven surgeries, radiation, and endless chemotherapy experiments, my mom had lived another four and a half decades with no breasts, her horribly mutilated body a mangled tapestry of skin grafts and scars, recurring bouts of inflammation and high fever, and a permanently swollen lymphatic right arm that forced her to become left-handed. Mom endured as a pioneer in the field of experimental breast cancer treatments and surgeries—never complained, seldom mentioned it.

I took her on that sunshiny, brilliant autumn morning to Balboa Park. At the Breast Cancer Awareness event, they honored Mom, ninety-three, as the oldest living breast cancer survivor in San Diego County.

cB

As Mom healed over the years and my grandparents died, my brother struggled in school and relationships. Dad's drinking increased. Two cases of Johnny Walker Black Label Scotch were delivered way too often to our back door. No outward complaints from Mom. Always simple acceptance and a beautiful smile that revealed an inner countenance full of love, compassion, and some denial, her coping mechanism.

ᘓ

"Spring break—my house!" I bull-horned with coed excitement to my gang of college friends in late winter 1960, my junior year of college. My parents welcomed all comers, and they were genuinely thrilled to entertain my group. Twelve of us caravanned eight hours from the plains of Lubbock to my home in Dallas.

ᘓ

All six feet four inches of Dad's athletic, lanky frame fell with a giant, crashing thud vertically across the Ping-Pong table, smashing the net. Paddles and white plastic balls went flying. The three other players, fraternity friends of mine from Texas Tech, jumped away from the table in unison, stunned and scared.

Immediately, fury at my father welled inside me. Sheepishly, he pulled himself up and off the table with the guys' help. And then that silly grin of Dad's—his badge of "no-honor" when he had messed up by over-indulging. His loopy look. How I hated it. A dismal end to our spring break celebration.

Earlier in the evening, Dad had grilled three-dozen thick, juicy, and expensive filets for my gang of college friends, captivating the group with his magnetic personality and tall tales. My saint of a mother had prepared a huge feast to serve alongside the steaks. Hungry students that we were, we eagerly piled our plates high with Mom's signature baked beans, corn, fruit salad, homemade biscuits, and more—plus, we each had our own steak. With great enthusiasm, we cut into what turned out to be bright red centers, still frozen; my dad's skill at the grill had been seriously compromised by his scotch.

Both Mom and I were horrified; my pals looked anxiously at one another. One by one, they finished everything on their plates except the meat and politely excused themselves.

When the last of them had left the table, Mom disappeared into the kitchen. I followed her, cried in her arms a few moments, and shortly returned to my friends. I'm not sure where Dad went, but all in all, he had made it miserable—mostly for Mom and me, but also for himself the next day, when the relentless hangover and guilt began once more.

CB

Five years later, I had married and divorced my first husband, one of the three fraternity boys who had pulled Dad off the Ping-Pong table that disastrous spring break, and was residing happily in rural Carmel, Indiana, with my second husband, Jack, and my two little sons.

It was five o'clock—dinnertime for Bo, my youngest, a tow-headed eighteen-month-old who was full of personality. Five-year-old Brent, sitting much too close to the cumbersome television, wore his omnipresent Batman cape, idolizing his hero in action. Jack was at work, broadcasting on the air—*Afternoon Drive*, 2 to 6 p.m., at Indianapolis's heritage radio station, WIBC.

Bo pounded his chubby little fists on the highchair tray in great anticipation as I approached with a plate of Vienna sausages and Kraft Macaroni and Cheese.

Quite unexpectedly, the doorbell rang. *Who on earth?* Living as far out of the city as we did, we seldom got unannounced guests. I opened the door. An irate taxicab driver confronted me, blurting out, "You owe me eighty-two dollars, lady." The driver's jaw clenched tightly, his anger oppressive. Behind the driver my dad swayed, looking haggard and wasted, brandishing that familiar, foolish grin.

Bo, getting restless, fussed and squirmed in his highchair, jarring me back to reality. I raced to the phone and dialed the hotline number.

"I need you, Jack. Come as quickly as you can."

I swept my little guy, one Vienna sausage in each fat little fist, out of the highchair and plopped him down on the floor by his brother. "Don't let him out of your sight," I instructed his big brother.

As I fumbled in my purse for the checkbook, questions pummeled my mind: *Why didn't Dad pay the guy? And why in the world did he come here instead of going home to Houston?*

I furiously wrote a check for eighty-two dollars plus tip, which depleted my meager grocery allowance but satisfied the militant cab driver. I grabbed Dad's well-traveled aluminum Haliburton suitcase from the front steps and pulled it and him inside. Reversing our roles, I admonished my drunken father, "Go to my bedroom and wait for me." He complied meekly.

I scooped two cups of Cheerios into paper cups to pacify the boys, turned, and started down the long hall. My heart hammered with a combination of fear and uncertainty.

I slowly opened the bedroom door. Dad sat slump-shouldered on the side of our bed and sobbed uncontrollably, mournfully. The late-afternoon sun cast filtered stripes of warmth across his bone-weary body. Instantly, compassion overcame me. I went to my father, my fallen hero, sat beside him on the bed, and put my arm around him. His damp shirt clung to his chest; his face looked puffy; his hands shook. I could smell the alcohol seeping from his body, which shuddered convulsively as he stammered, "Honey, if I don't do something I'm going to lose your mother."

My mind raced. Mom was alone in Houston. How much of this did she know? Why hadn't she talked with me? Did she talk to anyone? How much had she hidden? Had she forced his hand in some way?

In spite of my questions, my mind flashed to my little boys. I ran down the hall just as Jack arrived.

In his typical commanding fashion, Jack calmed and directed us through the next unbelievable hours. Quickly, he took charge of my dad, letting me give the boys much-needed attention and a bath. They were slightly upset but easily quieted with their favorite bedtime story, *Where the Wild Things Are*, and gentle good night kisses. Soon, they were asleep.

Heading back down the hallway, I heard voices, mostly Dad's, as he struggled in desperation to recall his past weeks in foreign bars and clubs and his ultimate arrival at our house.

During this three-week business trip to Libya and Egypt, Dad had apparently experienced blackouts regularly—so much so that it had scared the hell out of him. This and the fear of losing my mother had pushed him over the edge.

It grew dark as the three of us huddled in our bedroom. "It's alright, Mark," my husband said to Dad, comforting him. I tried hard to conceal it from my father, but I couldn't help but cry. At last, we were able to reassure him sufficiently so that he fell into an exhausted heap and slept, something he had not done since leaving Benina International Airport in Libya over thirty-two hours before.

While our young sons and my damaged father slept, Jack and I relived the trauma of the past eight hours. We debated over and over about calling

Mom. In the end, we decided to wait until morning. Jack and I were shocked at my dad's fear of what Mom might do. Never had she said a word to any of us about the escalating severity of his drinking.

It was late now; we pulled out the hide-a-bed, climbed in, and embraced one another, frightened and uncertain what the future would hold.

◌

The future began to unfold rapidly early the next morning. While I prepared pancakes for the boys, Dad sprang into action. By mid-morning, he had talked at length with Mom, made a plane reservation home to Houston, enrolled himself in a rehab facility in Arizona, and taken a leave of absence from the only business he had ever known, the oil industry.

Dad's life going forward was extremely difficult and heart-wrenching as he struggled to conquer his demons. Ours was a mix of joy and fear of relapse. He never took another drink of alcohol. He returned to the oil business; became a lifelong member of Alcoholics Anonymous; served on the Texas Council of Alcoholism for years; continued to serve as bartender extraordinaire when company came; and rescued many lost souls, most often in the middle of the night.

The inner strength and faith of my parents revealed itself more and more throughout my life. Over and over, I thanked God for my stoic, silent, strong parents.

◌

My father gave me many gifts in my lifetime, including his example of sober living for the last two and a half decades of his life, but his final gift endures as the most precious: after sixty-plus years of life in Texas, he brought my mom to live near me in Pauma Valley.

Chapter 20

Dad's Last Sunset

Slowly, Dad turned and faced us. A pink sheen fell gently on the shock of snow-white curls atop his head. His face beamed with a glow more brilliant than that of the sublime sunset behind him.

Ten short months before that April evening in 2000, my mom and dad had moved into their new home near us, in Pauma Valley, after living for six decades in Texas. We had begged, coerced, plotted, and planned. Finally, they'd come—to be near the golf course, the mountains, the orange groves, and us.

My dad savored more sunsets in those ten months from our broken-down deck than he had in his entire eighty-seven years before. He came whenever we invited him, and often came when we weren't home. "Just checking on things," he would sheepishly admit.

A week before this evening's sunset, a friend told us that once the bottom of the setting sun hits the horizon, only seventy seconds pass before it disappears. Dad really liked trivia, and I could tell he wanted to prove this theory.

"Sure, Dad, love for you guys to come for happy hour," I'd said when he'd called earlier. "We'll watch the sunset—"

"Can we bring the Jensens?"

"Of course."

"How about the Browns?"

"Dad, bring whomever you want. We love having your friends share special times with us."

Happy hour was indeed happy. Both Jack and I cherished time with my parents. Watching over them those past ten months had created a real awareness of a generational swing.

I smiled when I saw Mom signal to her devoted son-in-law for another white zinfandel by flirtatiously placing her empty wine glass upside down on top of her head. In the midst of the lively exchanges, I noticed Dad slip to the far edge of our sunset deck, just as the fireball hit the horizon. His head nodded in counting rhythm—fifty-five, sixty, sixty-five, seventy. At exactly seventy seconds the sun did indeed disappear, casting an extraordinary blanket of vibrant, warm hues above us and to the west.

Dad didn't turn back to us immediately; he lingered, relishing the majesty of the fiery sky. I couldn't take my eyes off him. Slowly, he rotated his head from side to side and then looked skyward, taking in every sliver of coral, pink, purple, gold, and blue this masterpiece of a sunset had to offer. I watched him take a deep, deep breath, engaging all six foot four inches of his slender frame. Then he exhaled slowly, bowed his head for a moment, and turned toward us.

In my entire life, I had never seen such an exquisitely beautiful face—so radiant, childlike in its innocence and purity. I believe the glory of God, of nature, and of the spiritual world filled my father in that moment. Not a word said. Not a word needed. His expression said it all.

ᘓ

At six-thirty the next morning my mom called, her voice full of terror. "Marilyn, I need you. Come fast. Your dad has collapsed. I'm so afraid . . . hurry, Marilyn. Please hurry."

Dad never counted sunsets again. He died three days later.

That night on the deck, I didn't realize it was his last sunset. But I believe he did.

ᘓ

My longtime hero gone; the void was beyond compare. Losing my dad thrust me headlong into full-scale adulthood. Forever, he had been the preeminent, respected ruler of our small family.

When my dad collapsed on that pleasant April morning in 2000, he had just finished a bowl of shredded wheat cereal and was about to head to Lindberg Field for a flight to Dallas, where he hoped, once again, to solve the ongoing problems of my brother's life. Instead, he went in an ambulance to the hospital in Escondido, where he died. It was the first death I'd experienced that exacted a part of my being.

When the dust had settled, I surfaced as counselor, CPA, companion, and caretaker to my grief-stricken mother and mentally ill brother. Only at this time did I realize the magnitude of responsibility my father had assumed all those years. A sobering understanding. How I wished he had leaned on me.

His death devastated me on so many levels. Grief counseling for mom, widowed after sixty-two years, was my main priority. My brother's condition, meanwhile, challenged me like nothing in my life before. As always, even though Jack grieved immensely at the loss of my dad, who had become not just a father-in-law for him but also an immeasurably close friend, he provided unending guidance, strength, and support for me as I crumbled.

Late on the day of Dad's death, Jack came to me, gently embraced me, and said softly, "Come on, M, let's take a ride."

I had never actually been on the Pauma Valley Country Club golf course where Jack, Dad, my son Brent, and my son-in-law, Bud, had long bonded over the little white ball. As we glided slowly toward the tenth fairway in Dad's golf cart, twilight loomed. One of Mom's favorite songs, "Twilight Time," about the splendor of deepening shadows that give way to fingers of night, floated in my mind as we approached the setting.

It would be twenty years later when my Chilean friend, Renato, would introduce me to the enchanting Spanish word for twilight. "It's *crepúsculo*, Marilyn, and like twilight it conjures up a poignant time of each of our days on earth." When he told me this, my mind instantly went back to that golf cart ride with my husband at *crepúsculo*, the day I lost my dad.

I sat as close as I could to Jack, experiencing a spirituality that emanated from the lush green fairways and the towering trees—silver oak, liquidambar, and pines. Shadows the deep blue color of lapis lazuli angled sharply from the trees toward us, stretching longer than the trees were tall.

Gradually, the sun set in the distance beyond. The golf course appeared as a cathedral to me. I tried so hard to be grateful for the ten months my dad had enjoyed in Pauma Valley with us, but excruciating sadness filled me knowing that his time here had ended. I huddled close to Jack and rested my head on his shoulder as I wept, mourning the most profound loss of my life thus far.

Chapter 21

The White Flower

Now living full time in our yet-to-be-remodeled home, Jack and I were finally settling into routine. Along with our burgeoning farmer duties, his included a daily radio show, golf as often as possible, and developing our wine business. I juggled sandwich generation duties and seriously pursued my passion for art and art history. At the time, this meant immersing myself in the life and body of work of Georgia O'Keeffe. More and more, as we continued to shed our big-city skins, Jack and I were each conscious of how art and nature figured prominently in our lives each day.

I drove the country roads around our property frequently. Jimsonweed, a regular along the highway toward Palomar, is poisonous if ingested. It populates roadsides and fields mainly in the Southwest, the part of our country O'Keeffe loved above all others. Chalk white and less than two inches across, its shape calls to mind a pint-sized trumpet. Its leaves are dull green, bordering on sage. It was an insignificant part of the landscape surrounding our home—or so I thought.

In my training program at The San Diego Museum of Art, I studied O'Keeffe, America's legendary woman modernist painter. She spent the first part of her long career teaching in God-forsaken West Texas, home of my alma mater, Texas Technological University. Both Georgia and I spent time in Palo Duro Canyon in that part of the state: me, at fraternity beer busts in the 1960s; her, memorializing the site in vibrant and bold abstract paintings three decades earlier.

When Georgia was in her early twenties, Alfred Stieglitz, the photographer and modern art impresario of the prestigious and innovative 291 Gallery in New York, heard of the diminutive, talented young woman in Texas. When he saw her work, it captivated him.

Jack, whose eyes often glazed over when listening to my art speak, "got into it" when I described the steamy affair between the photographer and the artist, a saga that still resonates with romantics worldwide. Over their time together, more than 25,000 pages of love letters were written between the pair. Much like our story, Alfred swept Georgia off her feet. He brought her to New York in 1918, quickly capturing international fame for both her and her body of work.

In 1934, Georgia first visited Ghost Ranch, a dude ranch north of Abiquiu, New Mexico. The stunning landscapes there provided new inspiration for the artist's work and she fell in love all over again. The grandeur and expanse of the majestic Southwest cast its spell on the artist.

For a decade or so, she lived and painted part time there, and when Alfred died, she made it her beloved home for the rest of her days. Her paradise.

Like ours, her daily existence was spartan and fulfilling. Given to routine, she ate protein in the morning; a large, leafy green salad for lunch; and wine and cheese for dinner. Jack and I often "ate Georgia style" at dinnertime, which we savored on our Sunset Deck.

The lone artist embedded herself deeply into the traditions of the area. She had her Model A Ford customized so she could drive even farther into the wilderness and paint each day. She selected the Ford because of its high windows, which gave her perfect light for her paintings. She removed the driver's seat, unbolted the passenger seat, and turned it around to face her "studio" in the backseat, which became the easel for her large canvas of the day. She created stunning masterpieces from inside the sedan. Purple hills, bones, crosses, cow skulls, and clouds—she marveled at the beauty of the simplest parts of nature, and her canvases emanate that beauty. During this time, my fascination with skulls and skeletons, which permeate my art collection now, blossomed. I thank Georgia for that.

The artist coveted another insignificant part of this desert landscape. Already acclaimed for painting giant flowers that some said smacked of great sensuality, she made certain that we could not ignore the beauty of the Oriental poppy, black iris, the common hollyhock, the morning glory, and everybody's favorite, the petunia. "Too many times, we ignore the smaller things in life," she offered. She enlarged these beauties of nature in brilliant color, most often spilling off the canvas. Hard to ignore her large-scale, iconic flowers.

Subscribing to her mantra, we found ourselves embracing countless small-scale and simple things in our life at The Orange Woods. Bud-break on the grapevines early each spring; the jaunty roadrunner pecking at our door early mornings; a lone hummingbird nest; a heart-shaped stone; spider webs in the sunshine; stars overhead in the dark—blessings of the nature surrounding us.

∽

I stood before *The White Flower (White Trumpet Flower)*, which Georgia O'Keeffe painted in 1932, at The San Diego Museum of Art; it was my research assignment. Because I like flowers and gardening, it surprised me that I didn't recognize this blossom, which I was told was jimsonweed, the tiny squatter along the highway. I learned that the flower, also called the Datura blossom, is a distant relative of the potato.

One day after receiving my assignment, Jack and I drove along Highway 76. I spotted some jimsonweed and urgently pleaded with him to pull over.

"That's Georgia's flowers—stop," I yelled.

Always accommodating, he stopped on the shoulder and smiled at me down and dirty on the side of the road, photographing the lonely jimsonweed with my Canon Sure Shot, which I kept handy in my purse for grandchildren's antics. I couldn't wait to share it with classmates at the museum.

In my research, I read how O'Keeffe lovingly related the pleasure she derived from the small white flowers sprinkled in the land beyond her porch in Abiquiu. She told about how, alone in her new, remote home, she lingered long into the dark night, appreciating the glow of the desert moon and the multitude of stars in the sky. She recalled being momentarily startled as teensy stars began to appear on the empty, forsaken land beyond her house—minute dots of soft white sprinkled over the barren land, looking very much like the star-filled sky above. It may have been the plant she had in mind when she said, "When you take a flower in your hand and really look at it, it's your world for the moment."

It didn't take Georgia long to discover that the little sparks of brightness in the evening, which grew wild without water, were worthy. Predictably, it didn't take her long to pay tribute to this lonely little beacon of nature in yet another of her oversized oil paintings, *The White Flower (White Trumpet Flower)*, which is in the collection of The San Diego Museum of Art in

Balboa Park. She painted several versions of this Lilliputian bloom. One version sold at auction in 2014 for a record $44 million, becoming the most expensive painting by a female artist sold to date.

Georgia did what she set out to do—make us take notice of this unique creation of nature. One of the most important and innovative artists of the twentieth century, she handpicked the lowly weed from the side of the road and elevated it to fine art status.

ଓଓ

I completed my research on Georgia O'Keeffe's masterful painting a short time after Dad died.

On a beautiful evening in May, two weeks after he died, I came home late after sitting with my grieving mother until she slept. As I walked into the house I heard Luis Miguel singing one of our favorite songs, "No Me Platiques Más." My husband sat waiting at our table on the Sunset Deck beyond. Candles flickered; a simple dinner and two glasses of wine awaited. A crystal vase filled with a dainty bouquet of flowers graced the center of the table. I went to Jack; he embraced me; I cried softly in his arms. Over his shoulder, I recognized the little white blossoms, slightly wilted, that he must have picked from the side of the road near our home.

Chapter 22

Steamer

On a freezing cold day in January two years after my father's death, Jack and I sat side by side once again, this time in the warmth of our brand-new steam shower, installed that morning. Aromatic steam filled the grand two-seater of the large, glassed-in space in our bathroom. The big decision of our maiden voyage: to infuse with eucalyptus, orange, or lavender oil?

Drops of moisture trickled from Jack's forehead as he happily related the morning's dog shopping excursion with Jamie. "She picked the cutest little black-and-white ball of fluff," he recounted, smiling.

"Bayley and Carly are going to adore that little doggie," I said.

"There was one puppy left . . ." he murmured.

I shifted my bare butt on the redwood bench, putting some space between us and doing my best to process what he said. Long pause. I looked at him. His eyes darted around the ceiling as he tried to appear nonchalant. The last thing on earth I wanted? A dog, much less a puppy. But something in Jack's voice touched me. Could he possibly want a puppy?

He did.

He returned for the lone remaining little guy that afternoon. He brought him home, and the magic of The Orange Woods skyrocketed instantly.

∞

Naming our new little black puppy began as a family affair.

Everyone arrived en masse the first weekend to welcome our new member. First order of business: the name. Jack and I had more or less settled on Reverend because of his black coat and because he'd come to live with us on Martin Luther King's birthday. However, it became immediately clear that the five little ones didn't relate and had ideas of their own.

"Neeny, look at him. He's wearing a tuxedo—let's call him Tux," eight-year-old Maddie pleaded. Bayley, also eight, considered his white paws and said to her doting grandfather, "How about Sox? Look at his white feet, Papa." Sophie, a born animal lover who often challenged the two older girls, chimed in with "Lucky" because he now had a good home. Four-year-olds Carly and Calvin were content just crawling in and out of the puppy cage. Other names were batted about—Midnight, Inky, and Carbon.

We were still undecided when the gang left. But after putting him in his kennel for the night—alone this time—Jack and I reminisced about the suggestions and the way our family had wholeheartedly welcomed our new doggie.

The more we discussed the name options, the more undecided we became. We sat in silence for a brief time. Suddenly, Jack surprised the heck out of me—and practically knocked me off the sofa—by jumping straight up and saying enthusiastically, "I've got it! Let's name him Steamer."

"Steamer? Why on earth?" I asked.

"Because, because think about it," he clamored excitedly, "he was conceived, or at least the idea of him coming to live with us happened, in our new steam shower."

I loved it. Steamer Woods; it was official.

cs

Steamer—an unbelievable creature with somewhat diminished brain power and a huge, overflowing heart—began his life as the sixth in his mother's seventh litter. We were told that the puppies were Akita/Lab mixes, but as ours grew, we suspected a Great Dane might have also been involved.

cs

Magnetism happened instantly between Jack and our new puppy—undoubtedly because Jack had rescued the jet-black, furry runt from the makeshift cage where he remained alone after his six siblings were chosen one by one. They continued to bond as Jack potty-trained and fed him.

Over the months, the two met each morning at Jack's big leather chair, where he gave the black dog a lengthy massage before he read the paper or drank his first cup of coffee. Jack's loyal companion reliably ended up next to his master wherever he sat or wherever he worked—in the vineyard, the winery, his office. When Jack left, his dog would sit patiently, sometimes for hours, at the end of the driveway, waiting for the return of the big Dodge Ram truck, Sirius NFL Radio blaring at deafening decibels. On Jack's arrival, the black dog would gallop full speed up the three-hundred-foot driveway alongside and dangerously close to the amused driver. In the garage, before Jack could open the door, all one hundred and ten pounds of canine would leap to the window of the cab, greeting his master breathlessly, tail wagging briskly. Theirs would endure as a lasting love affair.

From his humble beginnings, Steamer went on to canine fame as the poster dog for OrangeWoods Wine, immortalized by an oil painting done by our artist friend, Sue Turnbull, which became the Black Dog label. Each year of his life, three hundred cases of red wine were bottled, corked, and finally labeled with his portrait front and center on each bottle. The back label read:

Our black Lab, Steamer,
Proudly presents this, our latest edition of Cabernet,
Because he, too, believes
There's a California sunset in every bottle of OrangeWoods Wine.

Chapter 23

The Winery

Jack's lifetime thrills and honors were many, including interactions with countless celebrities (his favorites were Bob Hope and President Ronald Reagan). He prevailed as the premiere talent at some of America's most important radio stations, including WNBC in New York, WAVA in Washington DC, WKYC in Cleveland and KLIF in Dallas. His Pop Warner football teams won championships. At charity events, he worked alongside Jerry Lewis, Marla Thomas, Brooke Shields, Dr. Laura Schlesinger, and Mike Ditka. He interviewed Chet Huntley, Jerry Kramer, Dustin Hoffman and hundreds more. He was elected to the Texas Radio Hall of Fame and the National Radio Hall of Fame.

When Jack's glory days were over and he had become a farmer, he came in from the grove one day and said to me, "In the grove, repairing the sprinkler heads that the damned coyotes chewed up, I had a sobering thought: I am no longer part of the big world. I'm simply a guy who lives in the country and labors on irrigation."

Inwardly, I smiled as he removed his straw hat and wiped his face with his red bandana, his denim shirt soaked from his irrigation trials and errors. Then I gave my very important husband a big hug.

Our philosophical discussion continued well into the evening that day. I understood that Jack faced what so many dread: the realities of retirement. What on earth to do with one's time? How to find meaning? How to contribute?

Always the creative thinker and doer, Jack didn't lollygag in that purgatory of uselessness long.

He would become a winemaker.

First step: enroll in UC Davis's preeminent Winemaking Certificate Program, where he not only mastered the how and why of it all but also learned a new agricultural lexicon, vineyard establishment and management, vine nutrition and pest management, and an unbelievable amount of other stuff completely foreign to me, like malolactic fermentation. He lapped everything up.

Certificate in hand, he researched varietals for our vineyard, visited growers, and bought vines. Then we planted our grapevines. At the end of each row, we planted a rose after learning that roses, susceptible to the same pests and conditions, serve as an early warning system for vineyards.

As the vines grew, Jack, along with a very expensive consultant, began the two-year process of obtaining a commercial wine seller's license. He intended to make enough wine for not just our own consumption and that of our family and friends, but also for a handful of desirable clients.

He did get the license—the first and only commercial license in our area—and his growing list of clients turned out to be Pauma Valley's "world-famous" Lazy H Restaurant, which has a tree growing up through the roof in the bar; the Pauma Valley Country Club; Major Market in Escondido; and another in La Jolla. His sweetheart of a client—an eighty-five-year-old woman friend, Martha, who insisted Jack have a glass of wine with her after the delivery, no matter the time of day—bought ten or twenty cases at a time.

More research and, for me, surprises. Jack bought $4,000 worth of equipment—gulp.

"Where on earth will we put it?" I demanded in a panic.

"In the garage," he said. "It's three-car. We can easily make wine there."

Determined to drive home his point, he calmly reminded me of the book I'd given him about winemakers in France, *Judgment of Paris*. He retrieved it from the bookcase and flipped through pages madly until he found the one he wanted.

"Here, look. We are going to be 'garagistes.'"

Right there on a page in the book I had purchased, it said, "Garagiste is a term originally used in the Bordeaux region of France to denigrate ren-egade small-lot wine makers, sometimes working in their garages, and has been adopted by like-minded souls everywhere today."

We jokingly called one another garagistes from then on, saying we were making "vins de garage," and I thought that was the plan. But my husband, the newly minted winemaker, had bigger ideas. Methodically and diligently, he carved out his second career. There would be no garage winemaking involved. He moved quickly to build the winery.

Within six months, our storybook winery rose smack dab in the middle of our Valencia orange grove.

⅓

For Jack's birthday in November, we invited more than two hundred of our nearest and dearest friends, family, and acquaintances to the official opening of our winery. The invitation read, "We are having a 'Winery Warming.' Please come celebrate with us. BYOWG."

"Woods," asked his golf buddy, Tom, "what the heck does 'BYOWG' mean?"

There were a few wise souls who understood, without asking, that the instruction meant "Bring Your Own Wine Glass."

I had never seen my husband quite as thrilled as he was that memorable night. The winery was lit up like a Hollywood premiere; a neon sign proclaimed our love in living color, MARILYN LOVES JACK. The winemaker posed for endless photos. Wannabe winemakers huddled around the barrels savoring unlimited tastings, which Jack deftly appropriated straight from the barrels with a hand-blown glass wine thief.

Throughout the evening, Jack, wearing the wine bottle shirt Jan, his generous supporter and friend, had given him, held court—entertaining, as always, with his magical storytelling, as well as with his newly acquired expertise. Over and over and over, he filled his friends' wine glasses. The reviews were five stars all the way.

Jack Woods had become a winemaker.

Our Christmas card that year, 2006, read:

As many of you are aware, this is our inaugural year as Pauma Valley's first and only commercial winery. We have watched over the years as the orange groves have dwindled, the casinos have appeared, and we've struggled to maintain the peace and quiet of our rural paradise. With this in mind, we have created a small, boutique winery producing a limited yield—a little more than 250 cases—once a year. There are no directional engineers, neon signs, or flashing lights to lead the way to Orange Woods—just our secluded country lane, which we invite you to travel.

Chapter 24

Neon

The neon MARILYN LOVES JACK sign that illuminated the winery with a warm, colorful glow the evening of Jack's birthday, and every one that followed, had been an anniversary present.

Our anniversaries were always very special—blissfully happy times. A romantic dinner of crab legs with drawn lemon butter, spinach salad, and an expensive bottle of champagne became our tradition. Jack always added chocolate.

On our twentieth, however, fate intervened, and we were to be apart. An opportunity at a legendary radio station found Jack across the country in Washington DC, living in the dismal Oakwood Apartments, while I stayed behind in San Diego doing my best to corral three teenagers and sell our house. Sacrifices had to be made, including being apart on our wedding anniversary.

I struggled to come up with an over-the-top anniversary gift for the absent man of my dreams. I'm not sure what triggered the decision, but once the thought germinated, there was no turning back.

Neon—a neon sign professing my love—seemed a perfect symbol of our high-voltage, long-lasting love affair. An electronic affirmation of my devotion that would gleam in the dark loneliness of his sparsely furnished apartment.

Times Square's stratospheric light show of neon signs had thrilled me since my first visit to the Big Apple with my dad as a high school senior. And how often Jack and I had marveled together at the neon lights that dazzled in London, New York, and Vegas, loving the way they made cities fizz and crackle with life at night. We loved neon in the movies, too—*Blade Runner* and *Skyfall* and, way back in the 1950s, Alfred Hitchcock's *Vertigo.* But Sofia Coppola's *Lost in Translation,* the masterpiece of disconnectedness filmed in Japan, was what had truly hooked us. In it, Bill Murray, playing an American actor shooting a whiskey commercial there while in the grips of a midlife crisis, spends hours in the rooftop bar of the Hyatt Tokyo, wallowing in the neon glow. (Little did we know at the time that Bill Murray would go on to circle into and around our lives at The Orange Woods many years later.)

Neon art fascinated me, and I took it for granted until faced with actually creating a work out of the mysterious gas. How to execute? Who created neon? What made the color?

Soon, I found out. Neon lighting was invented in the early 1900s and was used throughout the century mostly for advertising purposes.

This was long before Google, so I researched neon via the Yellow Pages. Sure enough, in El Cajon, a company was listed—Mr. Neon. Off I went to a grimy, junky workshop crowded with an array of dozens, maybe hundreds, of bar, beer, and exit signs, rainbows and flaming pink flamingos.

Hard to explain how neon happens, but from Mr. Neon, I learned that it's basically a difficult process of bending fragile glass tubes. When connected to the transformer, atoms move around in the tube, hitting each other, transferring energy, and producing heat. (This is "neon for dummies." I dropped chemistry mid-semester.)

Working with the artist there to create my simple sign was a lesson in color theory. He explained how the warm colors enhance a woman's complexion and the cool colors—like my favorite, lime green—cast a "Wicked Witch of the East" pallor over one's face. So much fun selecting the colors. A Ferrari-red heart would link our names. "Jack" would be spelled out in block letters of boy colors—blues and greens with names like Blizzard Blue, Waterspout, and Spiro Disco Ball. My name would be in script in one color—Outrageous Orange, my new favorite.

I could hardly wait to pick up the love letter.

ᗱ

The day came, and my sign did not disappoint; it was very cool.

The package, however, was cumbersome—extremely lightweight, fragile, thirty inches in diameter, and oddly shaped. How on earth to get it from San Diego to DC safely?

A few days later, a week before our anniversary, Jack called.

"Babe, look out for Fed EX. I sent your anniversary gift early."

Anxiously opening the package, I found a round-trip, first-class plane ticket from San Diego to Washington DC. A Post-it note on top said, "Come—we'll celebrate twenty years!"

I exploded with excitement.

ଓ

I did my best to conceal my bundled, breakable carry-on as I boarded the plane, hoping I could rest it by my legs or in an empty seat next to me. No such luck—but fortunately the flight attendant, a hopeless romantic, stored it safely.

I will always remember the way Jack's face lit up when we plugged in the sign. The practical but depressing greys and browns of his dreary apartment were instantly ignited with excitement and the warmth of color—pure, exaggerated color like that of the French Fauvist artists.

Our neon sign would color our world for a long time—thirty years total, the last twenty as the centerpiece in our winery. We installed it before the first barrel, and we toasted one another in the neon shower of pure color many times.

Chapter 25

Art and Wine

Over and over, we added to The Orange Woods's art collection.

I purchased *The Harvest*—a painting of a sun-weathered, ample Italian couple sitting side by side on a low rock wall, surrounded by their lush vineyard and cradling large baskets of harvested grapes—as a birthday gift for Jack after the biggest setback of his winemaking career.

The two figures gaze inquisitively at one another, their arms full of rich red wine grapes, their oversize and calloused feet bare. He's dressed head to toe in worn denim; her warm coral work dress is threadbare. There is weariness on their flushed faces, exhaustion in their bodies. She looks longingly to him for guidance.

How well we understood the feeling. Our arduous few years as diligent grape growers and winemakers had informed us of the pleasures and disappointments of farming. Countless times we had remarked to one another how fortunate we were that farming wasn't our livelihood. It was our retirement folly. Folly, indeed. When you sink your heart and soul—and bankroll—into a project of passion, it's hardly folly.

The artist Tommaso Vei, well into his eighties at the time he painted *The Harvest*, had insightfully captured the very essence of the life Jack and I were living. Interesting, because he lived and worked in Cologno Monzese, a commune in Milan in the Italian region of Lombardy—two hours from Tuscany and more than 6,000 miles away from our property.

After his extensive research and study, Jack had determined that red grapes, which flourished in Tommaso Vei's land, would thrive in our vineyard. And they had—until we received an uninvited, unwelcome visitor after year four. When the sharpshooter invaded The Orange Woods and our grapes, we lost our entire crop, every beautiful, twisted, and so lovingly planted and tended vine. We were devastated.

No one was more despondent than Jack.

The Harvest, purchased just after that crisis, went right over the fireplace in our living room, overlooking our now pathetic collection of diseased vines. My birthday card read, "Harvest 2004. You worked so hard; the sharpshooter won." The painting commemorated—not celebrated but commemorated—our last harvest of Sangiovese grapes.

○3

I had been to Tuscany, but I didn't purchase *The Harvest* there. It came to me through an acquaintance who had struck a deal with the prolific Tommaso Vei, convincing him that she could sell his paintings in California, if only she could get a deep discount for the one she coveted. Thrilled with the possibility of an expanded international reputation, the aging artist agreed. The woman got her deal and within sixty days had sold a dozen of his paintings.

I couldn't resist the whimsy of my second purchase, *The Accordion,* done in Tommaso Vei's now familiar style—well-fed, usually mature individual characters or groups in scenes of everyday life portrayed with a visceral authenticity. In his working-class subjects' pensive faces, you can read the pain that reveals a lifetime of backbreaking work, unthinkable sacrifices, and an occasional bit of happiness.

In our new painting, again a loving couple, this time face-to-face on the dance floor with that same wistful expression of *The Harvest*'s grape pickers. No smiles in the funky dance hall, but the artist conveys joy and contentment in his figures nonetheless. No eye contact from the accordion player who stands with his sizable feet firmly planted on the ground and his eyes on his keys as he fills the room with rollicking music perfect for upright clinches and interesting dance moves. Two couples embrace in the background, near the bar. One guy, particularly amorous, nuzzles his curly-haired companion, his hand placed lovingly on her butt, subtly conveying a mark of possessiveness. "I'd rather be that guy back there," Jack often teased me. "To heck with the dancing!"

The dancing pair, engaged in a sort of wrestler's hold, are front and center, looking into one another's eyes, and both dressed in warm, butter-yellow attire—his a shirt over well-worn jeans, hers a soft cotton dress, short enough to reveal most of her chunky thighs. She has on a wicked witch's pair of dancin' shoes—bright red—that match her luscious lipstick.

Tommaso Vei's canvases emanate warmth, glowing colors, interesting and oversized figures, handsome and soulful faces, raw emotion, and life. As the artist said, "I paint 'Tales of Life.'"

Specifically, as it turns out, *our* life.

I framed *The Accordion* and hung it alongside *The Harvest*.

"Look, honey," I said to Jack, "this is how much fun we used to have before we became laborers."

He grinned and nuzzled my neck like the amorous guy in the painting.

ɔꙅ

Alice bought another Tommaso Vei painting, *The Farewell,* and surprised us with it as a gift at harvest time. "When it gets to be too much work, this will be you two, leaving The Orange Woods," she told us, laughing out loud.

Once again, the Italian artist's images hit home. In this piece, the couple is older; their shoulders slump dejectedly. Their hair is grey and partially covered with old people's rumpled hats. Still no smiles, just understanding and reassuring glances at one another—glances that reveal the kind of trust that results from years of devoted companionship. They walk close next to each other toward their new life together with a lack of tension and stress that equates to a feeling of nothingness. Behind the duo—hills, valleys, vineyard, olive trees, and blue sky, a perfect depiction of what we imagined to be our humble but perfect piece of the world.

A triptych of our life in art. To begin, our joyful, carefree life dancing our brains out in some dingy bar after work. Next, our laborious but astonishingly rewarding life as farmers, grape growers, and winemakers. Lastly, our life together when we would be too old to work in the fields and would be content with reading, watching old movies or *Jeopardy* together, or sitting on the porch.

For a very long and exceptionally happy time, Tommaso Vei's three paintings hung over what had become a very crowded space above the mantle of our stone fireplace.

We replanted our vineyard, this time with Cabernet and Viognier grapes, and we went on to harvest those grapes each year, make very good wine, and celebrate. Side by side, we were farmers.

It was serendipitous how often our two passions—mine art, Jack's winemaking—collided or complemented one another. One Valentine's Day in 2005 stands out with skin-prickling tenderness.

When I sat down with the newspaper and my first cup of coffee, a chocolate heart sat on the table next to my chair. Later, before our quiet, romantic dinner for two, I gave him the Valentine's gift I had purchased at The Festival of The Arts in Laguna. *Vintage Tastes* is an elegant oil painting of four wine glasses and three wine bottles of the red wines he savors. It's luscious in sumptuous shades of deep Bordeaux red, purples, sienna, and sapphire blue. Small, eight by ten inches. I could tell he liked it, holding it up against the walls around the dining room and wine bar, searching for the perfect spot.

"This wine looks good enough to drink," he offered.

My all-time favorite rock and roll disc jockey gave me a romantic card with two tickets to the upcoming Joe Cocker concert inside, a bottle of my favorite Fess Parker Pinot Noir, and a dozen gorgeous long-stemmed red roses for Valentine's. We were the perfect pair!

 CS

Jack and I read with a passion, often reading passages aloud to one another. In *One Hundred Years of Solitude*, a book he gave me one Valentine's Day long before we began our life at The Orange Woods, Gabriel García Márquez describes the paradise of shared solitude. When we lingered alone together in the majesty of our surroundings, often with both the sun and moon sitting in the sky, we occasionally read passages to one another. Our favorite: "They enjoyed the miracle of loving each other as much at the table as in bed, and they grew to be so happy that even when they were two worn-out people, they kept on blooming like little children and playing together like dogs."

Chapter 26

Steamer and My Dad

I don't recall when the thought first occurred to me; it came on gradually. Immersed in Asian art and religions—Hinduism, Buddhism, and Shintoism—at the museum, I studied reincarnation: the rebirth of a soul in a new body, a person or animal in whom a particular soul is believed to have been reborn. Raised in the Lovers Lane Methodist Church in Dallas, Texas, I scarcely knew of reincarnation before this time.

As a grandmother five times over, multiple viewings of *The Lion King* had reinforced my layman's idea of the circle of life.

I cherished my connection to our black dog. His devotion warmed me. His presence grounded me. He became a father-figure sort of companion for me. At some point after Dad's death, I began to have a notion that Steamer might be my father reincarnated.

Nah, that's ridiculous, I told myself.

And yet an astounding physical similarity was shared by the two. My long, lean, and lanky father had shiny black hair before it turned to a glimmering silver. In college at The Colorado School of Mines, he dominated the high hurdles. Steamer, also long, lean, lanky, and very black, once wowed onlookers by jumping off a twenty-foot deck and catapulting through the air in pursuit of a brand new red rubber ball—and ending with the ball and without injury. He took a bow as we applauded. He fervently loved to race our car from the gate to the ranch, romping through the fields. Many times, he won. Two high-jumping, super-fast runners.

Both, too, were gentle, vulnerable, and yet incredibly strong. They guarded and protected me, each in their own way: Steamer with a ferocious bark at an approaching stranger; Dad, the consummate gentleman, always on the street side, taking my arm as we walked.

Both reveled in crowds and festive gatherings, and frequently garnered the center-of-attention spot at such events: Steamer, so lovable as he performed his only trick, the high-five, shaking a paw with whomever asked; Dad, with his engaging storytelling, often laughing the hardest himself. Yet a shyness pervaded in them both.

They communicated in low, deep, resounding voices. Throughout my life, in their own time and way, they sensed my needs, how to make me laugh and how to stop me from crying. So many similarities.

But it was Steamer's face where I thought I saw my dad so often. A face full of understanding, compassion, and adoration. His dark eyes pleaded, warned, encouraged, and guided me. Often, I found myself looking to my loyal dog for an answer or opinion.

No way, I said to myself over and over. *How can this be? Marilyn, you are imagining things.* But when I looked at Steamer, there were glimpses of my father. Dad and Steamer. Both long, handsome faces. Long, lean bodies. Long on love and understanding. Adored by all.

I regularly entertained the possibility that my dad, or aspects of the man, were reincarnated in my dog. Possible? Probable? Doesn't matter. It seemed that way to me. Dad was gone; Steamer was with us. At times, it seemed they both were with me.

Chapter 27

Little Brother

My brother worshipped his dog, too.

His relationship with my father, on the other hand, was rocky from the beginning. My schizophrenic brother came every Christmas to California at my father's insistence. Reluctantly, he placed his little dog in a kennel each time.

After my dad died, my brother rarely came. When he didn't, I went to Dallas to spend time around the holidays with him. I'm always up for a taste of Texas; it restores my soul to go there.

On my visit in 2004, Mark stood across the gallery of the Meadows Museum of Art in Dallas, looking somewhat hypnotized, less than a foot from Pablo Picasso's *Still Life in a Landscape* painting. It intrigued me that my brother, whose mind so often played tricks on him, appeared to understand the complex Cubist work before him, a piece within which objects—a bowl, a mandolin, a glass and a stylized bunch of grapes—appeared as if they are being seen from a number of different angles at the same time. I smiled at his profile as he focused through his perpetually smudged glasses, his pants hiked up to ankle length by his omnipresent suspenders. His carrot-colored hair was thin now, but without a trace of grey.

As we walked among the masterpieces in the museum, at one point Mark sauntered ahead and stopped in front of a favorite of mine: *Blind Man of Toledo* by Joaquin Sorolla y Bastida, the great Spanish master painter of light. Again, he moved in close. The larger the painting, the closer he got. I thought of Mark Rothko, whose impassioned abstract paintings offer floating rectangles of color. Rothko encouraged the viewer to come as close as eighteen inches to his painting in order to be immersed in the emotion of it.

Mark spent an inordinate amount of time in front of *The Blind Man of Toledo*. I wondered if he identified with the solitary man in the black cape and fedora walking along a road that leads to an arched bridge. Mark existed so desperately alone himself; did he see himself in this figure? Or did he dream of retirement, now just four months away—did he long to escape to a faraway land?

ભ

"So, did you enjoy your first visit to an art museum?" I asked my brother as the server placed a huge bowl of guacamole on our table.

"I really liked the sculpture out front of the museum."

Instantly, I pictured the angst, panic, and upset balance of both the horse and rider in Marino Marini's *Horse and Rider,* the bronze sculpture at the entrance to the museum. It pained me to think that was what he recalled.

After our late lunch of Tex-Mex sour cream chicken enchiladas and limited conversation, I drove Mark home to his condo with the iron gates and his dog.

A short time later, I found myself daydreaming, parked across the street from the house on Wenonah Drive where the two of us grew up—a gracious two-story, set back from the street, with an expansive lawn of St. Augustine grass. Memories bombarded my mind. I pictured the two of us in, out and around the house, rarely together.

ભ

Markie, eighteen months younger than me, was an adorable, freckle-faced little boy with hair the color of a shiny new penny. Auntie Gwen called him "my little carrot-top." Painfully shy and nervous as a youngster, he probably already exhibited tendencies later identified by psychiatric evaluation. He obsessively sucked his thumb. Hated being outside; screamed if Mom forced the issue. He had very few friends, and escaped reality with Western heroes like the Lone Ranger—forever the cowboy.

School was always difficult for Mark, especially math and reading. And early on, telltale signs of violent anger began to surface. They escalated in his teen years.

C3

My head slammed against the front door, and my consciousness shattered. Mark's wild, angry eyes scared the shit out of me. At the top of his voice, he yelled profanities, his spit spattering across my tear-stained, horrified face. His entire body trembled as he kept mine locked in his fierce grip. His large hands clenched my shoulders in a powerful hold. Only my head moved as he violently shook me over and over.

I can't recall what caused my brother's explosion, an outburst unlike any I had witnessed in the past. Our parents were out for the evening. We were well past babysitter age. My brother was fifteen; I had recently turned seventeen. I don't remember much about my interaction with him that night. But at some point, he blew. We were talking, then disagreeing, and then he went crazy. With one final thrust, he slammed my shaken body savagely against the door. As quickly as it had begun, it ended. I fell to the floor.

Lenore, Mark's high school sweetheart, broke his heart with a Dear John letter when he served in the army in Germany. She was his first and last; he never had another girlfriend. The loss plagued him the rest of his life.

Alcohol became a problem early on. However, he stopped drinking after a Sunday afternoon brawl at an apartment swimming pool area in the early sixties. He gave up cigarettes the same way, cold turkey. He never gave up Diet Coke, though; he consumed at least four of those daily his entire adult life.

Compulsive spending, paranoia, part-time jobs, muggings, creditors, fights, and lack of friendship punctuated his troubled life.

Mark suffered a nervous breakdown in 1975. Hospitalized for weeks, he began treatment for paranoid schizophrenia, a condition that ruled the rest of his life. In some random twist of fate, Jack and I moved back to Dallas that year and stayed for a brief two years. My brother needed me; so did my parents. My humbled father wept at my kitchen table the morning of Mark's breakdown, saying, "They said he could have hurt someone, or himself."

From that point on, Mark saw a psychiatrist weekly and took powerful drugs—unless he decided not to, which caused major problems. Without his meds, he did to others what he'd done to me that evening when we were teens. But somehow, he managed to keep his job and routine, walking to work and caring for his dog he adored.

Although he enjoyed coming to The Orange Woods, Mark stayed home at Christmas two months after my October visit. At the beginning of 2005, however, my brother purchased a round-trip plane ticket for a summer visit to our place. A Post-it note on the airline's envelope read, "Go to Marilyn's June 26."

He didn't use that ticket. He died on a dismal January day five months before, not quite five years after we lost my father.

My brother labored in a paper manufacturing plant for thirty-nine years and forty-nine weeks. Three weeks shy of retirement at age sixty-five, he was felled by a massive heart attack. He collapsed as he lifted yet another heavy box in the Olmsted-Kirk warehouse. At one time, he'd run "the slitter," a big machine that cuts giant rolls of paper; that position had afforded Mark a badge of honor. But eventually, improved technology and Mark's limited resources had relegated him to the bottom rung of the ladder, so that he spent his final years pounding, lifting, and stacking heavy rolls of paper like the one that fell on him that day.

He wore a lime green plaid shirt and bright red suspenders the day he died. Three bottles of Strawberry Boost Energy Drink, two Diet Cokes, and the latest issue of *U.S. News and World Report* were in his briefcase.

C33

On the day my brother died, I went to the Nasher Sculpture Center, sat in the shadow of *The Hammering Man*, and wrote:

> I sit near a giant man—*The Hammering Man*. Huge in scale, made of steel, the figure is powerful, solid and black as night. He stands alone in the outdoor space, silhouetted against the skyline of Big D. Jonathon Borofsky, the sculptor, said, "With his head bent and motorized arm continuously moving up and down, he signifies both the drudgery and heroism of labor."
>
> Another giant man, my brother, not nearly so powerful, has died.
>
> Like *The Hammering Man*, his labors were full of drudgery, like his life, which he preferred to keep in simple routine.
>
> My brother could talk your ear off, scare you to death with his anger and rage, embarrass or frustrate you. He'd give you his

opinion, loud enough for everyone to hear. Fiercely loyal, honest and ethical, however. A scary soul at times, with a heart of gold. He conducted his life in an heroic manner. He did his job, endured in the most adverse world and asked for nothing.

Unfortunately, Mark wasn't thought of as a hero. But, on this day, as I sat near *The Hammering Man*, I remembered my brother as *my* hero. In his own private way, Mark signified both "the drudgery and heroism of labor." He exemplified the hammering man.

ଓ

After years of retrospection and endless Google research on mental illness, the puzzle pieces of my brother's crippling brain affliction continue to fall into place. Looking at it now that my brother and my parents were gone, I anguished with questions. What if he had been diagnosed as a teenager? How responsible had my family been? How culpable had *I* been?

Fifteen years later, I would attend a play at The Old Globe, *Benny and Joon,* in which the paranoid schizophrenic Joon's character was written and acted with such meaningful portrayal. I cried several times; the performance of the dynamic little actress, Hannah Elless, portraying a functioning schizophrenic whose occasional breaks from reality, rang so true for me. I identified clearly when she described her "nightmares in the daytime," which is what my brother described over and over to me.

As I continue to probe and ponder my life with a schizophrenic brother, I understand how blessed we were to grow up in an upper-middle-class environment where he could be protected and his condition sheltered. But as I watched Joon find Sam, another of society's "outsiders," I agonized over how Mark's life could have been different had he found someone with whom to share his life.

Chapter 28

The Sweet and the Bitter

Thanksgivings continued as my favorite celebration. Very special family times each year. Steamer particularly loved the chance for reunions with his dog cousins and hikes up the mountains.

The first year at The Orange Woods, always-creative Bo had provided two options: a fully cooked turducken and a deep fryer for a companion turkey to the twelve-pounder in the oddball orange kitchen.

In 2005, six years after Bo and Jennifer's wedding, a family horseback riding experience was on the agenda for Thanksgiving Day, just after the turkey went into the oven and before the football games began. We were surprised and puzzled when Jennifer, one of the most athletic and adventurous of us all, declined to ride.

"I'm not feeling too good," she said, declining politely.

"Come on, Jen," I urged, "Everybody's going."

"Nah," she said, "I'm tired. I'll hang out and read until you get back."

A short while later, Jamie's horse snorted as she rode up near me and asked, "Mom, do you think Jen could be pregnant? Did you notice that she didn't have a glass of wine last night?"

Our whispers of speculation erupted into shouts of jubilation later that afternoon when, together, Bo and Jen told us they were going to have a baby in the summer.

ଔ

Not quite seven months later, Jack and I went on an unforgettable trip with our good friends Alice, Steve, Faye and the Kessons. We spent three amazing weeks in Thailand and Vietnam, with plans to return a short time before the baby arrived in August.

In those days of unreliable Internet, we made Bo promise to send the news of the baby's sex when they were told. We searched for a cyber café the moment we arrived in Bangkok, in a frenzy to hear the news. We were eventually successful, and Jack sat himself down at the albatross of a computer there.

"You've got mail" thrilled us.

From Bo, it read, "*Sự chúc tụng. Cô sẽ có con gái.*"

"What? I'm going to kill that kid!" I yipped to Jack. After a moment, of course, we both were relishing yet another example of Bo's delightful sense of humor and his unending ability to create magic.

We began determinedly searching for translation; this became our most important sightseeing goal, more than any golden Buddha or ancient palace. However, we were in Thailand, and Bo had written his message in Vietnamese. We wouldn't arrive there for another eight days.

⊂ℨ

In Vietnam at last, as we dressed for our grand welcoming dinner at Cafe Indochine in Danang's French Colonial-style Resort, Jack assured me, "We'll definitely get Bo's message translated tonight."

At the welcoming happy hour, our group delighted when the hotel concierge, in his spotless navy and gold uniform, commented that I was "higher" than Jack—referring to my height, not my condition.

A feast ensued. Squid spring rolls on peacock, steamed fish with sweet and sour sauce, grilled chicken with lemon leaves, tortoise steamed rice—the flavors and aromas were exotic and breathtaking, especially for Jack and me, with our unadventurous tastes. Over dessert of Bánh Xoai, a sweet and savory mango cake, Jack approached the sommelier, a dashing sort named Thinh (the name, he had already informed us, meant "prosperous"). He delighted in translating Bo's message—finally! With a flourish of showmanship and a big grin, he announced, "Your new baby will be a girl."

The table erupted in cheers and great applause. I squealed with over-the-moon delight, jumping up and down, happy tears on my cheeks. Jack beamed and vigorously shook Thinh's hand, contributing to his prosperousness with a healthy tip. Within moments, a bottle of fine champagne arrived, courtesy of our appreciative maître d'.

We toured in two-person rickshaws the next day through the Citadel and markets with our friends. At day's end, our guide invited us to his home, a meager, dilapidated, wooden-covered gondola on the Perfume River where he lived with his wife, young child, and mother-in-law.

The only décor in the home was a tiny temple on a low table covered with ancestral offerings. No creature comforts. A dank, unpleasant smell permeated the compressed space. A paltry few cooking items were stacked on a shelf; one patterned blanket was spread on the floor. I assumed it was where the entire family must sleep.

When the mother, a slight young woman in a ragged dress, encountered our younger traveling companions, she turned hurriedly, grabbed her dark-haired baby, and thrust it toward them. Stunned, they leaned away from the woman in refusal. They were dumbfounded, as were we all, to realize that the mother was begging for her little one to be taken to America. The desperate woman spoke little English. Her face and gestures conveyed her daring proposition: a better life for her child. Our companions emphatically shook their heads in protest. "No, no, really, we can't," they said firmly, inching backward.

Our group quickly departed. Incredibly difficult to leave; impossible to take the child.

᚛

It was always good to go home, but the excitement of this return to California mounted steadily. Our newest grandchild would be arriving soon.

Our kids met us at LAX. I spotted Jamie, with her arms around Jennifer, as we exited customs; Bo stood behind them. Jack and I raced to them. As we embraced in a group hug, my daughter's entire body began to shake and she brought her hands to her face.

"Mom, Dad," she said in a muffled, tearful voice, "Jen lost their baby a few days after you left, shortly after Bo sent his happy message to you on the other side of the world."

My body went cold. As I turned to hug Jennifer, I began to hyperventilate. Her body shuddered. I couldn't hold back the tears, and soon we were all crying.

Jack pulled our little group tighter together amidst the travelers coming and going internationally through the world's fourth-busiest airport. The devastating news was unthinkable; I couldn't fathom losing a child. This little being who'd had no chance at life, no opportunity to be cherished and cared for by these devoted parents—how could this be?

We went home with Jen and Bo to their tree-lined Burbank neighborhood full of modest box-like houses built for WWII veterans in the late forties and fifties. They sat across from us on the sofa, staring down at their tightly clenched fists. Steadily, they recounted the painful horror of the past weeks. Their voices broke in the telling of the loss, which might have been brought on by a complication during her amniocentesis. They shared the name they had chosen for their little girl: Ella.

As I listened, my thoughts returned to the desperation of the woman and the little baby on the boat in Vietnam, so far away.

Some months later, I unwrapped the present we had purchased for Jennifer and Bo's fifth wedding anniversary. My shoulders tightened with the memory of our harrowing trip to Bor San, a rustic craft village outside Chiang Mai, in a rickety bus on a treacherous mountain road. The traditional fifth-anniversary gift is wood. A quiet artisan woodworker in a rustic shop we entered fascinated me. I had found the perfect gift. For less than ten dollars American, I purchased one of his carvings—a near life-size sweet baby child, kneeling with folded hands and a bowed head.

A long time passed before I could bring myself to give the gift to my son and his wife. When I did, we each shed tears. The wooden sculpture sits on their mantel today.

The sadness dissipated slowly over the next years as Bo and Jen went back to their life and jobs. Jack and I grieved for a long time as our middle son struggled. His heart is as big as the world we had traveled, and at this point—this life-altering point in his life—his brother and sister had beautiful families, five precious little kids between them. Jack and I longed for the same happiness for Bo and Jennifer one day.

On an extremely warm autumn afternoon three months after Jennifer and Bo lost their baby girl, I went to an Art Fair in Santa Ysabel, famous for Dudley's Bakery's delectable homemade pies.

I strolled the rows of booths filled with art, pottery, glass, weavings, sculpture, woodwork, and paintings. I stopped in front of a tiny image—pen, ink, and watercolor wash. Two inches wide by three inches high, the minute work of art grabbed me by my heart with an indescribable intensity.

Over and over I had prayed that Jennifer and Bo would have a baby. I looked at the art—an image of a tall, lithesome, blonde, and obviously pregnant young woman who looked very much like our Jennifer, standing near a gentle chestnut mare. Their heads met in the center of the small painting. The young woman wore no clothes; her breasts were full.

"Can you tell me about this watercolor?" I asked the artist, a gentle woman with a gracious smile who sat in an open tent surrounded by her art.

"Of course." She put down her paintbrush and wiped her hands. "Long ago, I prayed for a baby. It grew tiresome talking to others as the years progressed. My horse became my best listener. It took a long time, but I eventually gave birth to my baby, a delightful little boy."

I purchased the work of art for my collection, hoping that it might influence the baby gods once more.

03

Our family and friends spent wondrous Christmas Eves at The Orange Woods together; it was a time when there was magic not only for the little ones but also for the grown-up children. My father's Christmas Eve birthday celebration had for years rivaled that of Jesus. Dad delighted in the festive parties we threw in his honor, basked in the adoration and attention. He overflowed with pride and joy when Carly, great-granddaughter number four, arrived on his birthday. Sadly, he only shared her first birthday, and then was gone.

Tonight, Christmas 2006, there would be eight birthday candles on Carly's Peanut Butter Fudge Cake.

Jack and I had recently purchased an elegant solid walnut dining room table, ten feet long—a Thanksgiving gift to ourselves in November.

Tonight's repast—a potluck feast—along with candles in crystal holders, silver ornaments, and silky angel hair covered our long table. Jamie created a cheese tray, a work of art. Family favorites—Mom's traditional avocado and Texas ruby red grapefruit salad with poppy seed dressing, Laurie's Silver Palate Three Onion Casserole, Bud's Christmas goose from his October hunting excursion to Canada, and Barefoot Contessa's prime rib and baked potato wedges—were in abundance. Jack proudly interspersed bottles of his OrangeWoods Chardonnay, Black Dog Cabernet, and Zinfandel wines.

On the buffet at the end of the dining room was a smorgasbord of desserts, served with this year's Vin d'Orange, the French liquor we'd first tasted in Paris and then made with our own Valencias. Chocolate Heath Bar trifle, apple chutney pear tart, nuts, cookies, and ribbon candies clustered around a Peanut Butter Fudge Cake, the family birthday staple, with Carly's eight sparkler candles on top. The table overflowed with scrumptiousness. I was experiencing every mother's dream: a holiday home filled with love and family.

From my vantage point in the kitchen, I couldn't help but notice eight-year-old Calvin, head bowed in concentration, circle the table surveying the spread. Regularly, he grabbed a pickle or stuck his finger in something. I had to smile watching him cram the little Pigs in a Blanket, the frankfurter in a biscuit specialty from the fifties, into his mouth. Growing boy!

Cookies and milk for Santa and the reindeer were placed on the fireplace hearth after dinner. The five wide-eyed cousins jockeyed for a role in the process, knocking a few crumbs on the carpet in the Christmas Eve scuffle. When they were done, Papa gathered the cousin troupe together and they snuggled under a comforter near the Christmas tree, its evergreen scent still fresh. He read the Christmas story from the Bible. Goodnight kisses followed, and soon the little ones were put to bed with visions of sugarplums and the arrival of Santa Claus dancing in their heads.

Laurie and Jamie, mommies exhausted from orchestrating the entire holiday season, high-fived as they rounded the corner and bounced into the dining room. They helped themselves to bites of the still-bountiful spread on the table before plopping down side by side on the long, angled sofa. Thus settled, they smiled lovingly at one another, took a sip of eggnog, and breathed in a collective, weary sigh, relishing their few precious hours of downtime.

I closed my eyes for a minute, willing time to stop. James Taylor, the perennial family favorite, sang his mellow rendition of "The Christmas Song." I counted my blessings. Twinkle lights reflected in the floor-to-ceiling windows of our octagonal living room, which was resplendent with deep red poinsettias. Each year, right after Thanksgiving, Jack—never given to minimalism—visited the nursery whose commercials he had voiced for years and returned home with dozens of *Flores de Noche Buena* to begin the holiday season.

We gathered around the tree, which gleamed with tiny, sparkling lights and the colorful tin ornaments—angels, cactus, hearts, pineapples, pigs, and the Virgin Mary—Jack and I had collected on our multiple trips to Oaxaca, our favorite romantic getaway. The basket of pomander balls—oranges studded with cloves—filled the room with a sweet and spicy fragrance.

When he thought the time was right, oldest son Brent, slim and toned in perfectly tailored khaki pants and a green sweater, stood and announced, "Time for the presents."

Every Christmas, our family draws names for a lavish and lengthy gift exchange. Jennifer had drawn my mom's name but was not with us that night. This year, two years after the loss of baby Ella, Jennifer had gone home to celebrate her mom's birthday and the holiday season with her family in New Jersey. Bo, meanwhile, would be working Christmas morning on the air as the new kid on the block; radio doesn't close for the holidays. Jen would return on the twenty-fifth, and the two of them would have their Christmas together late that evening.

Tonight, Bo, wearing a denim shirt and Dr. Seuss Christmas tie, took great care in escorting his frail grandmother to the wingback chair she preferred near the fire.

"Can I bring you anything, Gigi?" he asked.

She demurred. We joined her in the living room.

Jamie plunked a Santa hat on Jack's head, and he sat himself down amid the gifts.

"Okay—first present." He pulled a shiny, emerald green–wrapped gift box from the collection under the tree and gave it to Jamie.

As she opened her gift, the family settled into our gift-giving tradition. Christmas Eve, adults. Christmas morning, all about Santa.

"Mom, I'm wild about these earrings—so cool!" Jamie gushed. The effects of the bourbon lacing in the eggnog were evident as she put the ruby red garnet studs in her ears and twirled happily in the center of the room. Her deep purple velvet skirt swirled as she turned.

As the evening progressed, I grew a bit annoyed at Bo. I didn't understand why he kept insisting that my mom wait for her gift. The matriarch should be at the front of the line, I reasoned, especially since she was nodding off every once in a while. Across the room, Santa, my loving husband, gave me a "calm down" look.

"I need a bathroom break," Brent said—but instead of going down the hall to the bathroom, he cornered his brother in the dining room, talked a bit, and then helped himself to a plate of cookies. When he returned, he gave one to his grandmother. She grinned and crossed her legs, still long and graceful. Content in her bright red Christmas sweater with jingle bells and holly on the front, she took a bite.

Most of us helped ourselves to gingerbread cookies and fudge from the Christmas platter Brent placed on the coffee table, casting the calorie count aside.

Not Bo. He sat awhile, then got up and paced nervously in the kitchen, around the dining room table, and in the hallway before sitting back down.

The gift exchange continued happily, with oohs and aahs as we unwrapped each present one at a time to make the celebration last as long as possible.

The phone rang. Bo bounded into the kitchen, grabbed the phone, and talked quietly for a minute or two before returning to the living room. He handed the phone to his grandmother.

"It's for you, Gigi."

Mom smiled. I smiled, too, as she finished freshening her lipstick. The noise level and laughter dazed her a bit. Slowly, she put her tube of lipstick back into her little purse.

"Gigi, the phone is for you. It's Jennifer," Bo said again, a little louder this time, before handing her the phone with one hand and putting his other around her shoulder.

The gift exchange stopped.

"Gigi, this call is for you. It's Jennifer," Bo repeated, leaning in. "She drew your name and she is going to tell you about your present."

Collectively sensing something out of the ordinary, the gathering around the Christmas tree grew quiet. Jack turned the volume down on the music.

Mom held the phone close to her ear. Her head bobbed slowly up and down; her eyes misted a bit. Weary and slightly confused, she let the phone fall to her lap. Jamie went to her. Mom, in a whisper, relayed the Christmas Eve blessing to her granddaughter.

Jamie shattered the stillness by screaming, "They're having a baby."

We soon learned that Jen had said, "Gigi, I drew your name and wanted you to hear our good news first. Bo and I are going to have a baby. You are going to be a great-grandmother again."

Bo and Jen were pregnant once more.

The noise level skyrocketed to a ridiculous level—whooping, ecstatic hollering, and hugging. Bo, no longer antsy, crossed the room, retrieved the phone from his grandmother's lap, and kissed her gently on the cheek. He held it out at arm's length, chest high, so Jennifer could hear our unabashed excitement and joy. He, too, had a tear in his azure blue eyes. True to form, he had delivered their message in a most creative, surprising, and romantic way.

03

Chesapeake, named for the bay where her parents fell in love, arrived eight months later.

As the adorable little baby girl with hair the color of marmalade learned to smile, unbelievable news came once again. Ten months and ten days later, her brother, Cash, named for the Man in Black, was born, and Bo's family was completed.

Chapter 29
Peanut Butter

Peanut butter, a comforting commoner's cuisine, has spread itself throughout generations of my family.

The golden-brown glob has surfaced and resurfaced since the time of the Aztecs, who mashed roasted peanuts into a paste. Since the dawn of the modern peanut butter age—which took place around 1885—a relentless debate has raged over which version, creamy or crunchy, has the best consistency. Smooth conjures up either a puddle of nut oil or implies a very pleasant experience. Crunchy, with random chunks of the peanuts it came from, comes across as more substantial. In my opinion, there is no bad peanut butter, just personal preference.

Jack and I liked the salty-sweet staple so much, we surrounded ourselves with it at The Orange Woods—not only in the pantry but also on the walls. We selected a rich golden-brown paint to mimic the land on the mountains and hills beyond our windows. We cracked up at the paint store when we read the name of our choice on the color sample strip: Peanut Butter. The walls stayed that color for eighteen years. Peanut butter is easy to live with.

In the dining room of my youth, dinners were simple: meat, a well-cooked vegetable, potatoes, and usually my brother's favorite salad: iceberg lettuce leaf, a slice of Dole pineapple (in syrup), and a half-inch layer of Ocean Spray jellied cranberry, topped with a large spoonful of Miracle Whip.

Peanut butter appeared in our dining room on one condition: if, when the plates had been served, my father somehow deemed the meal unsubstantial, he would excuse himself, head to the pantry, and return with the peanut butter. Mark and I would watch Mom as her face slackened and she fiddled restlessly with the crisp apron in her lap. Not a word was said, but we understood, as Dad carefully mounded a knife full of peanut butter onto his Mrs. Baird's white bread, that the meal lacked something.

Dad singlehandedly elevated peanut butter's status regularly on Saturday afternoons, following his weekly golf game at the country club. Looking back, I'm sure Bloody Marys fueled the game. Dad enjoyed his golf game, and the booze, but the weekend's highlight occurred afterward, with his creative and methodical preparation of "The Gardner Fried Egg Sandwich."

His performance offered great sound effects. Bacon frying to a crisp; tomatoes sliced on the pig-shaped wooden cutting board; eggs in the skillet simmering to a little beyond over easy to prevent a dribbling golden yolk; and the repeated opening and closing of the Frigidaire for iceberg lettuce and the Miracle Whip he slathered on the bottom slice of bread over a generous spread of peanut butter. When he completed his tower—bread, peanut butter, mayo, iceberg lettuce, fried egg, tomato, bacon, salt and pepper—he topped it with a second, thickly slathered, peanut-buttered slice of bread.

"Peanut butter holds everything together," Dad would profess, admiring his masterpiece. He would then pour himself a large glass of milk before settling into his lord-of-the-manor chair at the end of the table, his elation palatable.

A nap followed.

Dad's Saturday morning routine gravitated toward TV trays and no Bloody Marys decades later, but the creamy peanut butter remained a constant throughout his life.

⟨⟩

My love of California faltered once, when Jack received a job offer back in Dallas. Longing to be a Texan once more, I begged him to consider the position. He did—and we lasted a year and a half.

Our friendship with the neighbors next door turned out to be the best part of our brief return to Texas. Our six children quickly became good friends. Jeanine and I instantly became inseparable. It took Norm, her slightly offbeat husband, and Jack a little longer to warm up to each other.

Norm's inner silliness was infectious. He told my young kids, "When your parents take you to a big, fancy brunch, always go to the dessert table first. You won't need anything else."

A tall, fit marathon runner who wore dolphin shorts year-round, he drank vegetable smoothies made in his $300 Vitamix machine long before the world got healthy.

"The family has gone back to Nebraska on vacation and I've got to be away three weeks on business," Norm told Jack one day. "Will you take care of my pool? You know, triple-digit weather can do bad things to a swimming pool."

"Sure, neighbor, glad to," Jack said. "Where you headed?"

"Helsinki."

"Travel safely. I've got you covered here."

The next evening, network news reported, "President Ford departed this morning for the Conference on Security and Cooperation in Europe. He plans to be out of our country for three weeks."

Jack yelled at me from the living room, "Hey babe, interesting, Ford is headed to Helsinki and so is Norm."

We came to find out that neighbor Norm served five US presidents as a Secret Service Agent. The stories of strength, courage, discipline, and outrageousness he told us over the next thirty years inspired and entertained us. He was as regimented a guy as you'd ever want to meet—the perfect candidate to give his life for the president of the United States.

Our return to Texas brought us lifelong friendships, close family ties for my children with aunts and uncles and cousins, and an unforeseen opportunity for me to support my parents and brother when Mark suffered a nervous breakdown.

But the best part of our brief return to Texas? Jeanine introduced us to the fabled Peanut Butter Fudge Cake, which instantly became the family favorite.

Our love affair with the Peanut Butter Fudge Cake has endured forty years. It is dreamy any time, but it's especially delightful with coffee the next morning.

When my youngest and most affectionate grandchild, Cash, turned nine, Jennifer asked him, "What do you want for your birthday, Cash?"

With great conviction, he returned, "Peanut Butter Fudge Cake."

Jennifer called me for the recipe. When she tucked Cash into bed the night before his birthday, she told him she had gotten it from me. "As soon as you fall asleep," she said, "I'm going to make the cake."

"It won't be as good as Neeny's," he replied.

Gotta love that little guy.

It wasn't all smooth. I smarted one morning when six-year-old Carly watched me apply my makeup foundation. "Your face looks like peanut butter, Neeny and you are very tall and wrinkled."

Chapter 30

Country Road

I became an artist (and a farmer) during our Orange Woods years.

One cool autumn day, Jack and Steamer hiked ahead of me, walking together on a country road without a soul in sight, the stillness palpable. I took my iPhone from my backpack and snapped an unforgettable picture of the two of them—both unaware, both lost in thought.

A dense woodland loomed ahead of their path, and a clearing beyond; they provided a perfect background for my piece. Jack yearned to be in the woods among nature's abundance of trees. He grew up in a modest, square house on Waite Street in Gary, Indiana. There, he often escaped to the thicket of woods behind his house—a place where he could commune with nature.

Jack never got over loving the tranquility, privacy, and awe-inspiring beauty of a wooded space. Every autumn, without fail, he would be overcome with wanderlust, aching to return to the woods. It touched my heart to watch him and his beloved dog walk into the trees ahead of me on this pristine October day.

As I followed, I took in deep breaths of the pines along the road and the dampened earth below my feet. I relished the autumn season, too. "Life starts all over again when it gets crisp in the fall," writes F. Scott Fitzgerald in *The Great Gatsby*. I agree wholeheartedly.

Home in my studio later, I stared at the photo of my two favorite subjects. The effects of the light fascinated me, just as it had captured the imagination of Claude Monet and his renegade band of French artists, the Impressionists, over one hundred and fifty years before.

I experimented with the depiction of light as I composed my piece. This may sound simple, but it is darned difficult, at least for me. In a work of art, it is vital to interpret both the light source and its effects correctly. If the sun is shining on the left side of the tree, the shadow will be on the right side. Light can be blinding, can be diffused, can sparkle—and without a doubt can be the most significant element in a work of art.

As I painted the black dog and his master walking in the light of day on the lone country road, I gave the work a hint of a surrealistic effect, using unnatural colors—purples and teals—for the silent, beckoning trees. I painted the long, curving road coral and magenta, and shot it through with gold. A brilliant spray of light on the road beyond the two reflected back onto their figures, giving one side of their faces an ethereal halo effect. I loved that I had painted my humble guy in a baseball hat and his favorite worn-out red sweatshirt.

As they strolled, Jack and Steamer were bathed in the sunlight that emanated from the sky overhead and to their left. The light created a life-size shadow that fell on the side of the road to the right. It surprised me that the two of them morphed into a silent, single, ominous figure in shadow there in the gravel and dirt. A deep purple anthropomorphic shadow that looked like a large, irregular puzzle piece—their two images united there on that country path. They were connected, yet Jack looked far away into the distance, while Steamer, always obedient, looked down at the road.

Chapter 31

Bocce Ball

For a long time, I collected ideas to incorporate into our castle in the country. The inspiration for the stone fireplace, the lighting indoors and out, the wine bottle garden, the wide art gallery hall, and the entry all came from photographs and magazine clippings I had saved over the years. I stacked our firewood in a meticulous arrangement under a set of orange trees in a curvilinear design I had copied from Martha Stewart's magazine.

The idea for our bottle tree came from *Metropolitan Magazine,* which featured one a bit more elegant than ours at the end of a luxurious mansion's expansive tiled veranda. It took some real creative persuasion, but one autumn day Jack and I, armed with my magazine photo, visited a wrought iron factory in Rosarito Beach in Baja, ten miles south of the border.

"*Sí, señora,*" the man at the factory told me, "*puedo construirlo, sólo una semana. Sólo ciento cincuenta dólares!*"

We left and returned the following week in my SUV. When questioned by guards at the border, we told them the bulky and odd-shaped object on top of our car was our new Christmas tree!

Jack installed the bottle tree outside the winery and strung it with lights; I filled it with colored wine bottles, one on each iron branch. It was an unorthodox year-round Christmas tree, and I loved it.

෪

Steamer stood four feet high and weighed one hundred and eight pounds. Each time we added something new to The Orange Woods, like the bottle tree, he delighted in stationing himself nearby in some kind of show of ownership. He often wrapped his long body around the base of the bottle tree after its installation.

Early on, our long, lean black dog deduced that if he stretched out across a walkway or path, it would be impossible for either Jack or me to proceed without scratching his back or petting him. At his full horizontal elongation, he measured a tad over eight feet. His was a subtle way of seeking attention. At the entrance to the winery, we placed a photo, printed on metal, of Steamer—his right ear standing straight up, his frame fully extended as he slept in front of four wooden barrels. To get to the barrels, he stated, ask the guard dog for permission.

og

The idea of creating a bocce ball court began serendipitously one Sunday morning.

"Oh my gosh, honey, let's do this," I exclaimed. "A backyard bocce ball court—only five hundred dollars. Look here. It tells you exactly how to do it!" I thrust the article under Jack's nose.

"Babe, we've got enough on our plates right now," he said. "Let's wait a while."

My mind flashed to weathered Italian men wearing Panama hats and drinking jug wines playing the game on a sun-dappled afternoon. It looked very cool in my head.

"We don't have to do it," I pleaded. "Jesús can knock this out in a weekend."

Three Valencia orange trees gave their lives for the court, which ended up regulation size (13 feet by 91 feet), thanks to my persistence. "If we're gonna' do it, let's do it right," I reasoned.

Over the next three weekends, our workers dug, framed, and leveled the area and filled it with three inches of base rock. On top, a two- or three-inch layer of glistening white processed oyster shells, which we found at a feed store nearby that had been mentioned in the article. Over time, when the court needed refreshing, Amazon delivered the oyster shells to our door.

A month later, we christened the court and Jack informed me that the five-hundred-dollar "do-it-yourself" backyard bocce ball court had, in reality, cost us well over three thousand dollars, plus the three orange trees removed to make space. Our dream was never cost efficient, I'm afraid.

og

One of our favorite ways to entertain in the nice weather became happy hour and bocce ball games. One small pallina (the yellow target ball), eight brightly colored larger balls, and refreshments always promised a good time.

The best time we ever had on the court happened on Father's Day, a few weeks after its completion. Ahead of Dad's Day that year, 2006, we drew for names, teams of two. Ability doesn't matter much in the game—the way we played it, at least—so we paired one adult and one kid. Each team competed not only for the win but also for "Best Uniform" prize.

Jack and little Calvin, Grandpa and grandson in white straw hats, were "The Good Guys." Eight-year-old Carly, who had recently started wearing glasses, paired with me. On white T-shirts, we drew cartoon faces of girls with frizzy hair wearing spectacles. We were "The Four Eyes!" Uberhunter son-in-law Bud and ten-year-old Sophie—decked out head-to-toe in camouflage—ultimately took the prize. Sophie later went on to become a vegetarian.

Chapter 32
The Labyrinth

Creating our labyrinth ended up being less expensive than building our bocce ball court, and not nearly as confrontational as laying out the vineyard. It did involve a great deal of research, however. Turned out, the best place for our research was France.

Our second trip there two years after we became farmers convinced me that we needed a labyrinth at The Orange Woods.

After Paris, we visited a cathedral in the medieval town of Chartres that was built during the height of Gothic expression in France. I dragged Jack along on this pilgrimage. He resisted, saying, "But, Mademoiselle, I prefer to savor a bottle of fine French wine and *une assiette de fromage* at our favorite bistro on the Left Bank in Paris. *Oui, oui?*"

"Honey, please come," I insisted. "I need to show you what I'm talking about. A labyrinth would be the perfect addition to The Orange Woods."

Reluctantly, Jack came along, and the meditative aura of the intricate design of stones—set into the floor of the nave of the cathedral by unknown stonemasons in the twelfth century—pulled him in. Because of the cathedral's impressive size, the labyrinth itself is equally grand. A sense of awe came over me as we entered. Jack removed his sunglasses and breathed in deeply, as if to honor the hands that had created this masterpiece, beautiful, geometric, and sacred.

My determined quest continued in the south of France, where, several days later, we first experienced fields swathed in the fragrant mauve blooms of lavender at Notre-Dame de Sénanque Abbey. The majestic stone medieval relic sits at the bottom of a deep canyon behind the village of Gordes, where the Senancole River flows past fragrant pines, olive trees, and unending rows of manicured Provence lavender plants.

Our guide, a debonair French sort wearing a black beret, explained that the abbey was home to a quiet community of Cistercian monks who meticulously grew and cared for not only the lavender but also the honey bees. We hoped to get a glimpse of the monks, sometimes called The White Monks for their undyed white habits, but they stayed discreetly out of sight.

Jack and I stood silent, marveling at the expanse of mounds of lilac bouquets—slender, amethyst banners undulating their way to the walls of the stone abbey. I could not believe my eyes or my nose; a sensory overload of unbelievable aromas and vistas engulfed us.

"I read that Empress Josephine, the wife of Napoleon, favored lavender and used it lavishly in her home," I had told Jack at breakfast. "Supposedly she gave her husband a cup of hot chocolate flavored with lavender, thought to be an aphrodisiac, at night."

Now, gazing out at the fields, Jack whispered, "Napoleon would have willingly surrendered to Josephine here."

His quick wit charmed the pants off me right there in the lavender fields.

The smell intoxicated us. Once more, the poet Charles Baudelaire's words drifted through my mind: ". . . perfumes that fill my nostrils and my soul." I yearned to have this warm, heady scent drenching the air at The Orange Woods.

At dinner that evening, on my cocktail napkin, I sketched an initial plan for The Orange Woods labyrinth. It would be made Chartres-style, with rounded sides and eleven concentric circles.

"We can line it with smooth white river rocks and plant the lavender along the path," I said, plotting at high-throttle speed. "How about if we situate it right outside the French doors of our bedroom? Can you imagine, with the doors open on a summer morning, waking into the tantalizing, sensuous fragrance of our own backyard aromatherapy?"

Whenever I pummeled him with fast-popping thoughts and ideas in this way, Jack called me "Popcorn Brain."

ᴄ⳹

Just before the rainy season the following year we created The Orange Woods labyrinth, stone by stone. We had lots of help in the endeavor—enthusiastic in the beginning, reluctant as we progressed. Bayley and

Maddie were seven; Sophie, five; Carly and Calvin, three-year-old toddlers; Chesapeake and Cash, not yet on my grandchildren screen.

We invited ourselves to babysit the little gang one weekend with our labyrinth project in mind. For several weeks, Jack had hauled white stones from a friend's riverbed and dumped them near our proposed site. The last load filled the bed of his truck on this sunshiny Saturday morning. He and I had carefully marked the design of our labyrinth with blue spray paint in the half-acre plot beyond our bedroom doors. Several large Valencia orange trees shaded the area.

The paths of our concentric circles were to be four feet wide—wide enough for me to stroll hand in hand with a grandchild. When it was all laid out, Jack and I would plant the lavender between the white stones so we could enjoy the beneficial and pleasant scent of the lavender as we walked.

The kids were crazy about Papa's big truck. In the beginning, they were ecstatic to climb up into the bed and throw the white stones onto the ground.

Maddie, her blonde hair cut in a bob and her smile missing a tooth or two, assumed her leadership role as foreman, standing solo in the bed of the truck. As the others stood wide-eyed and eager on the ground below, she instructed, "Pick up a rock or more and take them to Papa or Neeny."

Predictably, mighty little Calvin dived into the project, carrying three or four rocks at a time. Carly, two months younger and a head taller than her cousin, went at a more leisurely pace, often strolling away from the construction site. Bayley and Sophie, good little worker bees at first, eventually protested, "Maddie, when do we get up there to throw rocks?"

Our little work crew soon became disgruntled. A pint-sized sit-down strike followed.

"Neeny, we're hungry," they chimed in unison. "And we're tired, too."

Half the stones were placed at this point, and Papa decided the little ones deserved a picnic. After they slurped the last of their root beer floats, I read "Wead It To Me Wufas, I Can't Wead" from *The Goody Good Book of Stories,* a coffee table–size picture book that was a favorite from my childhood. Written in 1943, the book is full of delightful illustrations of angelic, chubby little children much like the content little workers who snuggled together on the couch next to me.

Jack and I chuckled over the kids' contributions later that week as we finished placing the stones. In between the path's edging of white stones, as planned, we planted Provence lavender, two hundred plants in all.

 С3

Several years later, I watched as Sophie's hair—the color of creamy mashed potatoes—fell in silken strands onto the profusion of fragrant lavender piled in her lap. Her delicate hands worked gingerly to braid the long, fragile stems with pink satin ribbons. Her little nose was no more than four inches from her project, a lavender wand.

Maddie and Bayley had long since given up making their own wands and were snuggled close to one another in the family-size red porch swing near the fountain, telling secrets and giggling. Sophie, who had turned eight just as the lavender field spewed the summer's purple rain of alluring blossoms, focused on her task as if hypnotized.

What joy to have all the kids at The Orange Woods! I read once that it's the grandmother's charge to keep the cousins connected. I had planned a girls' afternoon, drinking lemonade, eating cookies, and making lavender wands while the guys golfed. Mom's arthritic hands had given up before the two older girls did. I worried that the project was too difficult, but Sophie worked with surprising diligence, following the instructions I had found in *Sunset Magazine*. It was perfect timing for this particular craft; I had picked bunches of the florets before the bees came calling earlier in the morning, and the newly harvested lavender flowers and stems were pliable.

Lavender wands were famously made by Victorian ladies who had leisure time to spend weaving intricate patterns with silky ribbons and long-stemmed lavender flowers. They would slip the wands into drawers and onto pillows or shelves to enhance their surroundings with the pleasant fragrance.

Sophie mastered her difficult craft, weaving the stems over and under the ribbons into an aromatic basket design. Her eyes, riveted to her project, exhibited her fierce determination and can-do attitude.

At the end of the day when the family gathered, Sophie sashayed into the room, head bent slightly downward, with her hands clasped behind the waist of her flouncy red skirt. Brent, flush from his win on the golf course, put down his beer and motioned his middle child to come close.

"What have you got there, Sophie?"

She sidled up to her dad and, after a moment's hesitation, pulled the lavender wand from behind and held it up proudly above her head—a mini Statue of Liberty. The smile on her face as she exhibited her finished masterpiece made every moment Jack and I had spent adding another bit of magic to The Orange Woods worthwhile.

ᴄ𝟹

Over the years, we did wake to the restorative, pleasurable scent of the lavender many mornings. We shared giant bouquets with friends. We made lavender lemonade, lavender bath salts and we made countless lavender wands.

One summer, Carly and I made satin scented eye sachets, silky soft eye pillows that we finished with a label that read "Made in Pauma Valley." (The label was made in China.)

Carly Mae, granddaughter number four, now a preteen, and I spent lazy days together over my mom's Singer sewing machine. First we sewed a muslin liner, then filled it with dried lavender blossoms and organic flax seeds, and then created a satin covering for it before hand stitching each one closed at the end. The Gift Fair was coming up at the country club, and Carly decided to sell her lavender eye pillows—fifty in all—there.

At the Gift Fair, Carly spread out a portion of her soft, lilac-colored sachets on the counter and placed her cash box nearby. Vendors selling art, fashion items, wines, and food items surrounded her. Her sales were lackluster for the first part of the day.

At lunchtime, however, a wacky golfer of sorts, clad in clashing wild colors, came off the course and into the Gift Fair. Carly's secret crush, the wacky movie star of *Caddy Shack* who called Pauma Valley home part time, Bill Murray, stopped at her booth.

"What are these?" Murray asked in his signature comic manner, juggling several in the air.

"Lavender sachets for your eyes," Carly replied in a nervous manner, trying not to act star struck.

With a dramatic flair, he removed his sunglasses, thrust his head back, and, with adoring fans looking on, arched his back, stretched his arms out like a ballerina and placed one lavender sachet over his eyes. In a stage voice he quipped, "Like this?"

He bought every one of her remaining eye pillows. As an extremely flustered Carly bagged his purchase, he leaned across the counter and lovingly pinched her nose. Much more intoxicating than the lavender, I could tell.

CB

The lavender lining the paths of our labyrinth brought great joy to our lives. Serenity, grace, and calmness, too.

In the end, our labyrinth, which burst forth with a mix of floral, sweet, and herbal scents each summer, became our quiet, hallowed place, where the simple act of walking offered us peace and solace. We shared time with family and friends there. We recuperated from illness and surgeries there. We were able to grieve there. A sacred space, it was our cathedral.

Chapter 33

Surgeries

For two longtime professional people accustomed to regular massages, manicures, and multiple annual mini-vacations, life in the country presented massive challenges. We demolished, constructed, planted, pruned, weeded, repaired, hauled, and rebuilt with great enthusiasm and energy. Our lives as retired working folks took its toll. Not surprising, when I look back at our Week of January 5, 2003 to-do list:

- Prune forty rosebushes
- Plant Asian pear and Santa Rosa plum
- Plant succulents under the oaks
- Spray grapevines with dormant oil spray
- Spray pre-emergence
- Fertilize camellias and azaleas
- Plant Mom's Mexican Blue Palm Tree
- Repair all irrigation under orange trees
- Reconfigure irrigation in sanctuary area
- Begin pruning of Sangiovese vines
- Wrap new cuttings in peat moss
- Pick up load of organic fertilizer for Valencias
- Distribute bags of fertilizer throughout grove for spreading.

Without a doubt, we were officially farmers.

CB

"Okay, I'm ready. Are you done?" I prodded Jack as we wrote our 2010 New Year's resolutions. I reigned as the consummate list maker. Him, not so much.

I persisted. "Should I go first?"

He nodded.

"My number one resolution—absolutely no surgeries. Stay out of hospitals all year," I read with emphasis.

"Whoa, that's a good one," he said, smiling at me. I'm sure my short list surprised him, since losing weight, reading more books, and spending more time with family were perpetually at the top of my resolutions.

"Not only for me—you too, buddy!" I said. "And we shouldn't make any other resolutions; don't want to dilute the focus on this one."

He crossed the room, picked up my coffee cup for a refill and gestured for a high-five on what had just become our joint resolution for 2010. Steamer sat up and raised his paw when he saw our high-five. Jack obliged.

Perhaps first-time farmers and vintners in their sixties should have taken it a little easier than we did. The infrastructure of our formerly healthy bodies suffered as our home and crops thrived. The hills were steep, the tasks backbreaking, and the equipment heavy. And all this just as arthritis came calling on our joints.

Between 2003 and 2009, Jack and I had donned the light blue surgery ensembles—one lightweight gown open in the front, a second gown open in the back, covering the gap in front; fuzzy socks with rubber treads on the bottom; and a billowy hair net much like the one the guy behind the salad bar wears—and been wheeled into the operating room eleven times. Never together.

The frequency and the severity of our combined surgeries in flash time finally got the best of me when I had my left knee replaced. When I was dressed in the Marilyn Blue Gown surgical outfit, Jack kissed me goodbye and the attendant wheeled me into the operating room area. Moments later, Dr. Bugby appeared at my side. Just as he began to speak, I burst into tears—the full-on, bawling kind. The anesthesiologist and OR nurses stopped motion as I sobbed out loud, uncontrollably. As soon as he gained his composure, the doctor leaned toward me, put his hand on my shoulder, and said softly, "Marilyn, what's wrong?"

"This is the fourth time I've been here," I choked out, "and I'm afraid I'm going to die on the operating table."

In the retelling, it's clear that I had worked myself into an irrational frenzy. My theatrics did liven the place up—and, minutes later, the anesthesia calmed me down. Still, the litany of surgeries that left us both bionic and guaranteed full-body patdowns in TSA airport screening lines for the rest of our lives stuns me even now:

2004   Jack, double knee replacement
          Marilyn, arthroscopic surgery, left knee

2005   Marilyn, left total shoulder replacement

2006   Marilyn, laminectomy
          Jack, left shoulder replacement
          Marilyn, double fusion L3-4, L4-5

2007   Marilyn, left thumb ligament reconstruction and tendon inter-
          position (LRTI)
          Jack, hernia operation

2008   Marilyn, right thumb LRTI

2009   Jack, right rotator cuff surgery
          Marilyn, left total knee replacement.

We marveled at our good fortune all year in 2010, the year of our resolve, and for another five years after that, we repeated the same number one New Year's Resolution each year: no more surgeries.

To help us keep our resolution, we did begin to use workers more for the heavy lifting.

ℭ

Jack's knee surgery—both knees replaced on the same day, by the same surgeon—was the first in our long line of visits to the operating room during The Orange Woods years. The prospect scared us both much more than we freely communicated to one another. I calmed my nerves by writing. I stayed by his side throughout the ordeal, and I wrote this on day three, February 1, 2004, in my journal:

> I married a Marine. Many of us have pedigrees, provenance and PhDs. He got his in Boot Camp.
> I married my Marine forty years ago. Over the years, Jack has assumed many roles, most notably—iron worker, salesman, disc

jockey, entrepreneur, father, talk show host, CEO, grandfather, friend, farmer and vintner. Through every incarnation, he has steadfastly remained a Marine.

I have tried to figure out what it is that is Marine about him all these years out of the Corps. The way he stands at attention when the flag goes by? The way he pleats and smooths his shirt in the back before tucking it into his pants? Or the way he approaches a crowd—no fear?

He and I have talked at length about it. We pegged it swagger, a word whose first recorded uses in the late 1500s are in Shakespeare's Midsummer Night's Dream and King Lear. Probably a form of swag, a verb meaning to sway or strut in a defiant manner.

A Marine swaggers.

He has always been my proud, strong Marine, until last Wednesday, when his sixty-seven-year-old knees (both of them) were removed and replaced with titanium ones. I cried when they wheeled him out of recovery. So ashen, so frail, so zonked. The whites of his eyes matched the whites of his teeth. No sign of a swagger.

The next two days were even worse. The fear of pain compounds the actual, excruciating pain. He shook, he moaned, he protested, he pumped the morphine. No swagger. Nauseated, dizzy, weak beyond words. When they tried to sit him up, he couldn't. When he finally stood, he shuffled like Tim Conway on the Carol Burnett Show. I could tell he had begun to believe that he (we) had made a dreadful mistake. The pain, far worse than the old knees had ever delivered, persisted. He'd never play golf again. He'd be in rehab for months, he mourned. We were each frightened, remorseful, depressed, and hopeless. We tried desperately not to let each other understand the extent of our secret fears.

Super Bowl Sunday came three days after surgery. I can't recall who played. Doesn't matter. Our own campaign went on in Room 608.

First came a wonder woman of a nurse who sat him up and bathed him from head to toe. She washed his hair—recently cut, boot camp style—shaved his emerging beard, and slathered him in lotion. The color began to return to his face, and his pearly whites began to glisten in a smile once more.

The physical therapist came next. He stood him up, wrapped a strong white belt around his waist, and off they went. "Out of the nest today," said super PT.

Before my watchful eyes, my Marine resurfaced. With amazing strength, he raised himself to a standing position, gripped his walker with both hands, and began to march. Ten steps to the door. Another twenty-five steps to the other side of the hall. He turned and plodded all the way back to the hospital bed that had been his cradle for the past eighty-plus hours.

Just before he maneuvered back to parade rest, he stopped by the side of the bed, clenched his right fist and, in a rapid downward motion, gestured with surprising emphasis and bellowed, "YES!" Under his breath, he avowed, "Semper Fi."

Jack understood in that moment that he had weathered the worst. Most importantly, he could conquer; he began to swagger again.

I got a glimpse of the swagger later that day. As Jack struggled valiantly to walk down the hall a second time, the back of his hospital gown came open. He flashed me as he swaggered defiantly down the hall.

Chapter 34

Good-byes

Rub-a-dub-dub—but actually, it wasn't three men in a tub. It was two men and a woman.

In reality, not two men and a woman but their ashes. And the ashes were in a tub for no more than an hour or so.

In the *Wall Street Journal,* I read that undertakers have coined the phrase "wildcat scattering" to refer to the practice of "love, honor, cherish, and scatter." The article said, "More Americans these days are scattering loved ones' ashes widely, with great purpose and often without permission. The funeral industry, obviously, suffers from this practice. It's a reflection of both the marked rise in cremation and the growing desire by people to find their own ways to ritualize grief."

According to the National Funeral Directors Association, in 2016, over half of Americans chose cremation over burial. The rates flipped in 2015. There is evidence, often revealed at cocktail parties, that choosing to scatter the ashes rather than preserve them in an urn or bury them in a cemetery continues to become more and more widespread.

None of this mattered to me before the Millennium. However, when my legendary, larger-than-life father died suddenly that year, it began to.

Together, as a family, we went back to Texas after Dad's death for a traditional, well-attended funeral at the Chapelwood Methodist Church in Houston, where my parents sat in the same front-row seat in the balcony every Sunday for thirty years, singing hymns—"Faith of Our Fathers" and the Methodist Doxology "Praise God from Whom All Blessings Flow." The pastor offered meaningful comments at the funeral, illustrating both his admiration and respect for my father. Dad's grandchildren's artfully crafted remembrances brought tears to the full house.

Before relocating to the Pauma Valley Country Club in our backyard in San Diego County, Mom and Dad had lived in Houston for over three decades. Ever practical, they had paid-in-full cemetery plots there. But with Mom, Jack, our children, their children, and me, his daughter, all living within thirty minutes of that same country club, it didn't seem right to put Dad in the ground back in Texas. Mom and Dad had been together for over seventy years; she needed him nearby.

In the days since my dad had died, Jack had reminded us several times what he'd said over and over: "If Charline didn't object, I'd ask you to scatter my ashes over The Orange Woods. This place is very special."

Collectively, we decided on cremation for Dad. He became the first in the long line of our family to be placed somewhere other than a cemetery with a modest headstone. His ashes were instead placed in an expensive, sapphire blue urn, Mom's brokenhearted selection at the crematorium.

Within a week, in a secluded spot at The Orange Woods, Jack and I had created a sanctuary: a memory garden on flat ground under the Valencia orange trees in a park-like setting behind our home. We planted a crimson red rose, the Chrysler Imperial, and Jack dug a hole two and a half feet deep as I sat nearby with Steamer at my feet. Occasionally, our dog would approach Jack's project, lie down, and put his nose at the edge of the hole, looking to his master for approval.

I leaned down and picked up a handful of the moist, fresh dug-up earth, took a moment to inhale its richness, and then let it stream through my fingers back onto the ground. Steamer pawed at the dirt, the fertile earth that tendered our oranges and grapes. Jack set Dad's urn to one side in the opening of the ground and carefully replaced the soil around it. When he was done filling the hole, he mounded soil, patting it in place, to mark the position. Steamer put his paw on the mound and looked up at Jack once again for approval. The three of us sat in silence.

We installed a wooden bench for Mom nearby. A few weeks later, she memorialized the site with a fake-concrete stepping-stone, purchased from her favorite catalog. It read, "If tears could build a stairway and memories a lane, I'd walk right up to Heaven and bring you back again."

When the family gathered the following Christmas Eve, Jack brought Mom's jade green pashmina to her and wrapped her in it. Gently, he walked her outside to the garden bench in the sanctuary. Inside, Christmas music played, and children did too. I walked to the sliding glass door in the hall and watched as Jack sat Mom down on the bench, took clippers from his jacket, and cut the single red rose from that lone tree, an extraordinary red flower in full bloom on my Dad's birthday, December 24. After cutting the thorns off, he returned to the bench, sat down beside my grieving mother, and handed her the flower. He put his arms around her and she lowered her head onto his shoulder as she smelled the fragrant rose.

My eyes teared a bit as Jack ushered Mom back into the house, cradling her affectionately and protectively. The glossy leaves of the orange trees shimmered in support. In Mom's hand, the red rose, a symbol of love.

03

When, four years later, the unexpected happened once again and I received the call that my brother had collapsed at work, I flew to Dallas immediately, arriving in the wee small hours. The fourth floor of Parkland Memorial Hospital looked deserted. The dark, quiet corridors, carved into my brain as JFK's final stop that November afternoon, loomed large, cold, and scary.

As I approached his room, Mark's heavy, labored breathing prevailed. Besides the sound of his breath and occasional beeping of the monitoring machines, an unnatural stillness filled the room. An empty sensation in the pit of my stomach overcame me as I did my best to calm my nerves.

At his bedside, I paused, lowered my head to his heart, stretched my arms across his chest, and embraced his near-lifeless body.

Mark, who had endured the most difficult life imaginable, even had difficulty dying. He struggled for another thirty-six hours before he died and lay in peace, probably for the first time in more than sixty years.

We cremated his body, got a license for transport, and brought his ashes, in a simple wooden urn, to California.

In sharp contrast to Dad's memorial observance, for Mark we held a simple, intimate service on a bright Sunday morning in our Memory Garden, just family. The flowers were red, white, and blue carnations in a design of the state flag of Texas, the only home he'd ever known.

Later that day, Jack re-dug the hole he'd created four years earlier and put Mark's ashes in the ground, close to Dad's. At last, my father and my brother could coexist in harmony.

CβЗ

Mom turned ninety, and Jack and I struggled with her driving. She regularly motored two-tenths of a mile across Highway 76 to the Beauty Affair, a salon straight out of Steel Magnolias. Twice a week—shampoo, set, and community. Her last excursion ended in a collision when she pulled out of the country club gates in front of a red hatchback car going 55 mph. The impact totaled Mom's Lincoln Town Car; three farm workers who'd been riding in the little red car left the scene on backboards in ambulances. When I arrived on the scene, I found Mom smiling, slightly dazed but unharmed, surrounded by police and EMTs.

After the shock of it all, Jack and I grappled with how to take the car away from Mom. At dinner the next evening at Lazy H, after rehearsing what we were going to say a few times at home, Jack began.

"Honey, you really need to think about not driving anymore. Both Marilyn and I—"

"Oh, thank you so much," Mom interrupted. She took a big gulp of her white zinfandel. "Every time I pulled to the front gate, I would stop a minute and say a prayer that I would get home without hurting myself or someone else."

I'm sure the loss of my father and brother accelerated Mom's decline. Within a year and a half after Mark's passing, she moved into an assisted living facility where she spent her final days. In the beginning, she played Bingo and enjoyed the visiting dogs and musical entertainment. That didn't last long.

She did continue to get her hair and nails done twice a week. Her hospice caregiver wheeled her to the beauty salon to have her hair permed three days before she died.

Frustration and depression filled Mom's final year, living in one modest room on a long hall. "It's living in a motel," she grumbled often.

Sitting with her in the quiet cafeteria one evening, Jack and I watched her play with her food, pushing the broccoli around the plate.

"More tea," Mom muttered to me; her shaky left hand held up her empty glass.

As I walked away from the table, she leaned close to Jack and in a stage-whisper said, "Get me out of here."

Her loving son-in-law put his arm around her and patted her hand. "Honey, you bet your life I would if I could. But you need to be here, where they can take good care of you."

After I brought her tea, he looked at her freshly manicured bright red nails and teased, "You look like a vamp."

Mom, the eternal flirt, coyly replied, "I am."

 og

She stopped eating on a Sunday afternoon in August. She simply turned her face away.

I had stayed with her the night before. After combing her thin hair, moisturizing her face, hands, and feet, and putting balm on her dry, cracked lips, I'd crawled in bed with her and hugged her. In the quiet, I struggled a bit, but managed to tell her good things—mainly that it was okay to go, we would be fine and that she had been the most extraordinary wife, mother, grandmother and great-grandmother. "You know, Mom, you're going to be with Dad soon," I whispered. My frail, fragile mother said nothing; her head nodded once, very slowly. We spent her last night curled up together in her twin bed.

The next morning, I tried to feed her breakfast. She refused and went back to sleep. Jamie came for a short while, so I could take a quick break and a shower. When she left to pick up Carly, Brent arrived. We had the entire weekend tag team set up.

On my way back to Mom, my phone rang. Brent, Mom's first grandchild, said through his tears, "Gigi's gone, Mom. She just stopped breathing."

Mom and I had talked a lot about what would happen when she died. After Dad's cremation, bravely, she'd insisted on the same. In her heart, I knew, she would have preferred a nice little gravesite with flowers, but I could never get her to admit it. Even now, her devotion to my father was unshakable. And so, we did as she said she wished.

Cʒ

We held the memorial for Mom at twilight, that precious time between daylight and darkness, on the Sunset Deck at The Orange Woods. Again, the grandchildren spoke their tribute and memories so eloquently. Jamie, who had been devoted to Mom, especially during her last decade in Pauma Valley—peanut butter and jelly sandwiches and a game of Spite and Malice two times a week—was the most emotional. Over and over, she paused and apologized, "I need a moment." Bo, also in tears, brought props—the Dallas Cowboy Cheerleader doll she'd made for him, and the broken glass cookie jar he'd always raided. Brent, reliably, spoke on a global level, inserting his grandmother into the history of the world during her lifetime. My game-playing oldest son ended his tribute to his grandmother by relating tales of her lifelong passion for games of all kinds. Their first game together: Parcheesi. Their last: bocce ball at The Orange Woods when she turned ninety-three.

My game-loving mother had started the Mah Jongg Club at the Pauma Valley Country Club. Her friends and fellow players were with us on this day, as were our dearest friends; they adored my mother.

As the sun set, the scene sparkled with crystal, silver, fresh flowers, and candlelight, like her home always had. Ten years before, five-year-old Maddie, wide-eyed and full of wonder, had whispered on seeing her great-grandmother's home in Pauma Valley for the first time, "Gigi's house is so fancy." At the evening's end, I smiled thinking to myself, *If Mom had been here, she would have turned her wine glass upside down often, signaling for a refill.*

Immense appreciation of my mother overcame me as her warmth enveloped me; I felt her gentleness comfort me. How on earth had I been so blessed?

Cʒ

Within a week, we began our steps to put my family to rest, together.

Jack dug up Dad and then Mark. In our greenhouse, he opened Dad's urn and removed the plastic bag containing my father's ashes. Continuing, he did the same with my brother's wooden urn. As he did this, I took Dad's now-empty blue urn to the crematorium.

"This is highly unorthodox, Mrs. Woods," the solemn gentleman in the dark suit said.

I insisted, handing him the gently used urn. When he returned from the inner sanctum, my mother's ashes were in my dad's urn and I returned home with Mom riding shotgun.

In the meantime, Jack rummaged in the kitchen and found my largest container, a big acrylic punchbowl, and my sturdiest wooden spatula. Returning to the greenhouse, he put both my brother's and my father's ashes in the round plastic container. He attempted to stir and combine them. However, after being in the cold ground for several years, the ashes were solidified. Jack had to do some major "un-clumping." Eventually, he blended an even combination of the boys. Mom, decidedly lighter than either Dad or Mark, went in with ease. My family, together at last.

Jack had a momentary dilemma when he finished combining, reluctant to wash his hands and send the residue down the drain. After some serious thought, he elected to rinse his hands with the garden hose, with the runoff going into the blueberry patch.

At the end of his greenhouse project, I thanked him and we embraced amidst the pots, potting soil, garden tools, and fertilizer, all used for creating new growth.

ഇ

And so began the scattering of my beloved family.

"Where should we start?" Jack asked as the sun began to set that September evening.

"I want them everywhere at The Orange Woods," I said.

We scattered a small portion at the entry, amidst the lavender in the labyrinth, up and down the rows of grapes, under some of the orange trees, in the raised vegetable gardens, and even a bit on the bocce ball court. Long, lanky, loyal Steamer followed close behind. Off and on, Jack and I cried. When we did, it made our faithful black dog extremely nervous—unsure what to do, how to help. He stayed between us, keeping pace as we walked and scattered. When we were finished and contemplating my beloved family from the Sunset Deck, I noticed an ashen smudge on Jack's cheek where he had wiped away a tear. I leaned over the table and wiped the smudge with my thumb, which only made it messier. I smiled.

ભ

As planned, we dispensed just one-fourth of the combined ashes that first evening. We had plans for the rest.

We designated the second fourth for Brent and Laurie's ranch, where the family gathers several times each year. After scattering the ashes in the cold November air, we warmed ourselves in front of a roaring fire, and I thought about my mom. She delighted in coming to the ranch, especially wearing her "cowgirl clothes," as she called them. On her last visit there, dressed in her flounced skirt with her silver and turquoise squash blossom around her neck, she'd cozied up in a big chair with her favorite Pendleton woolen blanket in front of the fire. When she settled in, she mused, "I'd like to die right here."

Together, Jamie and I scattered the third allotment of ashes over her rose garden on Mom's birthday on February 12th of the following year. Honoring her grandmother, Jamie made peanut butter and jelly sandwiches and decorated the table with little Valentine heart candies and cinnamon Red Hots. We toasted her with a celebratory birthday glass of champagne.

Still more "wildcatting" to go.

ભ

Never a doubt in my mind—they were going back to the house on Wenonah Drive in Dallas, my family's longtime home. The perfect opportunity came in April, seven months after losing Mom.

Jack and I planned to attend the annual Buffalo Gap Food and Wine Summit with our friends Janice and Frank. We arrived in Dallas to visit with them a few days early, allowing plenty of time for surreptitious scattering.

My young parents bought the two-story house I grew up in for $32,000 in 1949. The last time it sold, the asking price was $1.1 million. Those buyers did an extensive renovation soon after. Several years later, when

Jamie and I took Mom to tour the house, which the owners graciously agreed to, she "tsk-tsked" over the exquisite upgrades and unbelievable art collections.

"It's not as comfortable as when we lived here," she muttered a bit too loud.

I lived in a gracious and stately home third grade through my Texas Tech days—at least, that's how it lives in my memory. It was painted a unique color on the exterior—Lambert Green, a muted dark sage, the color of an aloe plant. There was a prestigious, high-end nursery in Dallas named Lambert's, and this was their signature paint color. The two-story, traditional house had always remained Lambert Green. Long before I knew the salad dressing existed, I called my house The Green Goddess.

My family's ashes needed to be there. Before we left California, I wrapped the last portion in a plastic bag, rolled them up in my pajamas, and placed them in my suitcase, understanding full well it was illegal to transport such contraband across state lines without a license.

In Texas the next day, Jack and I borrowed our friends' car, put our secret cache in it, and headed to Greenway Parks, the enclave in Dallas where our former home sits graciously on an oversize lot, one hundred yards from the street. We parked about a block away and strolled casually along the sidewalk, behind my stately house, which bordered the parkway toward 5362.

"Babe, are you sure about this?" Jack's hand protectively covered the small plastic bag that held the remaining portion of my little family.

I paused a moment, inviting childhood memories. I'd grown from a little girl into a slightly more mature college graduate there.

After a few steps, my home came into view. I put my hand on Jack's forearm, slowing our pace. "Hang on a minute, honey," I whispered as tears prickled my eyes. Sweetness and sadness combined to tug at my heart. Slowly, I approached my youth from so many years away. My breathing slowed as the memories took over. I lingered in the moment.

"I'm okay now," I finally said.

We continued walking. The sight of a dogwood tree in full bloom, highlighted against the deep grey of the neighbor's mid-century home, emerged in a spectacular fashion. Someone told us kids once that the tree was called "dogwood" because when the wind blows and the branches knock together, it sounds like a dog barking. Probably just lore meant to capture little kids' imaginations. On this day, the magnificent pink blossoms gave off a faint sweet smell and an onslaught of childhood memories.

We continued our walk—slow in the beginning but we soon picked up the pace.

As we neared my home, we furtively glanced around to be sure nobody lurked nearby. Jack scooped a generous handful for me, then poured the remaining ashes from the bag into his hand. Before we began, once again, to scatter—for the last time—I cupped my hands over the soft, ashen mound. *Good-bye,* I murmured to myself. Offering the last of the ashes to the land called to mind spreading fertilizer crystals, which Jack and I had done at The Orange Woods for so many years for oranges and grapes alike.

They (my family) went under the kitchen window, where Mom always had fresh fruit in the refrigerator and Dad's regular delivery of scotch showed up at the back door. They went in the grassy backyard, the site of my thirteenth birthday party while Mom recovered from surgery. They went under the huge oak tree, where my dad's grass wouldn't grow and both Buck, our beagle, and Cracker, our English bulldog, were buried. And the last bit went in the parkway, where Mark and I played.

Back at the car, before he opened my door, Jack stopped and drew me close in a warm embrace. We stayed that way for a long while. We had finished wildcat scattering.

∽

As we drove home after our son-in-law Bud's mom's emotional memorial service at Mariner's Church in Newport several years later, I asked Jack what he wanted in the way of a funeral or memorial service.

"Just hang me up in a tree someplace," he said.

Chapter 35

Inspiration and Celebration

There is artistry in the making of wine. It is often described as a delicate balance of art and science. Grapes are grown, harvested, fermented, aged, bottled, and finally consumed. While these winemaking basics are pretty much standard, many key decisions need to be made based on each particular vintage and the desired style of the finished product.

Jack, gifted in the art of winemaking, evolved as an artist with words. In retirement, he often wrote songs, poems, and stories. The winery, the vineyard, and nature inspired him to write:

Vintage

In winter's chill we start our quest
A generation is put to rest
Last season's shoots no longer here
Another spring, another year

The breeze is calm, the sunshine bright
It dries the fog that cools the night
The buds begin to break anew
The vines re-green, as spring vines do

Their arms extend with strength and love
Supporting shoots that climb above
And dainty blossoms now appear
Nature's vow for this new year

And as the warmth of summer grows
Into the fruit more goodness flows

Each cluster darkens and expands
As nature issues its commands

We walk the paths and view the leaves
The vines tug tenderly at our sleeves
And now at last the time is right
We pick from dawn 'til fading light

And so it goes as it's been planned
This gift to us from God's own hand
The nights turn cold; leaves disappear
Another wine, another year.

Jack's creativity inspired me. I painted a work, also titled *Vintage*. We combined our efforts, his writing and my painting, to create commemorative labels for our 2013 Cabernet.

ଓ

Celebratory times with friends and family at The Orange Woods shimmer brightly in my mind—fond memories spill out like jewels from a treasure chest. We delighted in sharing our home with others. My passion for people and entertaining came from my parents, especially Mom.

Mom and Jamie and I hosted a "Bring Your Own Rolling Pin" party the day before Thanksgiving one year. Five little cousins, armed with rolling pins, lined the large island in my kitchen as we distributed a big ball of pie dough and pie pan to each. Their wax paper and rolling pins were floured, and they began. Their contribution to the Thanksgiving feast? Five close-to-perfect pies. My kitchen? Looked as if the first snowstorm of the winter season had arrived.

When Mom turned eighty-eight, we staged a Princess Party. My granddaughters dressed up in a fairy tale combination of little Disney princesses, and my mom's octogenarian friends wore jeweled tiaras and silver shoes. Bayley was so inspired by the princess party that when she turned sixteen, she requested a "fancy party with the shiny crystal, silver serving pieces, and candles in crystal holders for my friends at Neeny's house at the Orange Woods."

We staged one of our most beautiful parties under the harvest moon in October, after Jack and I had visited Vermont with Janice and Frank. We had been spellbound there by a farm-to-table dinner under the stars. Jack and I invited his wine group and spouses for an al fresco dinner one evening. We rented long tables and chairs, enough for forty, and placed them in the center of the bocce ball court.

A gentle breeze wafted the sounds of Pavarotti and Friends from the winery. A collaborative wine tasting and pasta dinner, combined with friends and fellowship amidst the orange trees, produced a very special evening.

There were countless gatherings and festivities—special birthdays, graduations, Halloween costume parties, art shows and workshops, girls' nights out, fashion shows, slumber parties, golfing events—and so many holidays. For five years, Jamie, who lived in Valley Center, just miles from us, and I offered Art Smart Camp each summer. Young kids with drawing boards became mini–plein air painters and Jackson Pollock wannabes as they drip painted on the concrete floor of the winery. They delighted in making mosaic stepping-stones and self-portraits out of vegetables. Their favorite part? The morning's snack: ice cold Valencia oranges cut into "smiles." Two of our students became high school valedictorians and went on to graduate from Harvard University.

Many of our celebrations were just the two of us. Especially New Year's Eve. Early on, Jack instilled in me his premise that whatever we were doing New Year's Eve would be something we would do often in the new year. He managed to lure me into the bedroom every year as the clocks and calendars changed (actually, I went willingly).

Perhaps the most hyped New Year's occurred in 1999, as we anticipated the arrival of the new millennium. But as the build-up accelerated, trumpeting January 1, 2000, as the day our entire lives were going to be changed, we made the conscious decision to disconnect and spend New Year's Eve alone.

Because we were sequestered at The Orange Woods, I don't honestly know exactly what the fear was about, but I believe it was that the computers everyone depended on would malfunction. People feared that our electronic goodies would go dark and that we would revert back to living like the olden days, without any electricity, heat, or running water. People assumed that all of the world's computers would fail to function. I puzzle now, almost twenty years later—*Would that be a bad thing?*

When the year did actually change to 2000, computers barely had any problems. Jack and I, oblivious, ended our year dining al fresco under the light of the moon, slow dancing on the deck, and then we headed to our bedroom.

As I reflect, I realize the memories of my mom's devotion to friends and family and her dazzling talents for creating memorable gatherings and welcoming people into our home provided great inspiration for me.

Chapter 36
Cash's Birthday

September 4 will always be the day I lost my mother. Soon after she passed, however, the day became sad and heartwarming at the same time. Cash, my youngest and last grandchild, arrived one year later on the same day in 2008.

On Cash's sixth birthday, I wrote:

> My mother died seven years ago on my youngest grandchild's first birthday. My second son, his father, celebrates his birthday next week on the anniversary of 9/11, when the plane hit the tower, sending shards of terrorism through every American's being. As each year passes, I am struck by how new joy minimizes the fading grief. In the first years, I noted September 4th as the day Mom died. On 9/11, the horrific day, the loss for me, those close to me, and countless others throughout our world was unfathomable.

> Little by little, one sweet tow-headed boy in Arizona and one grown-up blond-headed man there too, marking the anniversaries of their birth and the resulting exhilaration, have overridden the excruciating pain. Now, instead of the day she died, I focus on my mom's February birthday, which she shared with my brother and Abraham Lincoln, and her beautiful long life. I reserve the day of her death, the 4th of September, for Cash's boyish birthday silliness and unending energy. And while the magnitude of 9/11 will never cease to cause my soul to shudder, the eleventh day of September is the day I gave birth to my son in Dallas, Texas, a whopping ten pounds and three ounces of a boy, who continues to this day to fill my life with surprise and pride.

> Today offers touching insight into the irony of life, at least my life, that unimaginable horror and fear can exist in tandem with sublime happiness and contentment; that the balance of the scales shifts, and the dichotomy is constantly changing. Happy Birthday, Cash and Bo.

Chapter 37

Losing Steamer

Steamer Woods
12/6/2002–8/31/2012

Steamer, our legendary black dog, died with the same humility and unconditional worship of Jack and me that had characterized his life with us for ten remarkable years. For six weeks, he had suffered from a "big dog" ailment—dysplasia, a very common problem causing pain and lameness in large dogs. He spent most of his time in his soft blue corduroy bed with his name monogrammed in large white script letters across the front, a gift from Santa. He had been limping and having extreme difficulty getting up and down and had lost some weight. We made an appointment with his vet.

Jack always did veterinarian duty, but something told me to go with the two of them on that hot August afternoon. It had been almost impossible for us to assist Steamer up into my SUV. His excitement over going somewhere with us, predictably, overrode his pain. As we drove to the Helen Woodard Animal Center in Rancho Santa Fe, I turned and patted his large head, memories of our gentle giant sashaying through my mind.

Steamer craved almonds and would wait patiently for one of us to share. Our lovable dog, impossible to ignore.

He would stay out all night about once every three months. Panicked the first couple of times, we eventually learned he would return.

Scared to death of the vacuum cleaner, he would bound for the opposite end of the house the moment it came out of the closet. Big, but not so brave.

He treasured play dates with his brother Speckles.

He hid brand-new toys the moment he got them. Jack always said, "Somewhere on this property, there's a huge mound of buried Kong toys."

Steamer never let us witness him poop. He had his own sanitation waste station somewhere out of sight.

Sunday evenings were his favorite time of the week. Together, the three of us took the trash down the long, gently sloped driveway to the end. I rolled the big blue recycle container; Jack precariously managed the other two, the trash and the green container. Inevitably, Steamer would lope happily along between us, regularly knocking Jack and the two big cans off balance. When the cans were set at the end of the driveway, overjoyed at our job well done, he galloped full speed back to the house and waited patiently for us.

We had a favorite "Steamer-ism": whenever we left him, as he looked anxiously up at us, sensing our departure, we would point one finger at him and say in unison, "We will be back in one hour." Whether or not we were to be gone for the entire day or a long evening, he trusted. True believer.

As we pulled into the parking lot for our three-thirty appointment, Steamer's tail began to wag excitedly. Even at this point, when he struggled with the fierce pain of each movement, he anxiously anticipated a new adventure.

The young doctor saw us promptly. Very pretty and petite, about the size of our diminutive sixteen-year-old ballerina granddaughter, Sophie, she must have weighed less than one hundred pounds. During the past three weeks, Steamer had lost weight, which put the two of them in the same light flyweight category. Also like Steamer, the doctor had jet-black hair and compassionate dark eyes. Instantly, he was smitten. His long tail wagged rapidly, knocking several medical items off the nearby shelf unit in the exam room.

In retrospect, the doctor most likely knew the diagnosis right away, but she suggested x-rays, giving us momentary hope that the pain resulted from arthritis or a hip that could be replaced. Steamer anxiously sidled up against her as they left the room, his tail still wagging. Fifteen minutes later, doc and dog returned. She placed the x-rays on the light machine and showed us our poor doggie's lower body. He looked at the light and wagged his tail. A large mass appeared near his left hip. His femur appeared less than half the normal size. The diagnosis: osteosarcoma, the most aggressive bone cancer of all.

Both Jack and I burst into tears. The doctor, unable to contain herself, began to cry, too.

As soon as Kleenex tissues were distributed and we composed ourselves, she delivered the rest of the news. "He probably has a few weeks. You can take him home, but that femur could snap at any time and he would be in excruciating pain. Think about how difficult it would be for you to help him if that happened. It would be almost impossible for either of you—or both, for that matter—to get him into a car. It might even happen when he roams alone somewhere away from your property, where you won't find him."

Jack grasped my hand with one of his and petted Steamer with his other, listening intently. My tears returned. Steamer never took his eyes off his new friend as she talked.

"If the cancer has not spread to the chest—which I'm sure it has," the vet continued, "we could amputate the leg and he might have a few months more."

Neither one of us could speak.

She gave us our final option: "Or we could euthanize Steamer."

Quietly, she left the room, leaving the three of us to make our heart-breaking decision.

Our loyal, lovable dog put his long jowl on Jack's thigh between us and looked anxiously back and forth at us both. He had this uncanny ability to sense our feelings. We both patted our dog, hoping to reassure him. The thought of Steamer lying alone somewhere in agony devastated me. I could sense Jack experiencing the same fear.

We sat together for a long while, weighed the options, and finally came to the decision we thought best for Steamer.

We spent some bittersweet time with our extraordinary dog in that examination room, saying the silly things he loved to hear:

"You are such a good doggie, Steamer Woods."

"How'd you get so smart, Steamer?"

"We'll be back in one hour, Steamer."

And then we left him with the charming, compassionate, pretty veterinarian. His tail wagged and he licked her leg as they left the room together.

At home that evening, we gathered his toys, collars, and leashes in a little altar near his bed. Jack opened a bottle of Black Dog Zinfandel with Steamer's picture on the label. We toasted him and spent the time until dark relishing our memories of the ten gratifying years we'd had with our big black dog. We cried most of the night.

Besides Jack, nobody idolized Steamer more than Cash. The big black dog outweighed the little guy by eighty-plus pounds, but our youngest grandchild always begged Papa, whom he also idolized, to let him help take care of Steamer. He especially liked curling up with his doggie playmate in the big blue bed, which had plenty of room for them both.

Telling four-year-old Cash that his doggie pal had gone to heaven broke my heart. As the little guy sat in my lap on Papa's big leather chair, I hugged him tight. His little chin quivered as tears fell. I removed his pint-sized glasses with the red frames and wiped his eyes as he pleaded, "But Neeny, I want him here. He's my best dog."

Every so often in the years that followed, the opportunity for another puppy or dog arose. In his quintessentially loyal Jack mode, my husband would reply, "No, thanks, I had a dog."

Two weeks after Steamer died, an emotional fourth grader, Carly, came to her grandfather with tears in her eyes and a folder in her hand. In it, her writing assignment for school that week.

Every morning I wake up to the birds chirping, reminding me that it is the start of a new day and anything can happen in The Orange Woods, my home. I live on a multi-acre orchard. On the orchard are our home, our winery, our garden, our labyrinth, and our vineyard. My best friend, Jack, is the owner along with his wife, Marilyn.

Today is a very important day at the winery because we are going to make a new type of wine. Our friends will come and help pick the grapes. A special machine smashes the grapes down into a juice that is stored in big steel vats until it is ready to be bottled. Once it's ready, the tubes pump it out of the machine and squirt it into bottles. For some reason Jack doesn't want me near the machines, probably because they are dangerous. I sit in the corner and see the red juice course through the veins of the machine. Once they're done putting the wine in bottles, they place each bottle in a box and sell them to different places and people like the world-famous Lazy H Restaurant and Bar.

Normally when Jack and Marilyn finish the wine, we go outside and eat cheese and crackers while Jack tells stories of his life on the radio. But today seemed different; they cleaned everything up and went into the house. Were they mad at me? So, I decided since there is a beautiful view of the valley from my house, I would go watch the sunset over the mountains.

After the sky changed from yellow to red to pink to purple, I decided to try to think what I might have done to upset Jack. Honestly, I can't think of anything. I start to walk towards the winery and hear music and laughter. I realize people are in there. A lot of people. It must be another party. As I creep through the doors, I quietly walk through the crowd of people and hear a voice. "The wine is delicious," says one woman. "How did you pick the name and the great label?" says another. Jack replies, "I wanted to honor the best friend I've ever had." He turned around, showing me the bottle and patted my head. It was at that moment I realized he was speaking of me. The label read "Black Dog Zinfandel." I knew that not only he loved me, I was someone's best friend.

In loving memory of Steamer,
Carly

Chapter 38

Radio Hall of Fame

After Bo's grief burst, I couldn't help but think about how good radio had been to both Jack and me and how awful it continued to be for Bo.

If careers have pinnacles, Jack's was, without a doubt, his induction into the National Radio Hall of Fame.

There were many high points along the way, but the one he always cited as the true highlight was emceeing the Beatles Live Concerts on their first US tour in both Dallas and New Orleans, where frenzied fans stormed across the field at City Park Stadium and broke through the police cordon, ending the concert prematurely. Jack, then a young Top-Forty disc jockey, did his best to quiet the crowd as limos rushed the startled, fresh-faced quartet away.

There were so many brushes with fame for Jack, the steel-worker-Marine-out-of-Gary-Indiana turned host-interviewer-commentator. He led a life sprinkled with politicians, sports celebrities, movie stars, musicians, artists, and writers. But this—induction into The National Radio Hall of Fame, class of 2014—capped it all. It was the culmination of a long career in radio, his longtime passion.

It's difficult to look back on the event; I don't think Jack was a hundred percent there. Melissa Etheridge headlined. She sang with Ingrid Michaelson, an engaging contemporary singer/songwriter. Ira Glass, public radio's reigning star, was also there, as was an impressive list of other radio legends, including Larry King, Dick Orkin, and Marion Ross, who inducted Agnes Moorhead posthumously. More radio greats, like Rick Dees, Jon Miller (one of modern baseball's legendary announcers), and Delilah, the most listened-to woman on radio in the US at the time, also attended. Radio's night to shine.

The friends and family Jack loved most were there.

He surfaced sporadically.

The black-tie, red carpet event thrilled us. Jack, true to his rugged farmer/cowboy self, looked fabulous in his black tux jacket, black shirt, black tie, black jeans, and black eel skin cowboy boots. In his pocket was a multicolored silk scarf, my gift to the honoree.

We rode in long stretch limousines to the Cicada Club in downtown LA as the sun set over the Pacific Ocean. On arrival, I felt I had stepped back into the 1930s. The historic Art Deco building and private club exuded speakeasy vibes.

The cocktail hour dazzled. Jack and I were separated by many famous faces, good friends, and glamorous outfits. Our girls were the most glamorous in this exuberant crowd of party-goers. Jamie, Jennifer, Jackie, and Laurie each wore black—they looked elegant, young, and beautiful. I had anguished over my outfit for weeks but ended up in basic black, too. Carly, looking more like a movie star than a high school senior, wore burgundy chiffon with stunning makeup, velvety red lips and glimmering eyes. Jack's eyes lit up when he saw her.

The Cicada Club's spacious lounge was dimly lit; golds and crystals gleamed. The exceptionally long bar was massive—a work of art crafted from rich polished dark wood. Between hugs and congratulations from our friends and well-wishers, I kept looking for Jack. *Where on earth could he be?* I knew he would relish a Manhattan. Cocktails, picture-taking, and chatter lasted an hour. My husband was still missing; a strong mixture of aggravation and concern began to swell within me.

I moved with the crowd down the stairs, doing my best to convince myself that Jack was backstage or being interviewed someplace.

My anxiety abated at the bottom of the stairs. Jamie, arm in arm with her father, came to me as we were invited to the grand ballroom for dinner and the ceremony. She had found him wandering aimlessly in the grand space set with tables for two hundred people, alone.

"Honey, where have you been?" I put my arm around his shoulder. "A lot of people were looking for you upstairs."

Abruptly, he brushed off my concern, saying, "I was looking for Harrigan."

The ceremony commenced just as the dessert service began. Lights, cameras, and giant TV screens surrounded the stage. A rumble of energy pulsated throughout the grand space. Jack and his team show partner—known in the industry by their on-air names, Charlie and Harrigan—were first on the program of six inductees.

Al Peterson, longtime industry journalist who introduced the duo, commented, "In these modern days of satellite radio, this pair is one of radio's most successful broadcasters and innovative pioneers. Coupled with continued dominance as a live two-man morning show in major markets throughout the country, this twosome syndicated this daily, four-hour morning show, *The Charlie and Harrigan Show,* in over forty markets in the US long before satellite surfaced as the common method of delivery in multiple markets. In the decades before shock and rage invaded the morning air waves, this dynamic duo presented an upbeat, informative and entertaining show to every time zone in the US."

My heart pounded with pride. I reached over and squeezed Jack's hand. He grinned, leaned over, and kissed my cheek. As the applause began, he rose and went to the stage.

Over fifty years, I had reveled in my husband's performances hundreds of times, often in front of thousands. Always commanding the stage, sharp, quick-witted, funny, he was a master of ad lib, confident and charismatic.

I did not observe that on this night. He began, and what I heard alarmed me a bit. This was not my usual Jack. What was happening?

Did anybody else notice? His split-second timing was off a bit. My eyes searched across the table to Bo. Did he feel the same way about his dad's timing and delivery? I looked at Jamie and Jackie. Did they notice anything? They both smiled and their eyes sparkled. Jack's remarks were good, but this wasn't his usual stellar performance. This was not my brilliant Jack. Did anybody understand that but me? When I look back at the photographs taken that night, there are some that break my heart—shots where he looks confused, even blank.

At the end of the festivities, we congratulated him and reveled in his accomplishment. He basked in the spotlight, his usual humble self. I tried my best to contain my wayward thoughts. But secretly, I hoped he wouldn't see the video replay.

Back at the hotel, he and I lingered on the balcony outside our room into the wee hours recounting the colossal evening's event. The night sky sparkled with crystal stars. Jack relaxed and put his arm around me.

We both agreed that the older you get, the harder it is to be thrilled like we both had been this night. We were knocked out by the festivities surrounding his induction.

But something didn't register right. My fierce pride in Jack's career accomplishment managed to temporarily quell any concerns lurking in my mind, but in my gut, I still wasn't sure.

Turns out, I was right to worry.

Chapter 39
Fresh Squeezed Orange Juice

Jack and I managed the next few years without Steamer. He left a huge void behind. Our home was never the same again but still blessed—until that daunting, unfathomable four weeks in 2015.

It began early on the morning of February 13. Unable to go back to sleep, I got out of bed at dawn. Jack's had been a fitful and puzzling night.

In the kitchen, I grabbed my coffee, my fruit-picking basket and clippers, and I slowly walked to the orange grove near the greenhouse. We cherished our Valencia orange trees—which, we had learned since buying the property, were believed to be a descendant of a sweet orange variety grown in China. Eventually, the orange was brought to Spain and named after the prominent city of Valencia. The fruit was introduced to the United States in the 1800s, but was not cultivated as a crop here until almost a century later.

I walked to the large tree at the end of the driveway so I could soak up the early-morning sun rising in the east over the mountains as I picked oranges. Small drops of dew glistened on the leaves. It was the middle of February, and another glorious day in our lives was dawning. Even with the disturbance overnight, I found myself relishing the pleasure of our lives at The Orange Woods. Jack, my bulletproof Jack, would weather this current storm of discomfort and we would continue our perfect lives in paradise.

A squirrel scampered around the corner from the grove. I looked at the varmint and then took in the three portly French Oak barrels lined up on their stands near the entrance to the winery. When Jack discarded them, I'd repurposed for an art project. On their circular wooden ends, I had painted grapevines amid script that read *Luxe, Calme et Volupté*, the line from Baudelaire's poem "L'Invitation au Voyage" that had become our motto.

Henri Matisse, father of the Fauvist art movement, reigned as one of the artists whose artwork I coveted most in my studies and on tours at the museum. His painting, also titled *Luxe, Calme et Volupté*, inspired me—a classicized scene of bathers in luxurious repose on the shore—painted in vibrant, unnatural colors, characteristic of the Fauve artists. About his art, Matisse wrote that he dreamed of "balance, purity and serenity, devoid of troubling or depressing subject matter, something like a good armchair which provides relaxation from physical fatigue."

Both the painting and the poetry had provided dreamscapes for Jack and me as we created our paradise over the years, a real sow's-ear-into-a-silk-purse project. Matisse's vivid colors blanketed our home and gardens. Baudelaire's lines became our mantra:

"Of living together there
Of loving at will,
Of loving till death,
There all is order and beauty,
Luxury, peace, and pleasure."

A hummingbird fluttered on a branch close by. My reverie ceased and I reached for one last perfectly shaped, almost ripe fruit overhead and placed it in the basket. I glanced to the south just in time to see our tenant, a male barn owl, swoosh into his box. His sharp, piercing call informed us he was a male; apparently, the girls don't shriek. Our guy stayed up late swooping down on unsuspecting prey in complete darkness. Jack had perched the owl house fifty feet high on a steel pole. It towered over the winery, bocce ball court, and that section of the grove. He had installed the box years earlier, with no takers until a few months before, when our feathered friend with the big eyes and ghostly white face came to live in the woods.

Walking back to the house with my basket full, the teak garden bench Brent and his family had given us as a housewarming gift beckoned me to sit a minute and bask in the early-morning sunshine. As I sat, I inhaled the mix of familiar scents—agriculture, earth, flowers, birds, and bees. My mind drifted back to our early days here.

CB

"Damn, M, that's the sweetest smell in the world," Jack proclaimed proudly as he pulled me close, turning his face skyward, breathing deeply. "Turns me on almost as much as you do!"

"You say that to all the girls," I teased.

The honeyed scent of orange blossoms signaled springtime. We stood on the threshold of retirement from our radio careers, about to embark on a new life together as farmers.

At the first intoxicating whiff of the sensuous fragrance, we had hurried outside to revel in yet another springtime blast of the divine magic of citrus. We had read that the Valencia, first named Excelsior, was the world's most important orange.

The fact we'd learned from our research that delighted us most was that both the snowy white bloom of next season's harvest and the richly colored fruit of the current harvest coexisted for a brief time on the tree. The long season required to produce the sweet, juicy fruit meant that by the next spring, we would still have ripe oranges on the tree at the same time new flowers were blooming.

We made our way to the center of sun-kissed Valencia orange trees laden with both flowers and fruit, taking in deep breaths, inhaling the heaven-sent enchantment. Nearly ripe oranges hung side-by-side with the delicate white blossoms responsible for our sensory overload and next year's harvest.

One friend described the orange blossom magic as "somewhat like wake-up sex on crisp, clean white sheets."

ༀ

An early-morning tractor rumble at the nursery down the road interrupted my daydreaming. Almost seven thirty; Jack would wake soon. He would be happy I had stayed home from my walk to share breakfast on yet another divine day.

Early evening last night, I'd woken him, and we'd had a bowl of minestrone soup together and watched *Jeopardy*. But shortly into the show, leaving half his soup, Alex Trebek, and me, Jack set his TV tray aside, saying, "Sorry babe, I'm going back to sleep."

He had been working on a few projects around the house, getting ready for company and the party, so I understood his uncharacteristic tiredness. When I went to bed a little later, he was sleeping soundly.

I'd woken with an uneasy start at four a.m. Jack wasn't in bed; all the lights in the house were on. Anxiously, I looked for him, hurriedly checking every room in the house, guest house, and garage. I didn't find him; alarmed,

I raced back to the bedroom to get my shoes to continue my search outside and in the winery. I'll bet that's where he is, I thought to myself.

He wasn't. I stopped dead in my tracks when I reentered our bedroom. There he lay, asleep in our bed. Had he fallen on the floor? Had he been asleep there while I searched? Had he turned on the lights? Had he gotten back into bed somehow without waking up?

Somehow, my dazed self answered my own questions. I concluded Jack had gotten up and roamed during the night, fallen when he approached our bed, and remained on the floor for a period of time. When I left the room to look for him, he must have crawled into bed.

Could something be wrong? Unsure and a bit afraid of the answer, I returned to bed and snuggled up, spoon style, as close to my warm, sleeping husband as I could.

I lay awake the next hour or two. At seven o'clock, I grabbed my sweats and shoes and left our room quickly. I glanced at Jack, who slept peacefully as the sunshine began to peek through the slatted blinds on our French doors. Most mornings, I walked with my friend, Sue. After the disturbance of the night, I'd canceled.

಄

Back in the house in my spacious, sunny, dreamy kitchen, I began to cut the plump fruits in half. The majority of our oranges didn't ripen until late March or early April, but the trees on the southeastern exposure gave us almost-sweet oranges much earlier. I would have to add sugar, but I wanted to make fresh-squeezed orange juice for Jack, and for our company coming from Dallas.

As I squeezed, the juicer hummed—the only sound in our home this early morning. The oranges were a tad sour, but full of drip-down-your-chin juiciness. I added several heaping tablespoons of sugar and began to clean up my mess.

As I dried my hands, I raised my fingers to my nose, taking in the piquant smell of orange peel, which lingered. The entire kitchen reeked of the tantalizing smell of our oranges. I poured the juice into Mom's crystal pitcher and placed it on the top shelf of the refrigerator.

Janice and Frank would arrive the next day—Saturday, Valentine's Day. We were having a party—"Come meet real live Texans," the invitation read.

I couldn't wait to spend time with my childhood friend from Dallas and her husband; Jack, however, was not so excited this time. He had been somewhat subdued for days—hadn't played his regular rounds of golf with Tom and Roy, and had slept most of yesterday.

I heard him approach the coffee pot shortly before eight o'clock.

"Good morning, honey. You sure had a busy night, didn't you?"

"Huh? I guess so," he said tentatively as he made his K-cup of coffee. His response was barely audible, not the chipper morning man's greeting his radio show listeners had become accustomed to over the course of decades. The refrigerator door opened and closed as he doctored his coffee with caramel macchiato creamer, his all-time favorite.

"I left the newspaper on your chair and there's a pitcher of fresh-squeezed orange juice in the fridge for breakfast. I picked the fruit this morning and squeezed the you-know-what out of it just for you," I chirped. "Are you better this morning?"

No answer. I listened to his footsteps as he headed to the living room.

No more than two minutes later, my husband wailed in a horrifying manner, unlike anything I had heard in my life. His voice, full of desperation, shattered the quiet and petrified me. "Marilyn, help me," he howled. "Where are you?"

I raced to him; we met in the kitchen. He looked dreadful, scared, and confused.

He pressed his hands to his temples, a contorted scowl on his face. "Babe, something is very wrong," he insisted urgently as I hugged him. "I couldn't read the paper. Everything blurred."

The tremors in his voice alarmed me. Terror-stricken, I watched as he convulsed. Disoriented, he began to babble strange, indistinguishable words and sentences.

"Fepar . . . chagrunt . . . blonight run so"—unrecognizable words spilled from my husband's mouth. The look on his face—pallid, almost ghostly—frightened the hell out of me.

Stifling the urge to scream, I put my arms around Jack and nudged him firmly toward the barstool. His knees buckled. I steadied him and sat him down.

"Sit here a minute, honey, while I run get my phone."

Frantically, I called 911 and tried my best to remain calm and give clear directions. Immediately after I phoned our daughter, Jamie, begging her to come. Then I threw my phone down on the counter and rushed back to Jack, who still pressed both hands forcefully against his head, his elbows pushing against the counter for leverage.

"Come on, honey, let's get you more comfortable," I whispered as I guided him to his chair in the living room. Newspapers were scattered on the floor all over the room. His coffee was spilled across his chair and the carpet.

"I'm sorry, M," he apologized.

"Honey, no worries. Tell me, what are you feeling?"

"My head is fucked up, Marilyn."

⅓

Jamie charged through our door within fifteen minutes. A flash of relief temporarily steadied me at her arrival. Two fresh-scrubbed young firemen from the barebones Pauma Valley Fire Department arrived shortly afterward.

The PV Fire Department is located in a modest concrete block building on Highway 76—no fire engines, just a van. I wondered if they recognized Jack, who came once a year to get his controlled burn permit.

The no-nonsense crew greeted him, hooked him up to a multitude of monitoring devices, and asked him questions.

His bizarre answers unnerved me even more: "Two tons"; "Olmace"; "Forn Barb." Tons made sense referring to grapes, and Barb was his sister, but streams of out-of-context, nonsensical phrases also spewed forth. A nearly comical moment occurred when he raised his hand in an emphatic gesture and barked, "No, Jack Ruby's not a friend of mine." (The killer of Lee Oswald, a hanger-on at the radio station where Jack worked in Dallas, had my husband's name in his wallet when he was captured. The FBI questioned Jack and quickly dismissed him. "That Ruby guy lurked around the station all the time—a real creep," Jack told the agents.)

His brain still has memories, I assured myself. *We've simply got to get it realigned.* Then came another torrent of high-volume, indecipherable, unconnected words: "phranx, boldong, minewest." A hollowing fear filled my heart when I saw the look of panic on his face.

"I'm really screwed. I'm lost. I don't get what's happening," my husband moaned as he rubbed his head in anguish. More gibberish. "Grabull out there."

I raced down the hall to our bedroom and got a sweatshirt for him, ridiculously thinking that he might be cold and helping him get warm would make everything better.

‹‹‹

The first set of summoned paramedics got lost on Sam's Mountain road, a dangerous, winding dirt road that was the long and wrong way to our house. Living in the country, we had always feared the length of response time of emergency assistance. As it turned out that morning, we'd been right in our reservations.

At Jamie's level-headed insistence, the head guy summoned a replacement team, and when they arrived on the scene, another interrogation began immediately.

"Can you tell us your name, sir, please?"

"Jack Lee Woods."

The normalcy of his answer placated me momentarily.

"How much do you weigh, Mr. Woods?" the head guy asked.

"One hundred and eighty," Jack answered, somewhat impatiently.

"What year is it, Mr. Woods?"

"One hundred and eighty," Jack barked.

‹‹‹

The ambulance ride to Palomar Hospital took forever, at least in my mind. Jack lined up as number seven in the ambulance check-in line on arrival. I surveyed a queue of shrouded bodies, strapped onto silver rectangles with braked wheels. The wait seemed like another eternity.

Before long, eight more patients lined up behind him. Had the bad luck of Friday the 13th resulted in this overload in the ER? A dark and crazy time at the new and shiny Palomar Hospital ensued—loud, crowded, unsettling—and compounded my already schizophrenic emotions.

Jack battled with bouts of agitation and severe head pain between intermittent signs of normalcy throughout the long midday.

I found myself comforted each time an attendant approached and my husband calmed. He had always enjoyed people, and maybe this love of his fellow man became even more important in this scariest of times. Nurses, technicians, social workers, doctors—he quieted for each encounter. The rare moments of peace settled me, even as the tension escalated.

Both Jamie and I advocated on Jack's behalf with fierce persistence, her more effectively than me. At some point in the early afternoon, they finally transferred him to a room. A momentary sense of relief engulfed us; we were more than grateful to be away from the chaos of the emergency room.

Jack dozed; Jamie and I relaxed a bit. "I'm gonna get a latte, Mom," my attentive daughter said. "Want one?"

She was back in minutes and, for a short while, we sipped and sat still together at his bedside. They had completed the initial examination and were processing his results and the doctors' findings.

Just as our latte cups emptied, the roller coaster ride revved up again. An officious neurosurgeon and his team entered Jack's room. A stiffness permeated my body. I stood at attention.

"Your husband has suffered an injury to his brain, Mrs. Woods," the surgeon said. "It will be some time before we ascertain the severity of your husband's condition."

A vagueness of nomenclature, disclaimers, and possibilities avalanched through my consciousness. I was scared to death but didn't want to shake up Jamie any more than she already had been. I needed my oldest son, Brent, here. I had hesitated to pull him away from his responsibilities—overseeing a company of more than two hundred employees—until I had something concrete to tell him. Screw the others, I thought now. I need him.

Jamie called for me. He said he'd be there in thirty minutes, then asked to talk to me. She handed me the phone.

"Mom, please try not to worry. I'm on my way. Everything will be okay."

The collisions going on in my head told me Brent might be wrong. As I returned from my phone conversation in the hall, I let out a silent plea for help to my parents. I became a scared little child who desperately needed to be a responsible, discerning adult.

I stopped outside the door to Jack's room and leaned against the wall. "Don't panic," I muttered to myself. "Try not to shake Jamie up. Be in control for Jack. This could be another false alarm. Calm down, Marilyn."

Eventually, an internist, a pulmonary critical care doctor, and a second neurosurgeon attended; we were grateful for their attention. A CAT scan, blood tests, and more followed into the evening for my confused, unsteady buddy.

Jamie stayed at my side all day, anticipating my needs and accelerating concerns. Much more nurturing to her father than I could ever be, she said in a gentle yet firm manner, "Dad, you need to calm down a little and you will be back home very soon. The grapes will wait for you."

Over and over, she straightened the sheets on his bed, gently patted his ashen cheeks, and caressed both his hands, roughened from work in the vineyard. A momentary flash of sweetness passed through my mind as I recalled Jack's pet name for Jamie—"Buddy Pal." More than ever before today, she clung to her forever buddy pal. She also kept the family informed, especially Bo, the youngest of her two brothers, who was stranded in bed at his home in Arizona, awaiting major back surgery and debilitated by pain.

What would I have done without Jamie by my side?

When Brent, my firstborn, walked in, I said a silent prayer of thanks. Jamie's face also showed great relief as her big brother took charge.

Jack, too, lit up instantly when Brent came near. From that moment on and throughout the agonizing ensuing weeks, he reacted obediently to anything Brent said—a heart-wrenching reversal of roles. This night, my son was exactly what the doctor had ordered, not only for Jack but also for me. He generated a sense of composure in both Jamie and me, but especially in Jack, who had continued to be agitated, cussing, and trying to get out of bed. With Brent there, Jack settled down.

Our son-in-law, Bud, arrived, and I worried that the familiarity of the hospital would upset him. He and Jamie and Carly, their youngest, had spent countless days in a hospital, first in ER and then a private room, when he'd lost his mother, Marianne, eight weeks earlier. But my son-in-law stood strong. Bud's big hug enveloped me with reassurance, warmth, and tenderness. I worship this man, the love of my daughter's life. She jokes that I love him more than she does.

Bud paused momentarily, took a deep breath, and approached his father-in-law's bedside.

"Hi, Papa." He leaned over and kissed Jack's forehead. He had kissed my father's forehead the same way that April evening in 2000 the night before he died. The memories were too clear for us. I hated that trauma struck so soon again for Bud.

Commotion shattered the quiet as Jack reared up once again, heading for God knew where. Brent strong-armed him back down on his pillow. "You've got to hang on, Dad, until they get you fixed," he said, patting Jack's arm.

After many long, frightening hours, close to ten-thirty p.m., we were summoned by the team of doctors. The neurosurgeon, in a godlike manner, addressed me directly: "Your husband has suffered a left temporal lobe stroke."

I don't recall exactly, but I think Brent led me back to Jack's room after that. My screen went black.

A sharp, piercing lightning rod split my body from head to toe as I stood alone on a remote, unfamiliar mountaintop.

I sensed my children circling. I heard voices.

"Nothing definitive yet . . ."

"Extent of the bleeding . . ."

"More tests . . ."

"Aphasia occurs suddenly after a stroke . . ."

"We will wait . . ."

"Jack, Jack," I wailed. I screamed without a sound, desperately, and dropped to my knees at my husband's bedside in bottomless sorrow.

From within my shroud of darkness, I heard Brent and Jamie question the doctors. At this point, they couldn't tell us what to expect, but in my heart, I sensed an epochal shift—that our lives had changed, maybe radically. Late-night fear and hopelessness permeated my being. As I began to resurface, I looked at Jack, who slept peacefully. Had they given him a sedative? Or had he finally worn himself out? Maybe he would be strong again. *Please, God.*

All was quiet in the hospital corridors as a new head nurse entered Jack's room and offered cheery greetings from the shift change. "My name is Lila," she said, "and I will be looking after Mr. Woods through the night."

With Brent immediately assuming the night shift for our family, Lila urged me to leave and get rest. My mind and mouth resisted, but soon my weary, frightened body gave in.

I felt dazed as Bud shepherded Jamie and me out into the cold February night.

℃

At home, the full pitcher of orange juice sat untouched on the top shelf of the refrigerator.

I dragged my weighted body down the long hallway to our darkened bedroom. With trepidation, I approached Jack's side of the bed. His worn brown boots lay angled on the floor. His pillow perched on the floor next to the nightstand. Was that where he'd last rested? I picked up the pillow and clutched it to my breast. My body dissolved onto the floor like wax overflowing from a candle, dripping slowly and steadily into a pool on the surface below. On the floor beside our empty bed, I pulled the familiar, battered boots he wore day in and day out toward me and savored the rich leather scent. I placed the soft pillow on the floor, put my head down on it and wept.

It was now Valentine's Day, 2015.

Chapter 40

Dual Brains

What transpired the first days after Jack's stroke remain mostly a horrific blur. Several days, however, are clear in my mind:

Day Three

"You can't be serious," I stammered in disbelief.

"Mrs. Woods, your husband behaved uncontrollably through the night once again," the nurse said. "The attending doctor has prescribed a restraining device; an enclosure bed has been ordered."

My mind reeled as I imagined my husband, the brick-solid man who had slayed the dragons and controlled our lives for five decades, cooped up, impounded in an "enclosure bed"—the medical term for a cage.

Day Four

"Can someone please review his meds? Please," I begged, hurling myself forward on the counter. "My husband didn't sleep at all last night. You caged him, which drives him crazy. He fights frantically to escape. He can't hold his eyes open and he's grasping his head in his hands like it's going to explode." I blubbered all this at a high-intensity pitch to a group of nurses clustered at the reception desk.

In a less-than-timely manner, a brusque doctor barged into Jack's room, leaned over him and barked, "Jack, open your eyes."

I couldn't catch sight of Jack's face, but the arrogant doctor turned to me and declared, "Jack opened his eyes. He's okay."

Before I could respond, he bounded out of the room without further comment. Jack thrashed in the cage, the mesh tent contraption connected to the frame of his hospital bed—a protective and calming restraint, they told me.

Separated from him by the enclosure, I leaned into the netting toward my stricken soul mate and said softly, "It's going to be okay, Honey. That guy's an asshole, huh?"

No response. Unzipping the tent at the end near his head, I touched his cheek and straightened the sheets before collapsing on the chair next to his bed.

I struggled with my thoughts, rubbing my temples. Within moments, a brooding fear slowly and surely permeated my body like a dark beast. I fought back tears as a frightening understanding of what might be happening closed in on me. From some altered state, I looked down and observed my hands wringing one another in my lap. I watched myself begin to rock in place, breathing hard. *What's happening to me?* I became wildly anxious; my head began to pound, and I fought an overpowering urge to run. All this time, I had been trying to fight, but my response now—flight!

I raced out of Jack's room, down the hall, back to the desk, and shouted as I shook, "I have to leave. For God's sake, please take care of my husband in 532."

I ran down five flights of stairs, out of the hospital, into the parking lot, and to my car. I drove way too fast and furiously home. In the driveway, I slammed on the brakes, escaped my car, and sprinted through the front door, down the long hall, through our office, and into our bedroom—our tranquil, empty bedroom.

I burst in and raced around to his side of our iron four-poster bed. Carefully, I bent over and moved his boots aside and gripped the cold, smooth post near his pillow with my right hand. I clutched the post with all my might for a moment, then released it and flailed myself forward toward the next pole at his end of our bed. Compulsively, I paced faster and faster around the bed, obsessively grasping each of the four poles before reversing. Around and around and around I went countless times, crying loudly, charging blindly, going nowhere in a repetitive, anxious pattern.

I have no idea how long I tramped madly around our bed in this way. At some point, my body slackened and the anxiety lessened. Eventually, like a wind-up toy running down, I slowed my pace. My body calmed. I lowered myself to the edge of his side of the bed. I slouched in the noontime sun, which shone through the half-open blinds, casting warm stripes across my body. I inhaled deeply.

Gradually, my mind began to swirl gently back into its normal space. I sensed composure. Time for me to return to the most precarious and alarming situation of my life. I needed to be with Jack.

Day Six

It was Paul's, Jack's radio partner's, birthday. Bud's fiftieth, too. How many celebrations had we had together?

Jack won't be aware of the birthdays this year. I woke up with this depressing thought. I walked to the French door and opened it to a gentle rain that turned the orange trees into glistening emerald green jewels. Were the trees weeping for us?

I tried to be thankful for the sweet surprise. We needed the rain badly.

Bud met me at the hospital and we tried to feed Jack breakfast. He steadfastly refused to eat, but when I told him, "Today is Bud's birthday, Jack," he smiled and mumbled, "Happy birthday, big guy." At that moment, at least, he recognized Bud and our life.

The rest of the day played out deplorably. I made a quick trip home late morning when Jack began speech and physical therapy. At his desk, reliably messy, I shuffled through piles of papers to separate bills, mostly unopened. Two insurance bills, our Automobile Club renewal, a golf club bill for both December and January, a doctor's bill from November, and Schwab General Fund in the red. Yikes, I needed to call Brent about this.

Added digging revealed our finances needed immediate attention. I became more and more disquieted as I realized Jack's head problems had been going on since Christmas or before. Ominous puzzle pieces began to fall into place. The accident hauling the wine bottles; the rush to the emergency room the day after Christmas; the lethargy; the withdrawal from his standing golf games; the near accident in traffic in his truck five days before his stroke; the disconnectedness. Was this all part of what was happening to him now?

I looked at the clock and realized I had to rush back to the hospital. His therapy would be over soon, and it would be lunchtime.

When I arrived, darkness filled Room 532; the curtain drawn and the cage zipped. Inside, Jack moaned and rolled his head back and forth. He pulled obsessively at his hospital gown, the netting, the pillowcase.

I hated this place. I chastised myself for leaving, even for a short time; he needed an advocate here at all times. I unzipped the end of the cage and patted him gently on the chest. He relaxed slightly. I kissed his face and talked quietly to him. His exhausted body gradually became immobile. He slept.

When Jack woke, I washed his face and put a clean gown on him. Scrubbed to a glow and back in the cage, he smiled and brightly said, "Hey, babe, where you been?"

Unable to answer, I unzipped the end of the netting, put my arms around him, and buried my head in his chest.

There were fleeting moments of joy. Jack smiled when my iPhone rang and I put it to his ear.

Bo's unsteady voice said, "Hi Dad, how are you doing today?" After a short conversation, Bo put little Chesapeake on the phone. Jack's head bobbed up and down as she chattered away.

After a short nap, at noon, I rolled him into the hall. "Why don't you wheel yourself to the lunchroom?" I asked.

He smiled, flexed his arm muscles in consent, and slowly began to turn the wheels, moving himself. My heart welled with faint hope. Could he be getting better?

At lunch, however, he refused the pasta, limp green salad, and bread and butter. He did take a bite of the canned peaches in syrup, but then he spit it out. I glanced quickly at the patients and caregivers at the other tables as I wiped the fruit from the table. I tried once more. Jack took the bite, sat a moment, thrust his head back, and, with a dramatic flair, spit the peaches out again, this time hitting me smack dab in the face.

Short-lived moments of joy. Prolonged hours of heartbreak. How long could this go on? I wasn't sure I could hold up. Scared out of my mind, I hung on by a fragile thread of nearly unbearable uncertainty and hopelessness.

Day Seven

Here's what I was certain of:

The human brain is mind-boggling.

I hadn't signed on for this crash course.

My husband was a tough son-of-a bitch.

Today, stroke plus one week, shaped up as another roller coaster ride of emotions, bizarre behavior, conflicting and confusing counsel, and unbelievable fear.

Brent, who had insisted on bedtime duty the previous night, called early and related Jack's behavior through the night, which ranged from vicious and turbulent to childlike and comatose. My heart sank at the disappointing report.

"I played a selection of classical music on my phone for him," my son said. "It settled him, at least for a while."

A beautiful idea, I thought. Jack is passionate about his music. "I'll download some of his favorites," I said. "Upbeat, happy stuff—Blake Shelton, Rascal Flatts, maybe even a little Lyle Lovett."

"Argh," said Brent to my country music playlist.

"You really are an elitist snob," I managed to joke. "Be there in thirty minutes."

Music emanated as a momentary answer, a momentary respite from my husband's dire struggle with whatever demons were jackhammering at his brain. That day, shortly after a botched attempt at breakfast and therapy sessions, I played his Garth Brooks favorite, "Friends in Low Places." I found it impossible to believe that just a few weeks before, Jack had electrified the karaoke crowd at a party on the terrace at the club with his spot-on rendition. There wasn't much of a performance element today, but his face did light up when the rousing anthem began. He threw his head back and sang. Every word—with attitude. This, on the same day he couldn't recall the color of his own truck.

Vince Gill's "Forever in Mind" visibly stirred Jack as well. His hazel eyes widened momentarily; he looked at me and pulled me close for a precious kiss. A tear trickled down my cheek after, and I looked upward in gratitude—just as a loud banging of his bedrail shook me back to reality.

Jack bolted upright in a show of infallible strength, violently shoved the hospital tray against the wall, defiantly pushed me aside, and lunged for the door. I grabbed the remote, pushed the nurse button, and screamed. Within moments, strong folks were in the room, restraining him. Once again, he sat placidly in his wheelchair. But as a nurse attempted to buckle him into the chair, in a flash, Jack bit her—hard—on the arm.

"Ouch!" she yelled as she grabbed her forearm and jumped away from her patient.

My gentle, affectionate, loving husband had just left his teeth marks in the forearm of a nurse. With great force, he pulled himself up again, grasping the end of the bed, turned, and kicked over the wheelchair.

Did I mention Jack was a tough son-of-a-bitch?

The injured nurse sprang into action, and within seconds three strong male nurses had restrained their savage patient, my amiable, thoughtful husband, and strapped him to the bed. Calming meds were administered, and the cage zipped once more.

When he finally slept, I reflected on this horrid day, which had unfolded as an exhausting emotional whirlwind. I made the decision then to move him to Scripps, a hospital in San Diego.

At ten o'clock, I packed up my bag of magic goodies I had hoped would jar him back to our reality—photos of Steamer and the little ones, a Butterfinger candy bar, a cigar, his wedding ring—and started my nighttime good-bye routine. I refreshed his water, made sure his meds were in place, tucked him in, and covered his face with kisses. As I touched his cheek one last time, he sprang upright from the pillow, busting my lip with the impact of his forehead, glanced around the room, and said with great enthusiasm, "I'm really getting a kick out of this place, M."

I wished I could have said the same.

ᴄ₃

I don't honestly know what transpired the rest of those first fateful days after Jack's stroke. We had him transferred from Palomar to Scripps Hospital. The time period—eight, nine, maybe ten days—remains a giant jumble of dogged fright, flashes of optimism, bouts of anger, and periods of extreme adrenaline countered by depressive slow motion as I slogged through the morass, my fog lights on. My head, like his, was so fucked up by this wild train wreck of aberrant, harrowing, unstoppable, bizarre actions from my unrecognizable Jack.

I received unending advice, counsel, and support from rotating strangers dressed in hospital garb. A multitude of family and close friends surrounded me, when my devastated self allowed it. I often wonder now if they recall parts I've forgotten? I haven't asked. I don't want their memories. I want mine.

As time has passed and the days after February 13, 2015, have continued to muddy, I have tried to jog my own memory. When I concentrate, a cannonade of hurtful, unthinkable images pierces my head—the caged bed, the wheelchair, IVs, steel cold MRI cylinders, monitors, EEG reports, relentless nurse call button beeps, CT scanners, a hospice team, and Jack, clad only in a hospital gown, his body withering, his brain twisted in agony.

Through it all, I stood powerless. An interminable brigade of medical professionals, charged with the ultimate care of my most precious natural resource, bombarded our daily lives. Who to trust? When to speak? What to ask? How to protect or anticipate? So much bewilderment, darkness, incomprehension, uncertainty, and trauma—not only to Jack's brain but also to mine. Dual brains knocked out of commission at the same time.

His didn't recover. Little by little, I would discover mine did.

As the months passed, I found myself looking into memory loss that had been frustrating the hell out of me. My internist explained psychogenic amnesia, also known as functional amnesia, is a disorder characterized by abnormal memory functioning in the absence of brain damage. It results from severe stress or psychological trauma on the brain. (Like when you are scared to death your husband is going to die?) There are two main types: global amnesia and situation-specific amnesia, which occurs as a result of a severely stressful event—which is what I guess mine is. A kind of protective PTSD, maybe?

The day before and the day of the stroke will be firmly planted in my psyche forever, I'm sure. Along the way, through my journals and conversations and tears, I have reconstructed as much as I can stand.

Chapter 41

The Oscars

I looked forward to viewing the Oscars telecast with Jack, even on the dinky TV in his new hospital room at Scripps. The transition—him via ambulance, me following—went well. I looked forward to indulging in our longtime Academy Award–winning movie tradition that night. We both appreciated good films and acting performances. We hadn't missed the ceremony in fifty years.

ၒ

Our first movie date happened two years after we married. We were dirt poor and had little kids, so the luxury of a movie evaded us until one day Jack said, "M, want to go on a date. Can you get a babysitter?"

Juggling Jamie's baby bottle and refereeing Brent and Bo's Tonka Truck fight, I asked, "Can we afford it?"

"The tickets are free," he said. "You handle the kids and get ready for Friday night."

The movie, *Arabesque,* starred a ravishing temptress, Sophia Loren, and Gregory Peck as a professor of hieroglyphics at Oxford. Jack had to nudge me several times as I drifted off to sleep, but what I saw of the film enchanted me. Sophia made me jealous—so sexy, so beautiful, so not tied-down, unlike exhausted me.

Five years later, living in Manhattan and a bit more secure financially, we began our Academy Award tradition. It lasted until three weeks before Jack's stroke.

Traditionally, most of the Oscar-worthy films premiere right before the Christmas holidays. Our little kids would be out of school and my parents in Texas were anxious to babysit, so we spent Christmas together, and then

Jack and I flew back to New York to spend a few precious days leading up to New Year's Eve alone together. During that time, we crammed in every film touted as a contender, usually two in the daytime and another at night. Classic movies—*Midnight Cowboy, Butch Cassidy and the Sundance Kid, Anne of a Thousand Days, True Grit, They Shoot Horses Don't They* . . .

Our popcorn, Milk Duds, and Coke habit premiered that first year and survived over forty years. The past fifteen, the Coke had become diet, but the chocolate, butter, and salt hadn't.

Our movie tradition changed over the years as we learned to record, binge watch, and miraculously order pay-per-view movies on our television screen—fabulous, since we lived thirty miles from the nearest movie theater during The Orange Woods years.

Sometimes, we treated ourselves to a nice hotel in the city. We checked in early, went to an afternoon feature then happy hour, followed by an evening feature. In the morning, we went to breakfast, a morning feature, a nice lunch, and, with a bit of luck on my part, did a little shopping before heading home.

Jack's last movies were *Birdman, American Sniper, The Imitation Game,* and *Selma*—our movie binge lineup in January before his stroke in February. I miss my husband madly in a multitude of ways, but never more than when I remember how he used to share his meaningful insights after a good movie or book or play. God, he was smart and perceptive.

⅓

My movie memories were interrupted by a volunteer carrying in Jack's bland dinner and a jar of Boost, strawberry, on a tray.

"Honey, guess what's on TV tonight? It's time for the Oscars," I said cheerfully, sliding the tray toward his chest—not too close.

I struggled to hear his indecipherable reply as he woke. He growled and rolled side to side. I tried to feed him; over and over, he turned his head and pushed my hand away. As I sat by his side, defeated, I realized he had no interest in movies, the television, me, or the world. I turned off the telecast, lowered the side of his bed, and lay close to him for a long time.

At home, keyed up from the long drive home in the dark and the stress of Jack's condition, I went to the television. It surprised me to discover I had actually programmed the darned recording device, which I had never done before. Recognizing pangs of hunger, I put a bag of popcorn in the microwave and settled in to watch the Oscars alone. The familiar smell of the popped corn permeated the house. God, I would have killed for a box of Milk Duds.

Midway through the show, Meryl Streep's "In Memoriam," a video montage in which the industry honors those they have lost in the year, featured a quote from Joan Didion's memoir. "A single person is missing for you. The whole world is empty."

I languished alone in an empty world.

Chapter 42

In the Middle

From time to time, I find the brain fascinating. Alone at home two weeks after Jack's stroke, not so much. His brain was monumentally fucked up, and mine was pissing me off. My friend, Gail, had asked me the previous day, "What kind of stroke was it, and how much recovery are the doctors expecting?"

This forced me to consider.

Sitting alone early morning in our inner patio, the one we call The Sanctuary for its spiritual aura, my mind reeled with questions and the heady scent of orange blossoms. The fragile, aromatic floral blooms last no more than three weeks. This year, he'd miss the experience, one of his most favorite times of year.

I'd bought a gift for a friend the previous month—Jo Malone's Orange Blossom, which Jack had given me that Christmas so long ago. The bottle describes the fragrance as Clementine flower sparkling over a heart of orange blossom and water lily, with warm undertones of orris and balsamic vetiver. To me, it was the fragrance of the magnificent blossoms of the Valencia oranges in our grove. Each day, I took the bottle of Orange Blossom perfume I had recently purchased, sprayed it around his pillow, and described the snow-white flowers that would turn into our cherished fruits very soon. Did he recognize the smell?

Gail's question planted a seed that had grown as rampant as the mint I'd mistakenly planted in my garden.

Maybe he wouldn't come all the way back. Maybe I was pretty much on my own now. Were we going to stop just short of fifty years? Perhaps the decades of shared storytelling was about to become a lonely monologue. My body tensed. I shook my head in violent refusal. I couldn't go there.

I'd always been a "glass half full" girl. Sometimes I felt myself slipping, however.

It embarrassed me that I'd erupted in tears in front of the damned Geek Squad guy the previous day—shocking the hell out of him, I'm certain. I had rushed home from the hospital to make a noon appointment; he showed up at two forty-five. Everybody came late to The Orange Woods, especially in *The Thomas Guide* days. What did it matter?

When I'd made the appointment a week earlier—a time when there had been so much more hope—I'd done so feeling I needed to make sure every TV and remote would be working perfectly, and that I could operate each one, when Jack returned for what I thought might be a long recovery at home.

When will he come home? Will he come home?

I secretly had spells of jealousy over the good times my friends and kids were enjoying and we were missing. Extremely selfish on my part. We should be leaving now on our "Golden Tour of the Golden State," celebrating our fiftieth, golden, wedding anniversary. We'd spent countless hours together planning the road trip after rejecting trips to faraway lands and a big, expensive party, opting instead for a California jaunt—Los Angeles, Ventura, Santa Ynez, Carmel, Monterey, San Francisco, Santa Barbara, and Montecito.

Jack had teased, "I'm gonna rent you a solid gold Prius, babe, so you can ride in style on this trip—on the road to our golden years!"

The ring of the phone startled me. I grabbed my coffee cup for a refill and went to answer. I started sobbing instantly when the case worker told me we needed to schedule a family conference for Monday. Without emotion, she said those who couldn't attend would be "welcome to join in on a conference call."

My mind only let me imagine the worst. I struggled hard to remain positive.

With warm coffee in hand, I returned to the comforting sunshine and sat in silence, except for the buzzing of the bees in the grove nearby. My reverie was interrupted once again, this time by a roadrunner who, upon glimpsing himself in the glass patio door, pecked vigorously at the image. I began to shake.

At that moment, I found myself longing for my mother and her gentle compassion. Scared and helpless, I pictured Mom at her sewing machine. A strong urge to sew a quilt or a dress came over me. Comfort food, I supposed. I smiled to myself at the image of Mom at her Singer; I could hear the sound of her machine. "The last model made without plastic parts," my dad boasted about her Christmas present that year. Over and over, as she taught me, she tried her best to slow me down and make me sew straight seams. Her Singer sits in the closet by my ironing board now.

The thought of sewing took me back thirty or forty years—simpler times, when I cut, pieced, and stitched a patchwork quilt for each of my kids for their beds out of their cast-off 100 percent cotton T-shirts—Little League, 10K walks, souvenirs from our vacation trips to Mammoth Mountain and Broadway, Stage 7 flash dance kinds of shirts, the Bee Gees and Earth, Wind & Fire concerts, and their favorites: Jack's radio station contest prize shirts with his image and logo on the front from KLIF, Mighty 1190, WKYC, KHOW, KCBQ and KFMB.

These days, my kids were wearing their kids' college T-shirts—Wesleyan, Whitworth, Davidson, Amherst, and Belmont. Still 100 percent cotton.

I drifted even further back, over fifty years ago, when my devoted mom, a gifted seamstress, made every article of clothing I wore up to and including my trousseau for my first wedding and honeymoon. Sewing is old-fashioned—so nostalgic, so uncomplicated. Would it be therapeutic for me now? Not stressful, like technology and GPS and stock portfolios and alarm system batteries and sprinkling system leaks and racking the wine and selling the truck and buying a car. So damned many things I didn't understand or care about; all the things he'd always handled.

Suddenly, a deep cold permeated my body. I shook. I began to cry again. For God's sake, how many tears did I have? Without a doubt, this was the most all-consuming meltdown I'd had in these weeks. My third. I was scared to drive, pay bills, turn on the oven, or use the washing machine. I was afraid to talk to anyone new, or anyone old, or anyone. I hadn't phoned his sister, or my cousin, or his radio buddies. I couldn't figure out what to say or how to say it.

To myself I said out loud, "Marilyn, you've got to calm down and be responsible. You've got to get back to the hospital." The shaking slowly subsided. Looking down to make sure the trembling had stopped, I noticed I wore a blue denim shirt, a little too large, with a "105.5 FM Thunder Country" logo embroidered on the pocket. I was wearing his shirt. I didn't recall putting it on. I saw a yellow spot, a little bit of mustard, on my pants. Costco Polish dog, no doubt. Didn't matter. He didn't look.

My body temperature warmed a bit. I breathed deeply. "Think about something else for a few minutes," I instructed myself. "Could help."

೧೮

More than anything, as a young woman, I longed to be a journalist. My heroine, Lois Lane, a Pulitzer Prize–winning investigative journalist employed at the *Daily Planet,* fooled around with Superman. Like Lois, I pictured myself as a first-rate, crack reporter, and eventually an editor of some prestigious news source. I also fantasized about having a Clark Kent kind of guy in my life. That part happened.

I got sidetracked and got into television first, where I wrote copy, and then into radio, where I crafted scripts for on-air personalities. At PBS in Washington DC, I found myself in administration—too far removed from journalism for my liking in the beginning, but as it turned out, the experience served me well, as I eventually, once again in California, moved into radio station management.

Somewhere along the way, I began to journal, which is Xanax for a writer.

I knew plenty about Xanax by now.

"But Dr. Arnstein, I don't need to take a tranquilizer," I'd said, crying hysterically into the phone, the previous week.

"Marilyn," she said, "fill the prescription and put it in your purse. If you start to melt, get the bottle out. Take a pill if you need it. If not, it's a pacifier—reassuring to know it's there."

Looking back, I realize how valuable it was for me to write through this horrid ordeal; the process has helped with the stress and fear. The writing I am drawn to most is storytelling, a craft I learned from Jack through years and years of listening to him on-air, and up close and personal in our daily lives. I listened as the master, who had taught many young students of radio, revealed, "I open the mike with a strong grabber—get their attention. What I put in the middle is essential—got to be fascinating, M. Never say one extra word—edit, edit, edit. And most importantly, I never, never open the mike without planning how I'm gonna get out! How you exit must leave a lasting impression. Make them crave more. Audiences hanker for a good punch at the end—shock, happy, sad, surprise, some strong takeaway."

After, with his amazing sense of timing and captivating grin, he would playfully simulate a drum roll on my knee, give me a quick kiss, and exit the room, leaving me craving more.

೧೮

An hour later, on the long drive back to the rehab hospital, which sat very close to the Pacific Ocean, it surprised me how clearly I heard him there, his signature smile of a voice oozing warmth and friendliness, telling stories to his listeners. It amazed me how often I felt he spoke directly to me over the forty-plus years of his broadcast career.

Reflecting on his wisdom and talent as a storyteller and entertainer took a bit of the edge off the severity of the current situation. But as I stood back at his bedside and watched him grapple with the demons in his brain, his monumentally muddled mind, I searched for answers. What had happened to his brilliant, inquisitive, fast-thinking, charismatic brain? Would it return to normal?

We were in the middle of this story. The beginning: the panic scene with the first responders, the stroke—certainly a grabber. What would the end be?

A journalist chronicles events. A wife's heart breaks and her brain gets screwed. It was late, and I couldn't think anymore.

As young reporter girls, Lois and I used to say, "That's thirty."

⁂

Jack grew more and more agitated as I prepared to leave later in the evening. "Babe, where are we?" he questioned, abruptly lifting his head off the pillow.

"You are at Scripps Rehab and you are here to get better," Joyce, an efficient soul, answered for me as she replaced a bag of some clear liquid on his IV.

I came to his side and gently lowered his head back to the pillow.

"Why are we here, Marilyn? I need to rack the wine," he said impatiently, ignoring the nurse, head and shoulders both off the pillow this time.

These moments of faint clarity penetrated my heart with torturous pain. As the nurse scurried out of the room, I bent my head toward Jack's and kissed his cheek, settling him once more.

"It's going to be fine," I whispered to reassure not only my husband in his convoluted state, but also myself.

Where are we? I wondered. Does he really want to know? Do I want to know?

Chapter 43

Two-Stepping

I was up bright and early to a foggy morning the next day. I arrived back at the hospital around seven-thirty to find him sound asleep.

Gina, the chipper night nurse, cautioned, "You have to stay close. He's fast—gets up and goes, has no concept of balance or weakness." She checked the monitors one last time before leaving us alone.

The breakfast tray arrived. I started with the oatmeal, raisins, and brown sugar, one of his favorites. Jack gritted his teeth, clenched his jaw, and refused every bite I offered.

"Honey, please," I pleaded.

At a meeting with the dietary staff later, I bemoaned the fact Jack wouldn't eat the food and continued to lose weight.

A helpful woman named Yolanda asked, "Any special requests? His diet is unrestricted—we can serve him anything you like, within reason."

"How about a hot dog?" I requested, thinking about his love of the Costco dog, which was our favorite meat treat after twenty-two years as vegetarians.

"Great," she said cheerfully. "A dog and some French fries for lunch. Maybe a chocolate shake? He ought to lap it up."

No luck with the frankfurter, either. Jaw stayed clenched shut.

After his afternoon therapy, they weighed him: 161 pounds. Good grief, he'd lost eighteen pounds. If this continued, he and I would weigh the same. As if it mattered.

The next day, I brought my Jambox to Jack's room. The tiny wireless Bluetooth portable speaker was much more effective than my iPhone for delivering Jack's favorite music. Even the nurses seemed to respond to our playlist. I noticed a little swish around the monitor by the night nurse as she checked his vitals.

He slept once again as George Strait sang "I Just Want to Dance With You," a song perfect for dancing the Texas two-step, which I first experienced as an eager college freshman at Texas Tech in Lubbock. I begged Jack to learn the two-step.

He mastered it many years later at the Buffalo Gap Food and Wine Summit, which happens every April outside Abilene near the center of Texas. It's a grand gathering of cowboys, restaurateurs, vintners, and musicians. Besides mouthwatering, savory food from the big state's best chefs (and less-than-incredible wines, compared with those of California), cowboy kind of folks whirl and glide on a Texas-size, open-air dance floor beneath live oak and mesquite trees and the colossal moon in the night sky. The moon is bigger and brighter there. As the dancers, dressed in leathers, suedes, denims, fringes, and silver belt buckles, float in a state of grace like skaters, musicians strum and croon under the stars, channeling Bob Wills and his Texas Playboys. *Texas Monthly* once commented, "Watching couples coast around at the honky-tonk may intimidate the double-left-footed, but heck, if a cowboy can dance, how tough is it, really? Two-stepping is just walking to a beat."

To me, this two-step, which has its roots in the foxtrot, is the most romantic dance of all; it is sometimes referred to as the "dance of intimacy." Jack didn't do many dances, but he did "the dance of intimacy" well. Resting my arm on the bicep of his strong frame, he led me as we danced the two-step, quick-quick, slow-slow, following the motion counterclockwise under the Texas moon. I can still picture him now—black Stetson, black jeans, black boots, and a smile that outshone the moon.

The rickety old wooden deck quickly became our dance floor after we moved in. The Titian sunsets we witnessed from our deck lasted for hours. A perfect scenario for dancin', the two of us alone under the boundless sky.

Without a doubt, our favorite artist—definitely country—was Vince Gill. His "If You Ever Have Forever in Mind" endured as our love song.

After dinner and a glass of wine—as the glowing sun set over the mountain and dipped out of our sight, leaving the most magnificent explosion of soft coral colors—we would dance. Just the two of us. I have no memory more tender.

I wonder, how long do old memories last? The thought of this frightens the hell out of me. Will I always clearly remember his methodical shaving routine; his love of black beans and rice; the foot-long scar on his left thigh, the jagged result of a steel mill accident? How he disliked tying bow ties, and loved his silver bolo? Will I ever forget the sound of him turning the corner at the end of our country road, his silver Dodge Ram 2500 gas-guzzling, mega-truck vibrating with the ear-shattering volume of Willie or Waylon or Garth, Steamer bounding along at his side? Will I always remember his captivating storytelling? His hazel eyes smiling like polished stones?

Alone at home later, as Jack memories glided through my mind, I forced my eyes shut tight and clenched my fists over them in an attempt to keep the memories locked within.

☙

When I arrived at the hospital the next morning, Jack had just finished his shower. A congenial occupational therapist, a young, muscular guy, had done the honors. The highlight of Jack's days lately was his morning showers. When the guy washed his private parts, Jack repeatedly said, "Thank you," exhibiting an emerging total lack of inhibition. No filters.

It embarrassed me even more when Jack said in a very familiar and sexy tone as Vince sang in the background, "Why don't you take your clothes off and come sit on my face?"

At this, a flush crept across my cheeks, and my heart welled with precious memories and affection that overrode any awkwardness I might have otherwise felt in front of the nurse as she prepared to administer his meds.

Delbert McClinton's "Two More Bottles of Wine" came up on the playlist next. Jack, now sitting in a chair and freshly bathed, reacted momentarily; his head jerked in a double-take as Delbert warbled about going out West and setting the coast on fire. Was Jack reminded of our first trip to the West Coast so many years before? Was that why he patted his hand in time with the beat? I swear he was into it. Even smiling a little. My cowboy.

Jack and I worshipped so many things having to do with the vast, wealthy space called Texas. Tumbleweed and turquoise. Buddy Holly, Larry McMurtry, and Janis Joplin. The Yellow Rose of Texas and the State Fair of Texas. Willie, Waylon, and the boys. The Alamo and springtime's bluebonnets. Barbecue, beer, and oil wells. Wranglers and rodeos. The two-step, the moon, and the eternal openness.

Jack lusted after Texas and everything Texas as much as I do. His go-to coffee mug was Dallas Cowboy blue and imprinted with Davy Crockett's "You can all go to Hell; I'm going to Texas" declaration.

Would he ever go there again?

Chapter 44

The Invitation

Mom, I'm sorry, but I can't be with Dad tonight. Can you handle it?"

Disappointed and exhausted to the point of collapse, I assured Brent I would be fine with the overnight duty. Then I asked, "Are you okay?"

His voice faltered a bit. "There's been a fire. Thank God, all the kids were out, but the entire second floor of 215 is destroyed. Police, fire engines, TV film crews everywhere. I can't leave Laurie and Sophie and her friends. They are shook up."

Waves of despair piled on top of my faltering hope for Jack's recovery as I recalled how nervous both Brent and Laurie had been agreeing to let Sophie bring eight college freshmen home for spring break, temporarily turning 215—their project next door—into a college dorm. Unable to resist Sophie's innate powers of persuasion, they had welcomed three young women and four active college men to the two-story Spanish Revival house, built in 1925, my kids had recently purchased, restored, and completely re-landscaped, five days before the fire. Sleek mid-century furniture filled the rooms; a smattering of fabulous art was on the walls. Laurie and Brent had just completed their latest preservationist project.

For four days, Sophie's friends—preppy young people with names like Will, Spencer, Daphne, Forrest and Garrett—had frolicked nonstop together at the beach, the ranch, Balboa Park, the taco stand, the swimming pool, and 215, embracing everything Southern California in the springtime had to offer.

A miracle had happened on their fourth night, the night of the fire: all of the North Carolina college kids, along with Brent and Laurie, had gone to a coffee house nearby in North Park to listen to Calvin, now in his last days of high school, and his band, Traffic Bear, jam. The concert lasted forty-five minutes. As they played, the unoccupied house had burned.

Both Brent and Laurie were visibly shaken for days after the fire. Their initial hesitation played out in a grave manner. What to do now? They no longer wanted the responsibility of the second house but resisted the idea of selling. They had dreams of it being a pied-à-terre for friends and family, especially Jack and me when we went on our city getaways in San Diego. Renting was an undesirable option for Brent and Laurie, both of whom had demanding careers.

Indecision about the property overwhelmed them, but shortly after Sophie and her friends returned to college, Brent returned to his nighttime duties—sleeping next to Jack, calming him during his restless bouts and fits of anger—and he and Laurie once more tackled the restoration of 215, the house they'd bought next door to theirs.

଼୪

Six days after the fire, more unsure of myself than I'd ever been, I walked into Brent and Laurie's backyard. Although I couldn't see the house next door, I could smell smoke and ashes. Centering myself, I settled into the grandeur of the park-like setting of their spacious backyard, a welcome contrast to the cold, sterile hospital. The spirituality of the setting engulfed me. Eight magnificent olive trees, freshly mown green grass, apples espaliered on stone walls, and a glassy horizon swimming pool full of perfectly still water surrounded me. I felt miniscule, insignificant, and alone. I sensed tears coming.

Quietly, Laurie approached from behind. "Let's have a glass of wine," she offered, putting her hand on my shoulder. My hand shook as I wiped a tear from my cheek and reached for the glass.

As the sun began to set behind their house, a slight relief from the day's oppressive heat took hold. Laurie, all one hundred pounds of her, looked cool in her sleek exercise garb. Looking at her made me realize how much I missed my regular morning walks with my buddy Sue.

Four low, cushioned lounge chairs were arranged near the pool in an intimate semicircle. As Laurie and I started for the grouping, a door slammed shut and Brent called, "Hi Mama." Now my lifeline of support, he pulled me close in a big hug and patted my back gently. A man of few words, not given to outward displays of either emotion or affection, he had pulled out all the stops during those last horrific weeks. My rock.

Calvin, my tall, handsome, sixteen-year-old beanpole of a grandson, sauntered in moments later wearing a stonewashed blue T-shirt. Tenderly, with head bowed, he hugged me and muttered a few indecipherable words. He had endured so much of the worst of Jack in the hospital—his teenage coping skills were indecisive and awkward.

The four of us spent a quiet, loving moment together in the wooden chairs, silently absorbing the magnitude of our situation. I sensed my optimism, my hope, my cheerleading waning. Today had loomed huge for me. I gazed into the sky above; an airplane floated across the horizon. Helpless, uncharacteristically out of control, waffling, indecisive, in denial, I was way off my norm. It didn't take me long to realize the others in our little foursome were in the same emotional lifeboat.

As if recognizing the need for a break from the gravity, Laurie disappeared to the kitchen and returned with our al fresco dinner—chicken pot pie, the ultimate comfort food—along with more crisp white wine. As steam escaped from the hole I punched in the golden crust with my fork, I smiled to myself realizing that had Jack, a longtime vegetarian, been here with us, he would have systematically spit every chunk of chicken out of his mouth toward Izzy, their dog.

After devouring our gratifying feast, Brent and Calvin, who had collectively struggled at times with what to say, what topics to avoid, or when to shut up since Jack's stroke, impulsively took off for ice cream.

Laurie, my caring and extremely strong daughter-in-law, took advantage of an opening while the boys were on ice cream run. She and Brent recognized the devastating truth I stubbornly refused to accept. Jack would never come home; even if he survived, he would live in a home with skilled nursing the rest of his life.

Deftly, she asked, "Marilyn, do you like the house next door?" Continuing her subtle sales pitch, she repeatedly said how much they would like for me to live next door.

Momentarily shocked and at a loss for words, I went silent. Tongue-tied.

She continued, "And your friends could come, too."

"Uh, I don't think so," I stammered. "I couldn't leave Orange Woods."

"But you could be here and there, too, for the time being. You two were thinking of selling. Wouldn't it be extremely difficult for you to keep up the property, vineyard, and winery by yourself?"

She dropped it when the boys returned with the ice cream—Ben and Jerry's Fish Food flavor, which sounded awful but tasted delectable. What is it about a taste of something sweet that can momentarily right such awful wrongs?

ଓଃ

Jack and I had indeed been considering selling The Orange Woods.

My mind returned to our harvest the autumn before. Hot, sweaty, and achy, Jack and I collapsed on the Sunset Deck with big glasses of ice cold Arnold Palmers, which we could hardly lift to our mouths, still weak from the physical labor of it all.

When we got to this point, the end of the vineyard's fiscal year, we debriefed. Each year, one or the other of us would suggest this might be too expensive a hobby or too much hard labor. Without fail, the other would emphatically refuse the idea, and we would continue as farmers. This year, however, within minutes of beginning this conversation, we looked at one another and read each other's minds.

"It's time," he said. "Too damned much work for old people." No longer in our sixties, being farmers in our seventies was taking its toll.

I nodded my head in sad agreement as he declared, "It's time to sell."

We were in the midst of those plans when the stroke happened. Now, I faced a huge decision in addition to all the other uncertainty in my life.

Chapter 45

The Saddest Sunset

Early morning four days later, March 12, I awoke with a sense of the world moving in slow motion and I still couldn't keep up. Deliberately, I dressed, grabbed a cup of black coffee and a chocolate peanut butter breakfast bar, and drove to Scripps Encinitas.

On approach, my glass neared empty.

Jack, overwrought and agitated, had slept little. The foot massage I had given him the previous night, which had put him to sleep, had no effect this morning. He thrashed wildly at times as I tried my best to calm him.

Throughout the day, he struggled restlessly in and out of consciousness, without any real recognition of his surroundings or me.

Helplessly, I stood guard over my savage beast. The so-often misquoted phrase from 1697's *The Mourning Bride*, "Music hath charms to soothe the savage breast," rang out appropriate today either way.

Desperate to soothe my tortured husband, I scrolled through my playlists to my newest one, which I had titled "Jack Rehab" and filled with his favorite songs. I caressed his face as I placed my Jambox nearby and pushed play on my iPhone, hoping his most beloved song of all, Carrie Underwood's "How Great Thou Art," would settle him.

As Carrie sang, I stroked Jack's forehead with my fingers, trying to erase the wrinkles there. He stiffened and pushed my hand away, knocking the phone to the floor. Trying again, this time I played "Every Time We Say Goodbye," by a very young Ray Charles—a song from our early days together. As I turned the volume up a bit, he settled back onto the pillow. Was he listening? Was he hearing the words we'd once made love to? Once he smiled, or at least I thought so.

◌

The long day grew worse. A welcome respite was lunch with Brent, Laurie, and Bud at a funky Mexican restaurant on Highway 101 nearby. Brent was slowly but surely assuming the patriarchal position, which I knew in my heart Jack would soon vacate. At lunch we analyzed, each in our own way, Jack's condition, gradually understanding the severity of what loomed in our very near future.

After lunch, Laurie and Brent took off to investigate more skilled nursing faculties, which seemed futile to me. How on earth could he ever leave this rehab facility? Bud and I lingered in the parking lot, struggling with both conversation and our uncertainty. He gave me a big bear hug as we parted.

ᙏ

I stayed by Jack's side all afternoon until early evening, when my stepdaughter, Jackie, came for a few hours. She hadn't been with her dad for two weeks and appeared visibly shaken and horrified tonight. She left the room abruptly. I followed, understanding she needed support. In the barren hospital hall, I hugged her as she shook, crying violently. In a way, I imagined, her grief was more difficult, since she wasn't there day to day. Jackie's daughter, Shanna, wasn't able to visit her grandfather in his last days and neither were Bayley and Sophie, both far away in college. Like Bo and Jen. My own heartache relinquished its hold momentarily as I tried my best to help her. No words were exchanged between us, just hugs. When the tears subsided, we returned to his bedside.

ᙏ

The wretchedness of this day became the proverbial straw that broke my back. Driving home was ridiculously difficult. Hard to navigate the freeway through an onslaught of tears.

Home, with a glass of Jack's wine in hand, I wandered aimlessly through the vineyard at twilight, up and down the neatly groomed rows of grapes. His grapes. Eventually, I found myself alone on the Sunset Deck.

The memory of him sitting in this very spot devastated me. As I prepared our dinner one evening, I watched as he stood near the railing and surveyed what he thought of as his manifest destiny. His patriotic stance and his gaze at the valley below and the mountains partially eclipsed by fog reminded me of American artist Thomas Cole's iconic painting *The Oxbow*. Cole, who inspired the generation of landscape painters known as the Hudson River School, aspired to what he termed a higher style of landscape that included narrative. The narrative outside my window at this moment involved a man who had a vision; cared for and loved the grandeur of his land; and, like an artist, created beauty on it.

Sitting at our special table for two near the wrought iron railing this evening, I realized I needed to put an end to the heartbreak. I couldn't take any more. But more importantly, I couldn't let him suffer any longer.

Sipping the wine, I wondered how many times we had slow danced to Vince Gill's "If You Ever Have Forever in Mind" in this very spot. I could hear the song in my mind. Overcome with tears, I shook violently and sobbed uncontrollably out loud. I always had forever in mind. Bottomless sadness overpowered me, greater than I had ever experienced in my life. I sobbed for a long, long time as the sun slowly set in the west; my body became lifeless. In my mind, the orange trees around me and grapevines below wept with me in unison.

At some point—I have no idea how long I sat there—I looked to the sky, ablaze with color. I pleaded in anguish to Jack to give me guidance. He had done so for fifty years; maybe he would even now. I prayed to God—whatever God—to give me direction. Aloud, I begged my parents, too, to help me. "Mommy, Daddy, please . . ."

In a matter of moments, the heavens appeared to open up. My body weight lessened. I experienced an unprecedented sense of a higher power. A flush came over my face and a soft pounding pulsated in my chest as the sunset turned into a glorious panorama that bled rapturous shades of crimson, coral, and deep blues.

For a time, I just sat there, enthralled. I received clarity.

The next morning, in my meeting with the palliative powers-that-be—after securing my children's acquiescence—I would direct, "Nothing artificial. No prolonged life. Let him be."

For the first time in weeks, I slept well.

Chapter 46
The Palliative Team

I woke up terrified on this frigid March morning in 2015, alone in my bed at home. Twenty-nine days had passed since Jack's initial stroke the day before Valentine's.

The previous day, driving the hour to the hospital, I'd listened to *A Farewell to Arms,* an audiobook I'd bought in anticipation of the upcoming trip to Spain I'd been planning with Sue and Linda, my best art-making buddies, and a group of docents from the art museum. I put the book on in an effort to take my mind off the hopelessness of Jack's condition. One of Hemingway's lines had haunted me all night, and it surfaced again this morning: "The world breaks everyone and afterwards many are strong at the broken places."

I headed to my husband's bedside to share every precious moment of our fiftieth wedding anniversary, March 13th, with him. The world was breaking not only for him but for me, too.

Brent, who, in our tag team rotation, had left Jack's bedside a few minutes before I arrived, called to tell me I should reinforce our directive and instruct them not to insert another breathing tube. This meant DNR, which, of course, alarmed me. Brent had met with a neurosurgeon who had recommended this course of action, adding the classic, "This is what I would do if it were my family member." Seconds later Laurie phoned and suggested we cancel the family dinner party at Jamie's planned for the evening, saying, "We should be closer to Jack."

Images of what could be flashed through my mind. Adrenaline spiked through my body. Panic and fear of the inevitable gripped my being. *What are they telling me? Please don't let this be true,* I begged God.

This started out as the worst day of the four full weeks since Jack's initial stroke. A horrifying roller coaster ensued—intubate, extubate, check vitals, family conference, chance, slim to no chance, non-responsive, palliative meeting, odds are, morphine, hospice, hope, little hope. Jack lay almost lifeless, on the edge of something horrifyingly frightening, in Room 301 at Scripps Encinitas.

It is excruciatingly difficult to relive, much less relate, those long, agonizing last days. Collectively, the family suffered from exhaustion, gripping fear, and unbearable sadness. But Brent, Laurie, Jamie, Bud, Jack's daughter, Jackie, and her husband, Tim, Jennifer and Bo—his after-major-back-surgery trials made all the more difficult by not being with us—and I managed to make some painstakingly difficult decisions together, with the guidance of the palliative care team.

"They've summoned us to a family conference, Mom," Jamie said when I arrived at the hospital. I shuddered.

An hour later, we assembled in a conference room around a long table—Jamie next to me, holding my hand; my strongmen, Brent and Bud, directly across from us. The room was sterile, with white walls, small windows, and no art in sight; it felt cold. I pulled my open cardigan sweater tight across my chest.

A team of three entered the room: a solemn young doctor, an administrative person, and the palliative nurse. They offered sympathy, followed by their report. We listened intently. They were properly cautious, well trained.

The words blurred together. I'm not sure who said what.

"Attending doctor's reports . . ."

"Our feedback from nurses . . ."

"He's struggling, flailing at times . . ."

"Assessments in combination lead us to our conclusion."

My mind flashed to the graphic words of conceptual artist Mel Bochner, painted large scale in bold colors, as part of the La Jolla Mural Project—"Blah, Blah, Blah." The text image cartwheeled over and over in my convoluted mind. I found myself looking at myself from some faraway place.

And then the words we hadn't heard before—"death is imminent"—jarred me back to the present, where the team of three nodded their heads in unison, eyes downcast. I don't recall who pronounced the sentence.

Strange to say, but deathly silence followed. A wave of darkness, like the tenebrism in a Baroque painting, engulfed my listless body; my troubled mind battled to get out of the somberness. Unable to speak or move, my jaw clenched, I sat frozen in place.

My small posse looked at one another. Searching my face for direction, Brent cleared his throat and requested some private time. The palliative team murmured their consent and quietly filed out of the room, one behind the other, closing the conference room door.

The room was still; more deathly silence.

At some point, we realized they were waiting and our decision had to be made. Should we remove all means of life support from Jack and begin to administer morphine?

"Mom." Brent leaned across the table toward me.

A slow dirge of a drum roll, deafening and painfully slow, beat in my head.

"Mom, I need you to talk to me . . ."

We faced an agonizing decision. The medical community would not and could not give us a definitive opinion in this situation.

Hesitantly, I shared my sundown revelation of the night before. This, plus the frightening talk of "quality of life," "short of a miracle," "a matter of time," "he can hear you," and "these are the numbers to look for," coalesced into our final decision, which we agreed upon solemnly and unanimously: we would begin the final process of losing Jack.

α

The next day, March 15th, was a blur. I spent it crying at his bedside, whispering, praying, trying my best to make sounds I hoped would be pleasant to him. In my head, I cussed some. A lot actually. On my iPhone, I played his music: Carrie Underwood, James Taylor, Garth, and Vince. When a harpist came to play for him, which sent me into a tailspin, I left the room while she performed some mournful church music not meant to be played on a harp—"In the Garden," I think.

It had been a day and a half since we'd given the palliative team our decision. I wondered if I could possibly change my mind.

α

The doctor—who, we'd discovered in conversations at the bedside, had listened to Jack on the radio for many years—came to his room.

"You cracked me up, Jack, with your stories," he said. "You always got my day started right. So many mornings for so many years. Thanks so much."

What a horrid small world.

In the hall, before he left, the doctor, with a gentle bedside manner, put his arm around me and told me he believed the end was no more than two or three days away.

As the doctor walked away and my tears began, I understood that Jack, my Jack, even as strong as he had always been, was failing. Morphine relieved his pain; he drifted in and out of consciousness, off any means of life support. No more frustrated gestures or unexpected bouts of anger or unrestrained bursts of random action. Just breathing in and out, slow. Soft. Every once in a while, he would open his eyes. I would speak with tenderness, touch his cheeks, kiss his lips. And he would fade back into a coma.

Brent, Jamie and I stayed throughout the next hours, covering for one another, always talking to him. "After all, Dad is the King of Small Talk," Brent quipped.

Jamie prayed.

Later over coffee, Brent teased her, "How come you never pray for me when I'm sick?"

Jamie's split-second response: "Oh Brent, I pray for you every day!"

The family gathered in the late afternoon. Three of my grandchildren—Maddie, Calvin, and Carly—were there, youthfully awkward and nervous, unsure how to behave. I was glad they had each other. They laughed some; they cried together.

Brent had made plans for us to get away for a quick dinner—a delayed anniversary gathering he arranged more for me than the others, I think. I had a Manhattan, which is what Jack would have ordered. An image of my husband holding up the cherry stem from his cocktail after he had tied it neatly in a knot with his tongue surfaced. The kids always applauded his feat; I found the process quite sensuous!

The family lingered together for a while. The spectacular sunset in Encinitas over the Pacific Ocean comforted, in a way. Soon, I excused myself and returned to Jack.

ॐ

In his room, the nearness of death felt ubiquitous.

The cold, cavernous nighttime space of the hospital room grew larger and colder as evening encroached. I felt my body shrinking into itself. The black panes of the oversize windows were menacing, closing in on me.

I sat quietly, touching his shoulder, caressing his cheek, holding his hand. At some point, I reached into my purse for my Jo Malone Orange Blossom Cologne. "Remember when you first gave me this, honey?" I whispered as I sprayed one soft poof above him.

Unbelievably, Jack wrinkled his nose a bit, slowly pushed his head upward from the pillow, and delicately inhaled the familiar scent.

Recognizing a slight, hopeful sign of life, I whispered, "Can you give me a kiss, Jack?"

Using every bit of strength he had left in his frail body, he pursed his cracked pale lips together and blew a faint kiss to me. I experienced a tender bit of bliss for the first time in thirty-three days. Leaning over him, a single tear fell from my eye onto his sunken cheek.

Brent came around the corner just then.

"Did you see that, Brent?" I asked. "He kissed me."

"Yes, I did, Mom. He kissed you." My son crossed the cold room and put his arms around me.

ॐ

Jamie returned from the restaurant and Jack returned to near lifelessness. A nurse summoned Brent and Jamie to the front desk. I stayed next to my husband, kissing his hand. My grown-up children talked in low voices outside the door; Jack's labored breathing was barely discernible.

A short while later, my kids returned to the room.

"Mom," Brent said, "Jamie is going to take you home for a few hours' sleep. It's important you rest; she needs it, too. I have an important meeting in the morning at eight, so I need you both back here by six thirty. They have upped Dad's morphine. He will be fine until you come back."

Reluctantly, I allowed myself to be ushered away, once again, from Jack's bedside, where he lay motionless except for the slow, slight rise and fall of his chest. Jamie put her head on Jack's shoulder and softly prayed for a quiet night, free of pain, for her father.

As we left the hospital and crossed the parking lot to begin the hour drive home, Jamie protectively embraced me.

"I don't want to leave, Jamie," I said. "Can we go back?"

Firmly and lovingly, my daughter insisted we abide by Brent's plan. A chill permeated my body as we walked into the darkness, which loomed in a threatening way.

"What is today, honey?"

"March 17, Mom, it's St. Patrick's Day."

Ironic. I thought about Jack, with his Irish heritage, lying in his hospital bed waiting to die clad in a green hospital gown.

A flood of memories spewed forth in my mind as we walked toward the car. Gerry's Irish tales of Rose of Tralee. Our wonderful years when Jack worked at NBC in Rockefeller Center, and we were among the million-plus spectators at the biggest St. Paddy's Day parade in the world. Green milk for my little kids' St. Patrick's Day breakfasts. One romantic night at the Buena Vista in San Francisco when Jack introduced me to Irish coffee. A green satin blouse purchased for a "Luck of the Irish" holiday party last year. My mom's crystal Irish coffee cups. Happy times over and over, celebrating the luck of the Irish.

A familiar Christian rock song played on Jamie's radio as we drove. I reached over and took her hand, noticing the tears in her eyes. So easy to get involved with my own heartbreak and forget she was losing her daddy. My children were such warriors. I needed to be strong.

We'd driven in silence for no more than five miles when my cell phone rang.

"Mom, I'm so sorry. Dad's gone," my heroic older son sobbed. He gasped, trying to contain himself. "It just happened. Dad stopped breathing."

My hand gripped the phone. The oncoming headlights intensified, blinding me. Unable to speak, I felt enveloped by a large black velvet curtain. My body gave way to its all-consuming coverage. Anxiety, sorrow, and horror permeated my head, heart, and body like shrapnel. Yet this sinister cloak, this shroud of darkness, was, in a weird way, comforting. I no longer discerned lights; an opaqueness glazed my world. My being steadfastly moved toward blackout.

"Mom, are you there?" Brent's voice echoed from my cell phone, now lying face up in my lap.

Stunned back to reality, I put the phone to my ear. "We'll be right there," I mumbled into the receiver.

I touched Jamie's arm. I didn't have to say a thing. She began to scream. As she wailed, she exited the freeway, stopped at the side of the road, got out of the car, and rushed to the passenger side to embrace me. We clung to one another. And then we returned to the hospital. Our luck had run out tonight.

ങ

Back in the hospital lobby, Brent waited for us. After the three of us cradled one another for a long while, he said, "Do you want to go back to the room, Mom?"

After a minute of thought, I said no. I remembered Jack's last loving gesture—the fragile kiss a few hours before—and decided that would be the memory I'd carry forever.

Standing in the empty lobby with Jamie and Brent, a lava-like rush of the finality of it all flowed through my body. I wondered if I would ever be strong again in my broken places. The three of us sat together on a couch well into the wee hours of the night, holding hands and barely speaking. It was final and frightening.

It must have been several hours before we stood and once again left the hospital. As Brent walked us to the darkened parking lot, Jamie remembered Gigi, their grandmother and my mom, had died on "Brent's shift" moments after I left and minutes before she arrived. Jamie punched her older brother gently on the arm and said, "Same as Gigi. Dad always liked you best."

Much later, weeks later, in a feeble attempt at humor, our family's lifeblood, I cautioned Brent in front of the group, "Don't come near me when I'm sick."

Chapter 47

Pink Moon

The day before Easter—April 4, 2015, nineteen days after Jack died—began as near to perfect as a day could be.

Early morning, I wandered out onto the Sunset Deck. The full moon of April, setting in the west as the sun rose behind me in the east, greeted me. Both the sun and the moon were sitting in my sky.

April's full moon is sometimes called the pink moon because its arrival heralds the appearance of pink flowers called wild ground phlox, one of the first spring flowers. However, this morning, it was my special moon—a stunning blush of soft, rosy hue, setting on the horizon in the west, partially eclipsed across the bottom. The pink, the romantic pink of the aristocratic French rococo artists, took my breath away, reminding me of the fragile kiss Jack had given me on his last evening on earth.

The night before, The Orange Woods had been full of people, friends and family, who had come to honor Jack. Many from his family had arrived from Indiana; my cousins had come from Alabama and Texas. We'd shared tears and laughter, tacos and margaritas, remembrances, and an extraordinary sunset.

Today, I needed quiet.

Even though my best buds—Alice, Steve, Sue, Ralph, and Nancy—were still with me, they too craved quiet, so we existed in stillness together for a while. Then we moved in unison to coffee, newspapers, and an amazing brunch, which Alice, a born short-order cook, prepared effortlessly. We talked, we cried. More coffee. More crying.

At some point, Steve read the New Year's resolutions Jack had written in Zihuantanejo three months before. Among others, Jack had resolved to "think before speaking."

Steve commented philosophically, "Isn't it amazing that after all these years, a guy is still reminding himself of something so basic and so important—trying to be better?"

Jack had done a much better job of keeping that resolution than the others which always appeared at the top of his list: "lose ten pounds" and "no creamer in coffee." He couldn't resist caramel macchiato or hazelnut or eggnog whatever in his morning brew.

At dinner a week later, when I recounted Steve's observation about Jack's resolutions, Brent offered, "Actually, Mom, he did achieve both of those in his last five weeks. In the hospital, they gave him no coffee or creamer, and he certainly lost more than ten pounds."

At some point, Alice, a dedicated gardener, brought up the vineyard. "We need to go there," she urged. They had all been with us in the planting at the beginning and at harvests each year.

"This is the time of voracious growth, Jack always reminded me," I related to the group. "Every spring, we worked side by side removing all but the strongest four or five shoots on each side of the vine, allowing the nutrients to go into the chosen grapes."

At high noon on this surreal day of his memorial service, Alice coaxed us to the vineyard to prune Jack's treasured grapes. The warmth, the sunshine, the vines, and the quietness in nature exuded what we all needed. We worked together without conversation for several hours; as we did, we almost forgot the gravity of the day.

ভ

At the Pauma Valley Country Club just before five o'clock in the afternoon, the two hundred and fifty chairs set up on the green facing the pristine ornamental pond seemed insignificant in all the majesty of nature that surrounded the setting. But as each one of those white chairs filled, the collective reverence matched, if not surpassed, the grandeur that is Pauma Valley.

Alice ushered me to the front, where my family surrounded me. Jamie sat next to me and handed me the program. On it, Jack stood, smiling, with his arms folded across his chest. Brent had taken the photograph, one of my favorites. On the back, three more pictures: Jack as a little guy with shirt and tie and his hair slicked down, parted in the middle; Jack in his first radio glamour shot, taken at KLIF in Dallas; and a close-up of him in front of an NBC microphone. He was smiling in each of the three photographs.

Jamie had selected John 14:27 to include in the program: "Peace I leave with you; my peace I give you. I do not give to you as the world gives. Do not let your hearts be troubled and do not be afraid."

Laurie had suggested Mary Oliver's poem "The Sun." Her words echoed the reverence Jack held for nature. "Have you ever seen anything in your life more wonderful than the way the sun, every evening, relaxed and easy, floats toward the horizon and into the clouds or the hills . . ."

I had found a quote by Thomas Love Peacock that reminded me of Jack, and had included it on the back of the program, under his radio pictures:

"He kept at true good humor's mark
The social flow of pleasure's tide:
He never made a brow look dark
Nor caused a tear, but when he died."

When I finished reading the pages, I lifted the program and kissed my husband's smiling face.

Soon, a meaningful, heartfelt, and brave tribute to Jack began. His nephew; his partner; his nineteen-year-old granddaughter, Sophie, speaking on behalf of them all; and his four children spoke. Over and over, I caught myself inhaling deeply and breathing out resolutely as I struggled to "be in the moment." I longed to preserve every last detail, to cling to every word said about the eternal love of my life.

They called him a hero, a warrior, kind and gentle, a compelling storyteller, the King of Small Talk, a proud Marine, a quick-witted comic, a rabid NFL fan, the master of the one-liner, and a bad golfer. They said he emboldened, mentored, inspired, and lit up a room when he entered.

So many tears from so many people. I loved these people because they loved my husband. Everybody adored Jack. I was the lucky one who had shared a lifetime of extraordinary happiness with him.

A party followed. There were many surprises—people we hadn't seen in many years. People who were our friends, our kids' friends, Jack's radio friends, old friends, and new friends. There were a few freeloaders, too, and even Jack's most favorite oddball film star, Bill Murray, happened by.

Bo's artfully crafted video of Jack the Entertainer's life entertained us all.

Why did it have to be like this? Jack would have loved being there on this day. He would have basked in the sunshine and reveled in the joy and friendship. He would have told stories.

He couldn't be there, but I believed he'd sent the pink moon to me that morning.

Chapter 48

Whatever Happens . . .

Seven weeks after Jack's first stroke, at his memorial service, my broken-hearted daughter, Jamie, stood in the late-afternoon "pink moment" of Pauma Valley, speaking to hundreds about her beloved father and the magnitude of her loss. She ended her emotional, moving tribute by vowing through her tears, "I'll never forget his last loving pledge to my mom. In a fleeting moment of clarity, he looked beyond the emergency response team crowded around him, determinedly pointed at her, and, in his signature radio voice that had spoken to hundreds of thousands daily over the years, promised, 'Whatever happens, I love you.'"

How could I ever have forgotten this? Until she said it, I had no memory of it. No matter what kind of shock or trauma I'd experienced, how on earth could something so beautiful be lost in time and space? Gone from my consciousness? On reflection, in all our time together, this remains the most meaningful thing he ever said to me—five profound words of devotion that I will carry with me forever.

Whatever happens, I love you.

CB

When we were planning the memorial, Sophie, granddaughter number four, volunteered immediately, saying she wanted to speak. She represented eight grandchildren—her brother and sister, Maddie and Calvin; Jamie and Bud's daughters, Bayley and Carly; the little guys from Arizona, Chesapeake and Cash; and Jackie's daughter Shanna from Chicago; and herself—with these words, written in her freshman dorm room across the country at Davidson University in North Carolina:

Everyone here probably knows that we are a family of talkers. When we all come together at holidays, birthdays, or other celebrations, lack of conversation is never an issue. In fact, sometimes the problem I have is getting a word in. You might imagine that after spending his life working as a radio talk show host, Pa would have been one of the loudest voices at the table, but surprisingly that wasn't the case. I think that to me one of the most important and special things about Pa is he knew exactly when and how to put a word in. I never recall Pa being an antagonist in one of our silly family arguments, but I will always recall his eloquent and meaningful way of saying grace, giving a toast, or expressing his gratitude.

He also had a habit of pulling each of us aside on special occasions to have a one-on-one conversation. Whether after a performance, a game, or a graduation, Pa needed us to understand how much he believed in us. When Pa wanted to talk to you, he made sure you understood what he had to say. Grandparents have a reputation of being proud and bragging about their grandkids, but this was altogether different. He would grab on to your arms tightly, look directly into your eyes, and make sure you understood him. There was soft shoulder shaking and gentle finger pointing, but most of all, genuine admiration and love.

It wasn't for anyone else to hear or understand, but I will always appreciate those moments that he insisted on. He was my biggest encourager, and I always felt loved and accepted when I was with him. No one ever believed so much in what I was doing, and that was truly amazing.

Chapter 49

Sorrow

After painting *Sorrow,* his poignant image of his working-class mistress, Vincent Van Gogh wrote the question "How can there be on earth a woman alone, abandoned?" across the bottom of the canvas.

With Jack gone, I felt alone and abandoned. The magnitude of this reality was staggering.

Edvard Munch's *The Sick Child,* 1907, touches on the fragility of life. It draws upon Munch's personal memories, including the trauma of his beloved sister's death.

Michelangelo's *Pietà,* masterfully carved from a block of Carrara marble during the Italian Renaissance, flickered in the candlelight of my mind. I saw the Virgin Mary in her utter sadness and devastation. She seemed resigned to her loss and becoming enveloped in graceful acceptance.

Was I seeing these sad works of art in my mind because I was supposed to exhibit graceful acceptance? Was I, through my appreciation of art, ever going to be re-sculpted into a new and capable me? Would I experience rebirth, my own private Renaissance?

03

The week after Jack's memorial service, a familiar-looking envelope arrived in our box at the post office, addressed to The Orange Woods.

When I opened it back at home, I immediately recognized the work of our muralist, MB Hanrahan. Although I found the title eerie—"Back By Popular Demand"—I had to smile just a bit. MB, once again naked, this time with an oversize decorated Easter egg—pastel pink, lavender, and yellow—on her head, and again, bunnies placed strategically on her still perfectly toned, sixty-year-old body. Momentarily, I experienced a tightness in my chest; the card trembled in my hand. I stood up from my desk, walked to the bedroom, and glanced at Jack's empty side of the bed. Slowly, I went to his side, opened the nightstand drawer, and put the card inside. My body slumped as I lay down on the bed and put my head on the pillow.

ᘓ

The idea of leaving The Orange Woods haunted me.

Jack died on St. Patrick's Day, four days after the chicken pot pies. Three weeks later, Brent, my oldest son who became my rock, escorted me on what he dubbed "The Suit Tour," which included appointments with our attorney, accountant, and brokerage firm.

I didn't see a reason for me to be there; Brent handled everything competently. When we stopped for lunch at a sandwich shop in La Jolla, however, he floundered a bit.

"Mom, we need to discuss the possibility of you moving to 215."

In his uncomfortable yet pragmatic manner, over a turkey club, he introduced three issues in rapid, bullet-point format:

"I work very hard, and I need my privacy. We can't be running in and out of each other's houses.

"It would be nice to have dinner with you but not every night. Once or twice a week would be good.

"I don't want any men in that house with you."

He's very good at bullet points. Trying not to react to the ridiculousness of number three, I concurred, and the deal was done. At the time, I didn't realize how difficult selling our property would be.

ᘓ

In the Orange Woods years, I would lose my parents, my brother and my husband, leaving me quasi in control of my roster of extremely capable children and grandchildren. Or, at least, they let me think so.

Chapter 50

Cars

Six days after Jack's service, my house emptied, leaving me alone. I stumbled into a new existence, solo.

Sitting in my car in the garage, I gripped the immobile steering wheel with a strangulated fierceness, my knuckles flexed.

"No," I moaned to the lifeless engine.

I pounded my fists on the wheel until they throbbed. Jack always handled car problems. He'd been gone only a few days, and here I sat with a damn car which refused to start. The life had gone out of it, too.

How many human years is 175,000 miles? I wondered. For dogs—one year for every seven. How many miles in a car year? I'd had my car—my dependable, efficient hybrid—for almost seven years. How on earth could it be unreliable at this very moment, the time when I needed it most? I ached for reliability in my life. I was journeying on a lonely road trip of unending heartbreak now, and I needed reliable.

Dead. My car was dead. Jack, too.

I went back to bed.

Ↄ

In the light of the next day, when everything should have looked better but didn't because Jack was still gone, I purchased a new car—something I'd never even thought about doing by myself before. In the early years, we'd bought cars together, but at some point I'd tired of the silly "let me go in to the manager and see what I can do for you" game and let Jack negotiate our new cars without me.

Turns out, buying this one was ridiculously easy. Who knew you could docu-drive a sales contract in a matter of hours? Could select your options online? Who knew they'd even deliver your new car? Especially to a place as remote as this?

Around eleven in the morning a week after my husband died, a polite older gentleman knocked on my front door and announced, "Hello, Mrs. Woods, I have your new car."

My chest tightened; I opened my mouth to speak. Nothing came out. Instead, I burst into weird, uncontrollable tears, which threw my gentleman caller completely off-kilter. He wrung his hands, glanced nervously at his paperwork, and meekly inquired, "Aren't you Mrs. Woods? Isn't this the right car?"

I babbled an apology and, after I settled myself into a modicum of composure, let him lead me into the motor court—a vast spread of russet-colored paver stones—where my new car awaited. The gleaming white pearlized SUV glowed in the noonday sun—birthday candle bright, shiny and spotless. The man behaved with caution, casting hurried glances my way as he walked me around the vehicle. He gave me a brief introduction, starting with the keyless entry and ending with the remote-open rear door. We came full circle to the driver's door, which he opened and gestured for me to sit in. After bidding me good-bye, he closed the door, spritzed the front windshield, and polished my rearview mirror before hurriedly climbing into the car that had followed him from the dealership.

Alone once more.

I closed my eyes and tried to stop my brain from convulsing with flashes of Jack—walking, working, driving, grinning, cussing, serious, happy, mad, gentle Jack. He liked cars—actually, any kind of machine. In the Marines, he was a tank mechanic.

I breathed in deep. I inhaled the new car smell—genuine, not the kind you get at the carwash—and leaned back against the headrest. An intoxicating mix of warm leather, shiny objects, and pleasant clean scents wafted over my head. I stayed still for a while, eyes closed. I sat in the driver's seat for a long time. As I ran my hand over the leather upholstery, the color of creamy peanut butter, a motorcade of car memories flooded my mind.

I took a moment before I turned my head and looked over my left shoulder—beyond the orange grove, toward Jamie's house—and thought of how many times Papa and Neeny had driven our two little granddaughters, Bayley and Carly, back and forth from their house to The Orange Woods. So many times, after they romped with Steamer, swayed together in the big red swing, played dress-up from the costume trunk, and picked oranges for their dad and a bouquet of lavender for their mom, we piled into Papa's "big farmer truck."

"Play it, Papa," they would squeal in unison to their doting grandfather.

Jack always laughed, knowing exactly what they wanted. They had memorized every word to their favorites from his crooner Dean Martin playlist.

The four of us would sing "That's Amore" at the top of our lungs—the girls shouting "like a big pizza pie," and Papa harmonizing, as always—over the hills and home.

Yesterday, I'd sold his big truck—too painful to see it sitting there empty. His side of the garage was now empty; his side of the bed, too.

As I turned back toward the house, I glanced at our mural, a colorful panorama of memories on the long wall of the guest house. I looked down. I held the spare key remote in my left hand and clutched the papers the man had left with me in my right.

I loosened my grip and, in a moment, recalled another little kid—my middle son, Bo—almost ruining a big car surprise at six years old. In New York, Jack had gifted himself a Corvette, Monaco orange (a less-than-subtle color choice), when he signed his NBC contract. Not one for delays and crowds, he couldn't handle the train commute into Grand Central Station (no control). He preferred to drive back and forth—over the pot-holed drives through the Bronx, along the east side into the city and Rockefeller Center.

After school one afternoon, Jack rustled up Bo from kindergarten and took him to the dealership to pick up the car. All the way home, he admonished, "Don't tell Mom, Bo. It's a big surprise."

At dinner, barely able to contain his excitement, Bo blurted out, "Dad got an orange—"

Jack's head snap and warning glare stopped Bo mid-sentence. After a pause, Bo finished with great emphasis, "banana!"

It took a split second for Jack and me to appreciate his adorable quick thinking. I ran around the table and gave the little guy a big kiss. With the back of my hand, I wiped the macaroni and cheese from my cheek. We called the car the Orange Banana thereafter.

My car in those days was modest. With three little ones, I didn't go out much except to the grocery store. I don't remember the make or model, but it was a silver-ish mauve color, sort of frosted, which appealed to me—until the used car salesman jabbed Jack in the ribs and, in a lecherous stage-whisper, said, "Like the color? We call it 'pussy pink.'"

We bought it, but after that I hated both the car and the color.

We went back and forth over the years with our car choices. Sometimes I got the fancy car and Jack got the utilitarian one. Other years, we switched. For my fortieth birthday, he gave me a butter-yellow Mercedes. Before that, I had a long history of station wagons. While I carpooled kids in the station wagons, Jack bought a blue—unbelievably bright blue—Porsche Targa. Before he got to the end of the driveway each morning, Willie singing "Blue Skies" filled the air as my happy husband drove off to the radio station, top down.

When three college tuitions loomed and carpooling was no longer necessary, Jack bought me an economical pre-owned Chevy Chevette, beige, which I "customized" with three racing stripes in my favorite colors: red, orange, and yellow. Although compact, the car exacted a mighty blast at random stop signs or traffic signals. The noise of the backfire practically lifted pedestrians off the sidewalk. I had never driven a stick shift before, and it's quite possible the backfires were operator error.

☙

Still sitting in the motor court midday at The Orange Woods inside my new white car, which I would later name Pearl, my reverie continued. A butterfly danced around my front window and landed momentarily on the glistening hood of my car. White—alabaster white—was the color of our first car, too, a sleek convertible we drove all the way from Texas to the West Coast on the trip that planted the California seed in our minds.

Fifty-plus years of automobiles continued their drive through my mind, carloads of memories.

I reached up and adjusted the rearview mirror. A pang of longing hit my heart. For an instant, I thought I saw him in his blue denim shirt coming up from the winery.

No one there.

I dragged myself out of the car and slogged around to the passenger side, my hand trailing along the exterior. I touched the door. Warm. I turned, leaned back against it, and basked in the sunlight, comforted.

As I lingered there, more car thoughts surfaced. I smiled, thinking about how Jack and I mastered the new technology of my last car—his idea.

For at least a month, at happy hour, he poured two glasses of wine and put a handful of salted almonds in a little dish, then motioned for me to follow him. Into the garage we went.

"Sit yourself in the driver's seat, babe," he offered the first evening as he leaned across and placed the two stemless glasses of Cabernet in our new cup holders. Next, he opened the second door and ushered an eager Steamer into the back.

The black dog tried his best to catapult all one hundred and five pounds of his scrawny, lovable self into the front seat with us.

"You be a good dog or you can't play with us," Jack reprimanded.

Our obedient Steamer lumbered into the backseat; Jack threw a handful of almonds his way. "It's such a beautiful evening," he said. "Let's roll the windows down before we start our lesson."

I tried my best to calm my nerves as I drove our brand-new vehicle fifty feet out of the garage to the motor court. Once we were situated, Jack began to thumb through the manual. In actuality, there were three manuals: one for the car, one for the navigation system, and one for the sound system. I sat behind the wheel, already overwhelmed but eager to learn.

Determined not to let the technology of this vehicle overwhelm us, we tackled one item at a time. Eco drive mode, parking assist monitor, AUX port, voice command, vehicle proximity warning—a litany of unfamiliar automotive terms barraged us.

"Hey, this damn car has pussy cookers," Jack said in his inimitable, racy way about the seat warmers.

I harkened back to the used car salesman in Scarsdale. Instead of lascivious, I found Jack's little joke amusing and familiar. I couldn't help smiling.

"Let's be sensible," my analytical copilot continued. "This is the same as learning a foreign language. We'll take it one section at a time."

Like we did with most technological wonders in our lives at the time—toaster, coffee maker, DVD, DVR, vacuum, television—Jack and

I persevered until we got the car to about 25 percent of what it could do. At this point, we were done. Our automotive happy hours ended in like manner.

As smart and logical as Jack was, he was technologically inept. In fact, he didn't like technology—resisted with vehemence most everything about it. He rarely made calls. He used his late-model iPhone mainly to send and receive text messages to and from his golf buddy, Tom, about their tee times. He used to say about his iPhone, "It will do everything but make a fucking phone call!"

Not only the iPhone but also the GPS system in our cars drove him nuts. When the GPS lady (and maybe herein lay the problem) gave directions to go one way, Jack insisted we should go another way.

"Recalculating..."

"She doesn't have a clue what the hell she's talking about."

He waged a constant debate, talked back, refused to agree with the GPS, preferring to wing it.

CX

I've never been a car person. But this car, my after-Jack car, took on new and unusual meanings in my life. The day after the home delivery, I slid into the driver's seat and closed the door. Vacuum-sealed. It transported me back to the womb. Safe and protected, I felt contained, isolated from the outside world I wanted to flee. On this second day of new car ownership, I began to drive. I drove over two hundred miles—over asphalt, around hairpin curves, down state roads lined with hand-crafted altars of flowers and crosses, across the Coronado Bridge, along Interstate 8, into the back country, and beyond.

As I drove aimlessly for hours, I mastered the car's remarkable audio system—and learned a lesson. Music, always my trigger, brought tears and an onslaught of memories of Jack. We cherished and shared music. So many special songs. Dreamy and romantic music—especially Luis Miguel, whom we had first learned to love in Oaxaca; Joe Cocker's funky and sexually charged "You Can Leave Your Hat On"; anything country, gospel, or blues; and our longtime favorite, the soulful Ray Charles. Jack listened endlessly to "America," Ray's stirring duet with Alicia Keys. Even now—perhaps even more now—whenever I hear it, I am reminded of Jack the patriot, proud to be a Marine and an American. So many memorable times together, all wrapped around music.

Near Julian in the east county, I turned the sound up loud—so loud the windows seemed to shudder. I whimpered first, and then bawled with reckless abandon. It's hard to drive one-lane country roads when you are sobbing. Between my bouts of tearful sadness, my head and heart pulsated with nonstop thoughts of Jack. The burning question—*What am I going to do without him?*—pounded with staggering ferocity in my head.

I drove for hours before I returned home to The Orange Woods from my grievous sojourn on wheels. Jack wasn't there. And even though I knew he wouldn't be, paralyzing grief slammed me as I started up our long drive-way. I ached for him to be there and hug me. I longed for Steamer to bound alongside my car.

A waning crescent moon made its way across the nighttime sky to the west. When I stepped out of the car, a shroud of darkness weighed me down, placing another stone on my heart. The darkness covered me through the night and most of the next few days as I lay in bed and nursed my stigma-ta-like wounds of loss and sorrow. Oppressive.

ᘓ

One week later, the morning began with amped-up, debilitating pain and sorrow. I resisted getting out of bed. Am I depressed? I wondered as I went through the motions of combing my hair. Jack had been gone two weeks now, and during that time I had been filled with more tears than I'd ever imagined were within me. It disturbed me when they flowed at inappropri-ate times, like in front of the poor man who delivered my car. Helpless to contain them today, I cried relentlessly throughout most of the morning as I read the Sunday paper and drank my coffee. My tears splashed on the crossword puzzle, leaving it soggy and unworkable.

José, one of our loyal workers, came to the door in the late morning. He handed me a simple bouquet of three white roses tied with a red ribbon. "*Para Señor* Jack," he said.

I cried some more.

Sue and I walked later in the day. Could this be my first step back onto the road that would be my life without Jack?

But at home again afterwards, a sense of panic began to settle in. Sitting alone on the sunset deck, I contemplated the life ahead. How on earth to jumpstart this different journey of mine?

Only two weeks, and it seemed an eternity.

Chapter 51

Things That Happened . . .

It was a gradual process. A shift from pleasure, gratitude, and extraordinary times to aloneness, unending confusion, overwhelming sadness, and heart-piercing grief. Without my husband:

- I overate regularly
- I cried incessantly
- I drank too much wine
- I hid under the covers
- I watched mindless TV, couldn't read
- I rarely calmed down, was never at peace
- I overspent
- I cried some more
- I refused grief counseling
- I suffered relentless stomach pains (ulcer?)
- I abhorred social situations
- I stopped reading the paper
- I didn't get an ulcer
- I drank too much black coffee—alone
- I avoided most eye contact
- I cussed a lot; words I had never used
- I learned how to use his drill
- I filled out endless forms, offering death certificates over and over as proof (really?)
- I slept in his pajamas

- I winced seeing couples holding hands
- I cried with his sister, long distance
- I stopped doing art, threw stuff on the floor and in the trash
- I gazed at the sunsets alone
- I gave away his socks and ties on Father's Day
- I read about the anxiety attack I experienced and its aftermath
- I coveted the full moons
- I dreaded the holidays
- I survived the holidays
- I sold his damn gas-guzzling truck
- I learned how to seal the wine bottles
- I gave his cashmere sport coat to his friend
- I polished his cowboy boots
- I started eating healthy
- I drank from his coffee cup
- I stopped eating healthy
- I renewed the winery license
- I got sick to my stomach over my portfolio
- I returned to my work at the art museum
- I took a trip with Alice to New York City
- I hired a personal trainer
- I started being moderate
- I cussed the realtor
- I worried about the price of oil
- I worried about irrigation
- I obsessed about pruning the grapes, wanting it done exactly the way he did it
- I downsized
- Sometimes I wasn't nice to my friends
- I stopped going to the personal trainer

- I stopped being moderate again
- I changed realtors
- I blamed both the Republicans and the Democrats for my house not selling
- I downsized some more
- I agonized over moving to the city
- I vowed not to cling to my children
- I forced myself to get out more
- I played more Duplicate Bridge, which became an escape for me
- I stayed inside
- I thought I'd go to movies by myself; I didn't
- I didn't enjoy doing anything alone or with somebody
- I cried some more
- I walked a lot
- I lost some weight
- I exercised some
- I texted my grandchildren; they answered, which pleased me
- I stared at pictures of the two of us
- I tore up some of those pictures
- I felt better, maybe.

Sometimes I wasn't even nice to my family. And they tried so hard...

I didn't belong anywhere. I hung, suspended, over my life. Floating aimlessly among anonymous people, places, and things. Sometimes I would land, and soon I would take off again. I didn't belong anywhere. I didn't want to belong anywhere. I ached to stay home. Or not stay home.

Writing in my journal released everything. An onslaught of soulful, arresting memories shackled in my head and heart. I was pummeled with sadness. I turned on music. The full moon arose in the sky. Everything else came crashing down. My chest ached with pain—the pain of despondency and despair. I was lonely, scared, and felt strange. But more than that, I felt so damned bad about how much he'd savored life and how much he'd marveled at nature and the sunset and the oranges and the grapes and the moon and the life we'd lived at The Orange Woods. I hated it that he wasn't there. I remembered how he'd worshipped his grandkids and dreamt about their careers and their weddings and their kids. He was going to miss everything going forward; terrible for me but devastating for him.

CB

Two months without Jack. Counting the four and a half weeks he'd struggled in the hospital to no avail, one-third of a year without him. And it seemed like most of my life.

I struggled with desperation to keep him with me—to preserve the feel of his skin next to mine, the small balding spot on the back of his head, and his roughened hands. I fought to remember his unending charisma, mind-boggling sex appeal, intellectual heft, and wit. I squinted my eyes to see his handsomeness, bright smile, and loving, inviting, tender way. I felt it got harder every day. I didn't want to let his presence fade one bit. I ached to smell, taste, touch, and summon everything back.

I slept in his pajamas. I clutched the last towel he'd used, sitting in the steam shower where he sat. I had never watched so much mindless TV. I couldn't focus or concentrate on other things. That week, I spiraled into a grand funk—so deep, so dark, and so frightening. I'd raced out of a very special friend's housewarming party the previous week as the floodgates opened. A recent lunch at Stone Brewery with my best buds, Lana and Tim, had also begun with tears—all three of us. And yesterday evening, as soon as I'd walked through the door of Jack's best pal, Tom's, house for his birthday party, I'd lost it again. A private beautiful few minutes during the tears (both Tom's and mine) had happened. Shutting out the revelry around us, we'd hugged and comforted each other in the midst of the celebratory crowd. In moments, loving arms had enveloped us both in a group hug. Ignoring her houseful of guests, the clinking glasses, and the laughter, Tom's wife, Jodi, had bent her head between ours and said a prayer for "Jack Jack." She'd spoken with such passion. We'd clung to each other for a few precious moments.

Moments like these made me question: should I be staying home all the time? I was so conflicted. What terrified me was the thought I might not come out of this state.

I wasn't angry. They say anger is one of the main stages in grieving. Was that coming? I was lethargic, unsettled, unsure of myself—but wasn't that to be expected?

I had this impression that if I could desensitize myself, it would get better. So, I turned up the music of Callas and Pavarotti, Chet Baker and Steve Tyrell, Garth, Vince, and Lyle. I played "Stay with Me" and "I Won't Give Up," sung tenderly by fifteen-year-old Carly. Her grandfather, her proud grandfather, had arranged a recording session for her at a local radio station and with great pride produced her four-song CD. Over and over I blasted the playlists, so loud it may have been hazardous to my hearing.

One morning, I arranged and rearranged his ties, contemplating who would get which one. I even ironed his wild, silly socks in preparation for Father's Day gifts—or regifts. After, I sat in the winery, thinking about how much joy being a vintner had given him. I stared at the neon sign until my vision blurred. I was thinking, *Eventually, it won't hurt so much. Maybe?*

Curious—I felt safer in crowds, groups where all were strangers. I embraced anonymity and isolation.

Why was I in this downward spiral? I'd felt pretty good for ten days or so after returning from glamping (glamor camping) at El Capitan Canyon near Santa Barbara with TTT. But now the grief had returned. Could it be the recent much-needed rain and the gloomy skies? Could it be that I was approaching the two-month mark? Could it be the fact that three of my best friends, quite coincidentally, were embarking on road trips with their spouses, something he and I had loved to do so much? Could it be the fact that one TV had just given out and I couldn't make the #@*!!^# volume work on the other one? Was it because I was eating healthy and not drinking wine? (I hoped it wasn't that last one.)

I can tell you what it wasn't: it wasn't because of lack of support from friends. Or a lack of undying support from my children, who were also grieving. Or because of financial concerns or inactivity. I had invitations, dinner dates, theater tickets, books to read, airplane tickets, and more. And I was healthy, blessed in these and so many other ways.

In a gem of a vintage book on surviving the loss of a love that Sue, my banker bestie, had given me, it said, "The process of healing and growth is not the smooth progression many people assume. It's more like a lightning bolt, full of ups and downs, progressions and regressions, dramatic leaps and depressing backslides. Realize this and know that whether you are 'better' or 'worse' than yesterday—or five minutes ago—the healing process is under way."

Intellectually, I understood this. Emotionally, I thought it was a bunch of bullshit!

I awoke the next day, Sunday, to find the barrage of depressing thoughts had dissipated, my outlook had become a little brighter. I changed batteries in the TV remote and, miraculously, it worked again. I had a delightful brunch on the terrace with Jamie, Bud, and Carly—who'd sung from her heart at church that morning—and Bayley, who'd arrived from college in Spokane the previous night. Maybe it was just the process.

At the end of the day, I read more in *How to Survive the Loss of a Love,* the grief book by Stephanie Kujack that had become my Bible. I had adopted a helpful tidbit from the author's counsel on how to evaluate oneself. I decided to lie down.

Chapter 52

Ten Weeks Adrift

Another Sunday. Creepy. Not a sound in my house. No dishwasher. No blowers outside. No TV inside. No Banda music in the groves. Not even my wind chimes. The silence stunned me. Mark Rothko said, "Silence is so accurate." Silence is conducive, sometimes, to productivity. And, sometimes, to tears. Today, there had been both. I sat down again with *How to Survive the Loss of a Love* and once more instead of evaluating myself I decided to lie down. It worked. A burst of productivity followed.

I cleaned out file cabinets and his closet, wrote long overdue thank you notes and placed an order for coffee and laundry soap online. Afterwards I took more time to rest and be sad.

The problem with resting? Memories bombard, exacerbating the reality. Instead of resting, I anguished.

We would never dance the two-step again. No more dancing. No more sex. No more turning to him to have him complete a memory I had forgotten. Jack and his bulletproof recall could always supply the date, the year, the location. "How on earth do you remember that?" I often asked in astonishment.

It didn't piss me off too much that I had to take out the trash. Or figure out which sprinkler is leaking or change a light bulb. I didn't miss having to think up something for dinner. Well, maybe I did. I didn't even eat dinner anymore. I had celery and hummus or apples and peanut butter for dinner most nights. I didn't miss the sex.

Yes, I did.

I did miss sex with Jack—bombastic, outrageous, mutually satisfying, gentle, loving sex, all of the above (not in the same session). Often. For years, our sex shattered the earth, blew the mind, and altered the mood. Steamy, heart-pumping sex. Jack was an amazing, loving, considerate, gentle, (sometimes not so gentle, when I craved it that way) partner. Creative, romantic, receptive, aggressive, hard to get, and, like I said, gentle.

We enjoyed said sex in some of the most amazing places in the world. On a quilt in the orange grove and in the neon light of the winery, on a Texas backroad in the moonlight, on the floor of a closet, on a balcony in Acapulco, in the Indiana woods near his childhood home, our dining room table, on the terrace as the sunset's colors shrieked in the sky above us . . . And did I say it happened often?

But like everything else, sex ages without mercy. It becomes more difficult and disappointing, I guess, because you have these incredible memories of what it used to be and is no longer. We, or at least I, harbored fears of becoming less desirable—old, silver-haired, wrinkled. The mirror showed that my boobs sagged and my butt did, too. How could I be sexually attractive in any way? Did he have these same feelings of inadequacy that are continually reinforced by the media? Did he fear a looming expiration date on his sexuality like I did? If he did, he never conveyed it to me. We talked about most everything. Not this. We found plenty of ways to compensate for the loss of whatever—testosterone, estrogen, stamina, youth, all of that and more. We discovered new ways to be close, to be satisfied, and to give to one another. God, I missed our sex—both ends of the spectrum of our fifty-plus-year sex life.

Jack and I didn't eat breakfast together often. We did enjoy our coffee-and-newspapers routine—the *Los Angeles Times,* the *San Diego Union Tribune,* and the *Wall Street Journal*—together every morning. We rarely talked during this morning time together. He did have to fight the urge to read to me all about the Chargers each morning, however.

On Sundays, our big treat was our joint effort on the *LA Times* crossword puzzle. I would start, filling in the easy stuff. Mr. Smarty Pants would tackle the tougher parts. Then back to me for another few words, and usually by Tuesday or Wednesday, he would finish it. Such a simple pleasure.

After the paper and coffee, we often went our separate ways. Most often, he went to the golf course or winery, and I went to the museum or art class. We reunited at the end of the day, always, for a glass of wine and our dinner. Dinner was never very sophisticated, and in fact could be nothing more than a loaf of bread, cheese, and wine—Georgia O'Keeffe's go-to evening meal—or a big bowl of cereal. Rarely did we have dinner apart.

I would miss the quiet nights at home after he smoked a cigar and we savored a glass of wine—his wine. I would miss sharing a glorious sunset and I would miss occasional sex as the sky colored above us. I would miss *CBS Sunday Morning, Jeopardy,* and *Sixty Minutes* with him. I would miss getting ready for bed together and reading our books until we fell asleep. We both devoured Eric Larson's and David McCullough's books. Jack always drifted off first. How boring and how beautiful the life we'd lived.

I liked to go away with my girlfriends or on museum trips, but I felt some guilt and hesitation about leaving. Jack had trouble sleeping when I traveled, or at least he said he did. When Steamer came to live with us, though, they both slept well without me. He and his big black dog were big-time pals, Steamer at his side constantly. So, I didn't feel bad leaving the twosome. But after Steamer died, I seldom went away. If I did leave, I left a piece of chocolate under his pillow, hoping he would have sweet dreams. The last time Jack traveled without me, on the pillow on his side of the bed, he left a "Reserved" sign.

Most often, however, he and I were together at the beginning of each day and at the end of each day. Each night, we went to bed together; neither one of us stayed up when bedtime came around, even when we argued.

It wasn't always that way; just during the fanciful Orange Woods years.

Nobody, and I mean nobody, could fight like me and my ballistic husband. We both had our signature styles. In the beginning, I cried and pouted. He, on the other hand, could cuss and yell and verbally dominate like the best of them, loud and repeatedly. Over the years, thanks to brutal, in-the-trenches tutoring, I learned to swear and yell with gusto as well.

We did not disagree much in those years—though there was that time laying out the vineyard—or at least, not out loud. From time to time, we both harbored disappointment or disapproval. It didn't matter as much as it had when we were young, feisty, and full of it.

Couples get that way, I guess. They morph into one another. They fuse; they become one. And when they are one, this amazingly symbiotic thing happens: two viewpoints seamlessly blend into one, without argument, without posturing, without one-upmanship. There is a caring and a respect that overrides any ego in a good marriage.

Was that why I felt ripped apart? A severed part of a whole?

As my mind wandered and my coffee grew cold, I recalled Dr. Laura Schlessinger, an outspoken, opinionated talk show host of the 1990s and 2000s. She broadcast on my station, KOGO, in Ventura about the time my children were reaching adulthood and finding their mates. I caught what I thought was a profound comment from her one day, one that adjusted my thinking in a most positive way. "Whoever it matters to most," she said, "handles it."

Jack had never turned off a light in his life. I'd constantly nagged. But after hearing Dr. Laura's comment, I no longer pestered my husband. I simply turned off the lights myself. It's not scrubbing pots and pans or scouring the shower, I reasoned, it's the flick of a damn switch. This small act delighted him. Me, too. As my children married, I passed on this insightful snippet of wisdom.

A delicious bit of universally good advice . . .

Was I reinventing our history? I hoped not. I longed for every memory to be crystal clear—not only for me but for all those who loved him.

ᘓ

My phone timer buzzed and I realized I had promised to show up at a reception for a local artist. In my car, I continued to think about my Jack. Not the technologically challenged, impatient, cranky, and wiser Jack in his later years; the Jack I desperately tried to bring back into my consciousness was the stud I'd married.

When we were young, I'd lusted after him. We'd had furious chemistry. He'd been movie-star handsome, brilliant, sexy, strong, and in control. His street smarts had fascinated me. The way he purchased tickets, a car, or a house; how he made a reservation, understood politics, balanced budgets, figured out solutions to everything.

Trained as a tank mechanic in the Marines, Jack could repair anything— an electrical problem, a broken pipe, a bankrupt radio station, or a skinned knee. Two days before his stroke, he'd spent hours, literally hours, working on the lighting behind my large decorative pots in our inner courtyard, refusing to give up. Tonight, the lights would shine brightly behind the pots that illuminated that fountain area.

Ad lib sponsors waited in line to take their turn on his radio show. Cars, groceries, new tires, window replacements, vacation getaways—whatever they offered, Jack and his phenomenal voice and vocabulary and bit of theatrics could sell a product. Jack could buy and sell anything. He was a crack salesman, no doubt a function of his grandmother's training. She had the little charmer selling chickens, strawberries, and brooms made in Arkansas by her blind brother by the time he was seven years old.

I always marveled at what I called his "magic red pencil." Long before computers and calculators, whenever we were in debt or needed money for an emergency or a new project, Jack would get out a yellow tablet and a pencil and go to work. He always worked it out. He could solve any financial conundrum! He had that kind of a brain.

Both world history and politics were passions of Jack's. I adored the way he put a current event or happening right into the context of the entire world history.

When I married him, he was a staunch, rabid Democrat, a real JFK man. When he began to make money, he became a Republican but not a close-minded Republican—a fair-minded thinker. So many times, in this despicable political climate we live in, I have pondered what Jack's allegiances would be. Would he share the constant disillusionment about our government that I experience?

As I drove, countless Jack-isms took a turn in my mind.

"How'd you get so smart?" I often asked him.

"Hanging out with you," he reliably replied with a heart-melting smile.

Over and over I told him he should be in Mensa, the high IQ society. His scores qualified him for membership, but he never made the move. Not a joiner, that husband of mine.

He was the son of an entrepreneurial guy who swept out railroad box-cars for a living and good-as-gold Mabel, a checkout lady at Wise Way Grocery Store. From the beginning, Jack's opportunities were limited. He used his smarts to get himself out of the steel mill and into the Marines (after his father told him to join the Air Force), to get himself into Columbia School of Broadcasting in Chicago, to grow from small to medium to major market on-air talent, culminating at NBC in NYC, to convince a group of sophisticated New York investors to buy radio stations in Ventura/Oxnard and Monterey/Carmel, CA, and to create a second career developing our property, planting grapes, making wine, and build a boutique winemaking business. He used his smarts to negotiate contracts, and to deal with extremely important people as well as relate to the most common of laborers. They all gravitated to him.

What I'd relished most was the magnetic field of his body—his strong, warm body. I'd adored the way he enveloped me in his arms. Now I hung untethered, so unprotected. I longed to be hugged.

The previous day, I'd done something typical of the new me. As I drove, my mind had wandered—and I had, too. The Miramar Road exit startled me and I'd realized that I was driving the wrong direction on Interstate 15— away from my house. I was fluttering in a fog. Another world. A scary world.

After getting off the freeway and returning on the other side to head north, my head had hammered with feelings and thoughts I didn't like. I didn't feel I belonged anywhere. In my mind, I floated balloon-like over my life, over different groups, people, places, projects. Sometimes I would land, and momentarily I would take off and fly again. A desperate attempt to escape this reality. I didn't belong anywhere. I didn't want to belong anywhere. I wanted to stay home, or not stay home. I was conflicted.

So, I went home. And the daunting, unnatural emotions continued—a flood of emotions released. Everything. All the memories galvanized into a penetrating steel projectile into the labyrinth of my grief. At home again, I listened to music as the spectacular full moon rose in the night sky. A monumental mix of melancholy and mourning came crashing down on me. I sat alone in the cool evening air and sobbed softly. I stared at the silhouettes of mountains, their purple shades darkened to navy. Our Orange Woods years had been heavenly. Spiritual. Beautiful. *Why can't I simply be grateful?*

I stepped inside and brought a candle out to the table. Its flickering light illuminated my thoughts in the twilight.

It might have been as still as I had ever known it to be. Everything was settled. Not a leaf moving or a speck of dust in the air. How could it be so quiet? Perhaps it's quiet, I thought, because it's time for me to be alone with Jack.

"Jack, how many times have I sat in this very spot and mourned the loss of you . . . begged you to hear my pleas . . . missing you with all my heart? You loved times like this so much. Just you and me and the mesmerizing grandeur of nature unfolding privately before us. It made us feel so special—like we were chosen in some way."

It broke my heart that he wasn't there with me. He had such passion for life; he found God in nature. He religiously marveled at the sunrises and sunsets; the seasons of the oranges and the grapes; the beauty of our surroundings and the life we lived there. Often, he said, "M, take a break. Come sit with me and savor our life."

I was a sucker for that invitation.

I hated it that he'd missed everything after February 15th. He'd looked at me that day, pointed his finger, and said with all the conviction he could muster, "Whatever happens, I love you." He'd known, I was certain he'd known. He had to have been frightened but he hadn't shown it—couldn't show it. I'm sure he sensed himself plummeting toward some unknown end and been scared to death. But in his last desperate moments of clarity, he reassured me that he cherished me and everything would be okay.

It wasn't. It was horrendous.

Chapter 53

Heads Above Water

It had been nearly four months since St. Patrick's Day.

All of a sudden, I was out of control again. I had begun to come out of the trauma of it all and now, once more, I was overwhelmed again, frightened and sick to my stomach. I wanted to throw up. My normal low blood pressure had skyrocketed up to 165 over 110 in those four months, which my doctor attributed to the radical change in my life.

Bo and Jen invited me to come to their house for Mother's Day. I went. Cash and Chesapeake were exactly what I needed, such adorable, tender little children. Bo, on the long road to recovery from his back surgery, beamed as he showed me the gift he'd received from one of Jack's radio friends: a Texas Radio Hall of Fame ring inscribed with Jack's name and induction date, 2004. The silver ring was large and impressive, just like Texas.

"Honey," I said, "keep it on your finger. He would want you to wear it."

Bo and I, in our shared grief, needed each other. For a brief time, we were happy.

Driving home from Bo and Jen's house in Arizona, however, my heart became heavier and heavier as I approached the long, curved drive to our home. He wouldn't be there when I arrived.

The same sensation would happen three weeks later when I went to Alice's in Ventura. How long would this continue? I could escape the horrific reality for a few moments in a different surrounding, but heading home, the impact gutted me.

After an on-again off-again night's sleep, I woke one morning sad, filled with feelings of isolation and missing my roommate. The pillow on his side lay wrinkle-free; his boots still sat on the floor where he'd taken them off before lying down that night. I wanted to stay home that day, sequester myself in bed and be quiet. However, I had made an appointment to take friends to an artist's studio a few weeks earlier. I needed to make myself go.

CB

As it turned out, it pleased me that I fired up and went to Michael Stutz's studio, although my overspending continued. That day, I bought my first work of bronze from the charming thirty-something artist from Tennessee who was carving his reputation in public art installations.

I'd learned about Michael from my alma mater, Texas Tech University in Lubbock, and the important public art program there. His installation, four immense bronze faces, seven feet tall, stood in a courtyard near the Boston Avenue entrance. Stutz's innovative, signature, larger-than-life bronzes represent individual personalities like the students on the campus. About his work, the artist said, "What I like about these pieces is that the differences in gender and race became more and more blurred the farther in the process the faces went."

The graceful sculpture I purchased from Michael was still in process, unfinished, when I first saw it, but I wanted it the moment I spotted it. The movement and airiness made the piece, about the size of a car steering wheel, appear to soar, which I desperately hungered to do. The piece exuded lyricism and a freedom to me. I wanted it. So, I bought it. Screw the budget.

"You can pick the color of the patina," Michael told me.

As he started for the color chart, I said, "Can you finish mine in the same as *Four Faces* at Tech?" This subtle connection to my college days soothed me.

CB

Driving south from Ventura after a restorative visit with Alice, Faye, Sue, and Nancy, my TTT circle of close friends, my car hugged the coast of the majestic Pacific Ocean. Nearing San Diego County, a pulsating vibe of familiar, all-encompassing dread came over me. I lifted my shoulders, inhaled deeply, and pushed my left hand down hard on my left thigh, attempting to steady myself, as I neared Scripps Encinitas, where Jack had died three agonizing months before. As I did, I found it comforting to catch a glimpse of the late-afternoon sunshine sparkling on the water to the west.

It hadn't occurred to me before this moment: Jack had died in this sterile, modern white edifice that shouldered the ocean. He was not a beach guy. Couldn't swim. Detested waves, water skis, canoes, even rafts.

When the kids and I would beg for a day at the beach, he would tease us, saying, "I've got an idea. Instead of going to the beach today, let's make it easy. I'll go to Handyman and buy a big bag of sand. While I'm gone, you guys put on your bathing suits and slather on suntan lotion. When I return, I'll spread the sand in the back of the station wagon. You can roll around in it, and we won't have to go to the beach."

The little kids would groan and race off to get their boogie boards and pile into the car.

Jack didn't like the beach, but he did appreciate the beauty of nature, especially his beloved sunsets in the west, over the Pacific. His were humble beginnings in the steel mill hub of Gary, Indiana. He ended his days in the arms of the extraordinary Pacific Ocean.

⁓

The freefall of grief bursts in my life continued to pummel me. One day, the grief was Bo's—which, of course, made it mine.

Bo, all his life extremely close to Jack, had lain debilitated by his back surgery while the stroke, the horrible weeks in the hospital, and Jack's death had transpired. Coming to terms with the loss itself, but also his absence through it all, magnified Bo's pain.

Late one Thursday evening, my son phoned. He burst into tears the moment I answered and said, "Mom, I can't do this without Dad." An assault of agony, angst, and upheaval burst from his broken heart. "I need him so badly."

I had never seen a man cry so freely and so openly as Bo did, repeatedly, over his father's death. When he could talk he said, "Mom, Dad and I were so close—we loved broadcast so much. I will never have anyone in my life like him. Ours was such a symbiotic relationship—so full of reverence, respect, and radio. And he always had my back."

Bo and Jack shared a tight bond, mainly because of their passion for radio. But, it evolved as so much more than that. Jack was always patient and supportive of Bo. And he was the same to Jack. The older Jack got, the more important Bo and his hero worship and companionship became.

Bo called Jack at least three times a week, many weeks more often than that. Every aspect of the radio industry filled their conversations. Jack often joked, "Our exchanges last longer than a dozen stop sets." (A stop set, in radio speak, is the time between music that a disc jockey talks open mike, typically three to five minutes.) They both loved the business—so incredibly generous and gift-giving to Jack, so heart-wrenching for Bo, whose career began as deregulation of the industry did.

Bo had followed Jack's path into radio, only to find it a business controlled by banks and bottom lines. No place for the upcoming talent, the blossoming personality. Satellite had destroyed these opportunities.

The morning after our late-night phone call, Bo was fired from his radio position.

Jack had been fired once, only once—from his position in Davenport, Iowa. "You're too good. You'll leave us soon," said the General Manager. Jack would have been the first to tell you that, on reflection, he understood it to be the best thing that ever happened to him, career wise. He never looked back.

Not so with Bo. Radio's contemporary demands from banks and bottom lines had resulted in his being released several times. He'd entered the radio business as it was being leveraged out of the ballpark by mergers, acquisitions, downsizing, and cost-sharing.

Curiously, Jack had been one of the pioneers of satellite delivered radio programming. Now, small markets where a young talent could "practice his craft" had disappeared. Satellite and Sirius had taken care of that.

One of the most charming things about Bo is his naiveté—he's a dreamer. He is also a loving father and husband, entrepreneur, excellent at finances, and definitely a survivor.

I called Bo again the next day. He sounded upbeat when we talked. He had been up and exercised, and once again filed for unemployment. I got goose bumps when he related his morning conversation with Jennifer.

"You think your meltdown last night was a warning signal from your dad?" Jen had asked him.

"I believe Dad signaled me," Bo told me on the phone. "Tried to prepare me. I believe it, Mom."

Every inch of me tingled. Jack had loved radio. It had thrilled him for Bo to be part of the radio industry. He'd been very protective of our son and constantly mentored him. Had Jack tried to protect and prepare him for this morning's cutting session? I wasn't sure—but with amazing conviction, Bo believed he had received a very special message from his "consultant."

ം

It took a long time for Bo to come to grips with Jack's death. Throughout his long and penetrating time of mourning, it devastated me that I couldn't fix it for him.

It's interesting—and, I guess, predictable—how we all ultimately handled Jack's death. Brent, the most mature and beneficent among us. Jamie, forever nurturing and compassionate. Bo, emotional and devastated. And me . . . I kept keeping on, understanding I was blessed with my children and their families.

Chapter 54

Little Blasphemies

Four months. Four long months without my soul mate. Seven short months after his Radio Hall of Fame induction. Was it getting easier? Maybe a little. Was it blasphemous to say such a thing?

Truthfully, I was learning to exist alone. I wasn't crying twenty-four seven. I still struggled fiercely to hold on to him.

The most glorious light rainfall happened one morning. Early-morning lightning and thunder were welcome surprises. The orange blossoms were aching to bloom; they needed water badly. It rained slow and soft most of the day.

Thank you, God, for this beautiful gift. You keep me hanging on.

More unexpected rain came that July Sunday. Rain in July is extremely rare in Pauma Valley. I received a Flood Alert on my cell phone.

By design, I stayed home alone on this rainy, rainy day. I had so many things that needed my undivided attention—projects in most parts of the house going all at the same time. But I kept coming back to my journal and pictures of Jack. I yearned to touch him and have him touch me. The memories of how his skin felt; even though his hands were rough from laboring every day, his skin was so soft, his feet, so tender. He never went barefoot. I adore going barefoot. One of our many opposites.

As he aged, Jack's hair, jet black when he was a young man, turned shiny, silvery grey. "Smilin' Jack," they dubbed him at one radio station. His huge smile radiated wherever he went. Even his hazel eyes smiled. And that dreamy voice. I loved hearing him as he talked to thousands of radio listeners each day, and I giggled when he whispered in my ear.

Maybe I shouldn't look at his photographs, I thought. It hurts so much. Especially on a rainy day at home alone. I kept thinking about that warm, cozy Sunday we'd spent together the previous January. It had been freezing cold outside, so we'd stayed home together. We ate unhealthy food—nachos piled high with cheese, hot dogs, and ice cream, binge-watched *Mad Men,* and caught up on movies—*Whiplash* (starring J. K. Simmons, who married Jamie's best dance buddy from Stage 7 in San Diego) and *Chef* (feel-good fare featuring Dustin Hoffman, whom Jack often ran into on the elevator at NBC in New York). Today would have been one of those "together" days. There hadn't been enough of those.

ം

Perhaps the image of my mother and her best friend, Sweeter, both ninety and newly widowed, riding in a golf cart at the Pauma Valley Country Club and shooting their collective middle fingers at an unsuspecting couple holding hands as they walked nearby remained too clear in my hard drive. I felt the urge to do the same damn thing way too often these days.

There are five stages of normal grief that were first proposed by Elisabeth Kubler-Ross in her 1969 book *On Death and Dying.* One of them is anger.

Up to this point I had not been angry, except when I had to take out the trash, but in recent times a cumbersome fury had begun to creep into my daily life.

"The anger may be aimed at inanimate objects, complete strangers, friends or family," Kubler-Ross writes.

Lately, my anger had been aimed at complete strangers. It made my blood boil to peer at happy couples strolling hand in hand—infuriated me, in fact. This began to manifest itself in unbecoming and unfeminine ways that would have horrified my ladylike mother.

I had to do something. These poor people have done nothing to me, I reasoned. Why do I want to take a sledgehammer to those coupled hands?

Of course, I got it. Holding hands with Jack—not an option for me anymore.

In the summer after my husband died, two very good friends and fellow docents at the art museum lost their partners—one after a long, debilitating illness; the other, shockingly and suddenly before a hike in Oregon. Kathee, Margaret and I became circumspect soul mates as we slowly, painfully, and unsteadily worked to rebuild our lives. Once a month, we would get together for "Happy Hour Salon." In the beginning, this consisted of wine and tears. Over time, strong bonds of friendship, some laughter, and art speak emerged alongside our collective whimpering.

In my mind, a sixth stage of the grief progression began to unfold—a black humor stage. A sort of sacrilegious line of thinking, if you will.

Walking among the crowds in the mall one day, I saw, straight ahead, a devoted, lovestruck, mature couple with hands locked coming toward me. As they passed by, I whirled around to follow closely, fumbling to get my iPhone out of my purse. I snapped the perfect shot from behind the pair and forwarded it to Margaret and Kathee. One word in the subject line: *Shit.*

Within the hour, they began to return similar images with similar subject lines, and soon we were enjoying a much-welcomed break from the overpowering sadness of being lost and alone.

The exchanges continue.

Chapter 55

New Year, New Me

The holidays blurred by, my first without Jack. My Scorpio's November birthday, then Thanksgiving, Christmas, and New Year's Eve. I suffered serious heartache all the way through.

I had always written New Year's resolutions, but I couldn't bring my depressed self to do it as 2016 began. About ten days into the new year, I half-heartedly came up with a list.

- Write diligently
- Save even more diligently
- Be with people often
- Be with family—just enough
- Sell the Orange Woods
- Move to San Diego
- Keep Pauma Valley connection
- Preserve Jack's memory with passion.

ↄ৪

My life without my husband offered many new and often scary opportunities.

Blindly, I stumbled into what became a grief counseling session for me. On January 25, three and a half weeks after the beginning of 2016 and just over ten months after Jack died, I enrolled in a Personal Narrative writing class. My eight classmates—strangers until this time—along with a little dynamo of an instructor, Judy Reeves, became my quasi-therapists.

To begin, Judy asked us to say something about ourselves as a way of introduction. "Something to make you stand out in my mind," she said.

My chest constricted. Across the room, someone boasted, "I'm a ballroom dancer and a private pilot."

"I joined the Peace Corps at eighteen."

"My family has three sets of twins."

Think of something, Marilyn—not that. But try as I might, as the introductions skipped merrily around the table, I couldn't stave off the inevitable. My lip began to quiver uncontrollably.

"I played semi-pro baseball for Milwaukee," the guy next to me offered as he turned toward me in a sort of visual handoff.

Panic first, followed by rampant tears as I blurted out, "I lost my husband last spring. I'm a widow."

My unexpected outburst stunned my classmates. Judy—who, I would learn much later, had experienced exactly what I was going through—sat without speaking in the center of our group, her head down. She paused before she asked, "Are you alright, Marilyn?"

A few deep breaths, and a handful of Kleenex later, I was.

ଓଃ

Over the next eight weeks, I learned that I wasn't the only one with something to cry about in our group. Together, we touched on tragic accidents, financial ruin, alcoholism, 9/11, kidnapping, incest, loss and more loss, the environment, third-world countries, and profound devotion.

And at the end of the eight weeks, I had ventured back into a habit of writing and moved into the acceptance phase of my grief. Slowly, I crept—baby steps—back into life. A life without Jack. The extraordinary thing is that I began to make this transition with these nine new friends, souls who had supported me and opened their lives to me.

I'd found a world of talent and compassion in Room 240 at UC San Diego.

ଓଃ

I had clawed my way through the caverns of sorrow and solitude for almost one year. I had dragged myself through the arduous landmarks along the way—his birthday, my birthday without him, Mother's Day, and Father's Day. Thanksgiving, Christmas, New Year's Eve, Valentine's, and our wedding anniversary. Now I was squeezed tightly between that date and tomorrow's anniversary: the anniversary of Jack's death. I felt like I lay in a vise, a screw turning relentlessly. I floundered on the eve of the one-year marking of his death. How could I navigate the sheer drop into the second year?

I moved on autopilot through the morning until a strong urge to flee, to change something, came over me. At some point in what evolved into an otherworldly sort of day, I began to move as if on autopilot. I found myself in my car and headed to the hospital—the place where we'd gathered at his bedside one year earlier. The pilgrimage back made me remember it so clearly, even though I didn't want to. The scenario churned within me, and I supposed it would always lurk there. It might be getting a bit easier; I was somewhat better, not feeling so lost and full of despair. But it wasn't "good" by any means; how on earth could it ever be good?

Justin Timberlake sang of a cold and broken Hallelujah as I approached the large complex nestled between the 5 and Coast Highway 101 near the Pacific Ocean—the hospital where Jack died three-hundred and sixty-five depressing days ago tomorrow.

In the parking space, my warm, sweaty hands gripped the motionless steering wheel. An involuntary bouncing of my right knee signaled me to turn off the ignition. I stared through the windshield at the multi-story building, blocks of white and tan with a long, narrow portico at the entry and extended wings on each side. Inside, the colors of the design—sand and blue—were said to evoke the tranquility of the ocean. I'd never felt tranquil in this hospital.

I don't recollect doing it, but I got out of the car and walked toward the entry. A blue and white banner waving in the breeze above me caught my attention—Scripps Stroke Care, it said. I winced, wishing it said Stroke Cure.

The closer I got to the entry, the more upset I became; flashes of the Room 153B window, the sterile equipment up and down the cold halls, the beeping of the nurse call buttons, and his anemic frame with little consciousness pummeled me. I took a few almost drunken steps and then cowered backward.

Images of a horrid time, a helpless time, and yet a hallowed time, flailed about in my mind as I stood statue still. We had made the decision to let him go. He hadn't been gone yet, but on morphine he'd been peaceful, without the frustration and anger and edge that had driven him crazy for four and a half long weeks. He'd relaxed as nature took its course. I hadn't.

I am eternally thankful that my children and I were so close through it all. I know they were frightened and scared and traumatized, too, but together we made the right decision—to stop clinging to false hope and keeping him alive, because he couldn't live.

Aware once more of the warmth of the sunlight, I balked at going into the hospital. Instead, I retreated to a bench in the center courtyard, nestled among magnolia trees. In the middle, a tall, graceful kinetic sculpture moved with elegance in the wind—the same wind that spread the scent of salt air from the ocean over me. The titanium sculpture's gentle arc replicated itself in deep blue shadow on the pavement beneath my feet. I had sat hypnotized by the sculpture's silver facets and slow, circular motion here outside the hospital many times when Jack went to physical or speech therapy, or when I desperately needed to flee. At this moment, I couldn't look at the sculpture's dedication plaque nearby; the piece had been donated in recognition of a couple's sixtieth wedding anniversary.

As I sat alone at the threshold of the hospital, waves of doubt and sorrow washed over me. "I'm not okay and it's not over," I protested out loud.

Stupid to think it was. I shouldn't have come here, I thought.

When I calmed a bit, I wondered, Am I going to move into a different part of the grieving process? Is that why I came here today? To close a chapter? Does one year, coming up tomorrow, somehow make it different? My rigid posture gave way to a slump as I leaned back, letting the sunshine wrap me in momentary composure.

I don't know how long I sat there. Images, year-old images, trounced through my head. I sensed the world speeding up again. A heaviness engulfed my chest. I heard my own heartbeat thrashing in my ears. I tried to steady myself, but I lost control once more. Tsunami waves of grief battered me. I needed to leave. Get away from this monument of my loss.

Adrenaline surged through my body as I escaped, driving way too fast in the passing lane. I'd gone right back to the beginning, to the saddened-to-death square, and I hadn't even gotten $200 when I passed go.

Fuck.

૭ঙ

Then it was morning once again.

March 17, 2016. Exactly one year after.

I opened my eyes and stretched out of my drowsiness. I swept my arm overhead in an arc. It landed on the crisp linen pillowcase on his side of the bed. My hand searched.

No, I told myself firmly. *He's not there. And he never will be again.* I stayed with that for a few moments before rising.

I walked around our bed to his side and leaned over and picked up those boots he'd worn on his last day at The Orange Woods. I cradled them in my arms, inhaling their still-present scent of leather, then walked to the closet, where I put them on the shelf.

I went back to the French doors and opened them both to let the sunshine spill in. A golden mean of warmth and peace of mind materialized within me as a fresh breath of March welcomed me. I let my eyes wander about the landscape, embracing the power of the earth and sky.

Beautiful words written by Judy Reeves, My inspiring writing teacher, chasséd in my head:

"It was winter when she became a widow. In the orchard at the bottom of the hill the citrus ripened—the grapefruit, the lemon, the orange, and the last tree on the farthest row, his favorite, tangerine.

"Neither of them knew its Latin name, they knew only that in January came the sweetest fruit. Standing at the end of the row, they'd pluck the fruit and tear away the skin like they sometimes tore away their clothes. Then leaning over, they let the juice sluice down their chins, over their wrists, sticky up their fingers, their lips. How sweet their tangerine kisses.

"It was winter when she walked down into the orchard, her hands full of ashes, and let the wind claim them, let them sail like so many seeds, to find their place among the roots of the grapefruit, the lemon, the orange, and at the end of the farthest row, the tangerine."

I found great solace in being connected to people who had experienced loss like mine.

A pristine day had risen in my small world. I'm sure it was my imagination, but I heard a soft chorus of comfort emanating from the orange trees as a gentle breeze shivered their leaves. My eyes watered. I bowed my head. *Thank you, God, for letting me get through this year.*

Chapter 56

Relocating a Broken Heart

I began year two. A wave of resignation and a glint of hopefulness united within me. At times, I felt optimistic. Other times, not so much. My decision to move to San Diego coalesced during what I realize now was the bottomless trauma of loss. When I was deliberating the pros and cons, my decision-making mind wasn't functioning well. I had said yes to Brent and Laurie, but a tentativeness hung over my scattered thoughts.

If I ever sold The Orange Woods, I could move to a nice condo within the gates at the Pauma Valley Country Club. Many friends nearby. Closer to Jamie. But still so far away from the city life I longed for and my volunteer work at the art museum. I wrestled with my options endlessly before deciding to leave Pauma Valley and live in San Diego. Bo wholeheartedly encouraged me to move away from the isolation of the country.

Making the decision weakened and panicked me and thrust an even bigger fear into my consciousness. The thought of telling Jamie made me sick to my stomach. A knot of anxiety twisted in my chest. After all these years of living fifteen minutes apart, there would now be an hour's time between our houses. And I would be living next door to—just steps away from—Brent and Laurie.

Like all good procrastinators, it took me several weeks to get up my courage to tell her. Clenching my fists, I mustered my courage and said, "Honey, I am going to move to San Diego."

My daughter, my grieving daughter, burst into tears as she drove down the freeway. The shrillness of her wail erupted with a force that reminded me of that dark night as we left the hospital. "Mom, I lost my daddy," she cried. "And now I'm going to lose you, too?"

Pangs of indecision and guilt returned, violently. I reached for her hand. At first she pulled away, but she soon relented. We both cried the rest of the way to the shopping center. We bantered in a superficial manner over our Chinese chicken salads for a while.

I saw my loving daughter take a deep breath before saying, "Of course I want you to move to San Diego, Mom. It's the absolute best thing for you, and that's exactly what I want. But I'm coming to your house all the time." She gave me a brave smile.

How on earth did my daughter get to be so unselfish? I wondered.

Since that time, both Jamie and I have realized that the hour between us has enriched our time together. Instead of dashing in and out of one another's houses for a quick sandwich or a glass of wine or to look at a newly purchased outfit, we spend extended times with one another—all day, overnights, even weekends. Nurturing, quality time.

When Jamie and I finally got over our separation anxieties, I began to understand what my move to San Diego meant on a much deeper level. From the first night Laurie mentioned the idea until that September afternoon in 2016 when I began to live both in San Diego and at The Orange Woods, the entire process of consideration, declaration, preparation, and finally relocation was a wonderful diversionary tactic. Moving became another focus in my life—a focus besides the omnipresent grief and loss of my roommate.

ॐ

A week later, in the process of moving smaller items, carload by carload, from The Orange Woods to my new home in San Diego, I stopped at Michael's studio in Fallbrook to pick up my bronze sculpture. The effusive and talented artist had completed the finishing process and carefully wrapped it for transport.

That afternoon, as I sat by myself at the rickety card table in the empty house (the movers were to come with my first load of furniture the next day), I unwrapped the bronze carefully. Instantly, my heart broke—my sculpture was broken. The rhythmic, flowing burnished ribbons with their Renaissance copper patina had separated, come apart into two pieces.

A panicked call to Michael's cell phone allayed my fears. With measured calm, he told me he had designed the piece to be two parts.

"They can be joined, intertwined, or separated, your choice. As a whole, the piece is quite beautiful, but when the two pieces are separated, therein lies another kind of beauty . . ."

He went on, but I barely heard what he said. The tears flooded down my face and pooled beneath the sculpture. I put my head down on the table. A revelation came over me. Jack and I were separated now. But in the quiet of private times, we came together. I felt close to him. Often, I sensed his presence—even here, in a place he'd never visited. Maybe my horizon had shifted. Was it possible I would someday be whole again?

☙

It didn't happen as much these days, but once in a while, I got broadsided.

I entered the winery gingerly that morning, planning to survey its contents for the eventual sale. I slowly opened the oversize double glass doors with the graceful OrangeWoods logo on the front. I recoiled momentarily at the glow of the neon across the way—the MARILYN LOVES JACK sign.

The moment I entered, an infusion, as the wine snobs say, of mingling aromas—dark fruits, a hint of vanilla, and tobacco—embraced me. I closed my eyes and took a deep breath. It smelled of Jack. I sensed his presence as a warm, velvety feeling engulfed me. The blood in my body rushed rapidly throughout. A sense of lightheadedness filled me. I swirled, much like the rich red wine in a long-stemmed glass. Grabbing hold of the counter, I steadied myself. I glanced to my left, across the winery.

Stacked rows of French Oak barrels stood like formidable wooden soldiers across the cavernous space. I had always acknowledged the wine in the barrels, our precious inventory, when I entered the winery, but this time they struck me differently. Inexplicably, my eyes were drawn to the end of the lower center barrel.

Cab, 2012 was inscribed in his handwriting—in chalk, white chalk. My eyes moved slow in automation from the end of one perfect oaken circle to the next.

Zin, 2013. Cab, 2014. Zin, 2014. These were his casual handwritten documentations of the varietal and the year of the contents of the barrel. I pictured him, chalk in hand, writing.

Jack was a denim kind of guy. No designer duds for him, he was a Levi's man all the way. It was amazingly clear to me how cool he looked, Marlborough Man rugged and strong, when he came in from working in the winery in his faded jeans and work boots, covered with bits and pieces of the grapes and smelling like the full-bodied cabernet wine. And always, that smile. Quite an aphrodisiac!

On this day, I stood in momentary shock, riveted in place, an empty feeling in the pit of my stomach. I moved closer to the barrels. His handwriting. He had actually picked up the stub of white chalk in his strong hands and written on this barrel. The same hands that had caressed my body with tenderness over and over. I ran my fingers over the barrel, following its curved form. For a guy, Jack had very nice handwriting: bold, a bit free-form, and somewhat legible. I smiled thinking of how he, too, was bold, a bit free-form, and so transparent, open, and honest.

I touched the writing but jerked my hand away, a surprising reflex. Turning my hand over, I saw a faint imprint of white chalk dust on my forefinger. The impermanence of the chalk writing—some of it already brushed away in these past, awful months—struck me. Before my very eyes, vanishing, one particle at a time. At some point, it would be gone. Just like him.

The realization grabbed hold of my heart and shook my universe. I burst into tears. *When on earth will I stop this volcanic spewing of tears?* I couldn't stand to focus on the fleeting moments of the past—the time when he systematically documented what he had so artfully produced in French oak. More importantly, I couldn't dwell on the fact that he was gone. I needed to savor the precious memories.

I cried a long time in the winery. Evening approached. The neon sign glowed in a bizarre, haunting manner. *Marilyn loves Jack.* As I closed the doors behind me, I stood in silence and vowed to make sure that Jack's legacy did not vanish like an inscription written casually in chalk.

CB

It was twilight time again, my day's most tender and sorrowful moment. Earlier, I'd read and reread parts of my journal, reliving divine times of bliss. Now, sitting in his chair, I stared at the impressive painting across the room, the first work of art we purchased for our walls at The Orange Woods. Looking at the painting evoked so many memories of our rapture together. The setting sun, shining through the window behind me, cast a warm, pink-gold spotlight on the art. Impulsively, I grabbed my journal to reread my entry about the painting, *Lost Love*, a story that proved to be both romantic and prophetic.

ଔ

Ojai, California is a charming gem of a little town set inland twenty miles from the Pacific Ocean at the foot of the Topa Topa Mountains. Each year, the artisans there hold an Art Studio Tour where they open their studios to the public.

Jack and I were particularly drawn to one artist's portfolio on this lovely October afternoon. We lingered in the open studio in front of one large mixed media piece, captivated by the emotion and the energy. The colors— rich jewel tones of reds, teals, blues, and purples—of the piece enthralled us. We struggled to understand the complexities of the subject matter, however. A man and woman dominated the picture plane, falling away from one another. In the upper right-hand corner, a group of dining room chairs exploded out of their setting.

As we stood in front of the painting, a woman approached from behind.

"Hello and welcome," said a gentle voice, introducing herself. "This is my art."

"Can you tell us about this one?" I asked.

She spoke with hesitance in a soft voice. "The title of this one is *Lost Love*."

Turning around, I realized her eyes were beginning to fill with tears.

"This is the first painting I created after my husband died a year and a half ago," she said.

We both turned back to the art. Indeed, she had captured the magnitude of the sadness and grief she must have been experiencing as she created. Dressed in black, the man fell backward. The woman fell away from him, reaching in desperation, agony in her face, her long, golden locks flowing behind. The artist explained that the chairs were, indeed, her dining room chairs, "the symbol of the family and life we had shared for forty years. With his death, that had blown up in an instant."

Jack and I were stunned speechless. As much as we liked the painting, so full of expression and passion, we exited gracefully after managing a few polite words. In the car, we concluded we could not have this visual testament of separation, loss, and grief in our happy home.

Over the next few weeks, however, *Lost Love* haunted me. I could not shake the intense emotion it projected, could not get its magnetic force out of my mind. The vibrancy, the drama, the desperation, the longing—it was a powerful and emotional piece. I began to rethink the painting. Part of what appealed so much was the way the canvas emanated fear, overwhelming despair, and helplessness. The impact of sudden separation gave the work its power. The artist had painted the magnitude of losing your life partner—how it would be if I lost Jack, I imagined.

I decided to purchase the painting as a birthday gift for Jack, spinning the message to "this is how I would feel if I ever lost you."

One problem: if it wasn't to be a joint purchase, I had to be creative. I contacted the painter, reintroduced myself, and asked if she'd consider a layaway purchase, to be completed over the next ten months until November and his birthday. "Of course," she replied.

Over the next ten months, I regularly trimmed the grocery budget and sent my payment to the artist in Ojai. The remarkable bonus to my experience of purchasing the painting in this way was witnessing what happened to the heartbroken artist and her work over this same period of time.

On my first visit, about twenty months after her husband had died, she had begun a series of oils; the first one featured a tiny, dark house on a hill under a dreary night sky. A few months later, another canvas showed the same house with a warm light in the window and a hint of a moon. By the time I had paid off *Lost Love,* close to a year after first meeting the artist, she had completed the series. In her last painting, hearts in the blue sky, flowers in the garden, and happy babies under the bright yellow sun overhead surrounded the same little house.

The painter had a new romance in her life, and it showed in her work. To witness, the therapeutic power of art was heartwarming. I bought a painting and shared a memorable catharsis with the artist.

Lost Love hung in our dining room until the end. Many times, we told the artist's story. Many times, there were tears.

ঙ

I continued to love art, but sometime during year two I realized I was no longer creating works of my own. The wooden box of soft pastels had not been touched. Colorful acrylic paints dried up in their containers; my brushes were stiff from lack of use. I refused to go into the studio.

Making art had been such an integral part of my life—a part that had surfaced soon after my career in radio ended. I'd sold a bit, exhibited some, hung out in galleries and museums, studied art history, become a docent, and taken lessons from Richard Stergulz, a brilliant young teacher.

But when I lost my biggest admirer, my ability and desire to make art had vanished.

Jack was a devoted fan. I lapped up the reception he gave when reviewing a completed work of mine. He had his routine: he would take my latest effort, prop it up on the floor-to-ceiling bookcase at the end of the large open space that contained our sun-splashed kitchen, dining room, and living room, turn on the LED spotlights to illuminate my work, pull up a chair, and slowly enter my painting. With thought and careful observance, he studied my work, and eventually asked about my inspiration. Seldom did he offer anything but praise and encouragement. My forever fan.

Now he was gone, and so was my passion for making art—a passion we shared throughout our lives together.

I floundered a great deal in the beginning. But in time, I began to write. Writing released me as it made me go deeper, made me hurt beyond comprehension as I relived everything. I found myself in my own private grief counseling sessions. Just me and the damned keyboard. Writing served as both my salvation and my passion. I wrote about him, I wrote about art, I wrote about wine, and I wrote about grief. Quite mystifying how interconnected they are.

Chapter 57

Día de los Muertos

October came again. I was depressed about my house and property. Overwhelmed. I decided to take it off the market when the listing expired that weekend. Politics had paralyzed the country; I'd watched the Republican debate for a short time the night before, but politics just kept getting stranger and stranger.

No one was looking at my house. I wasn't sure whether to relist with my realtor or go with the guy in Valley Center Jamie and Bud were recommending.

I was sure dismantling our dream house was a big part of my depression.

When I went back to The Orange Woods, everywhere I turned, he was there. He'd lived such a joyous life there, religiously savoring nature. Life in the country thrilled Jack. Over and over his dad had told him, "Start driving out of town. When you get to the place where they are quoting by the acre, buy."

Nineteen years had passed since we'd bought our acres fifty miles northeast of San Diego. When we sold off the back acreage, we'd built our winery and done the major remodeling. Lots of impulse and spontaneity on our parts. From my vantage point today, maybe not such a wise decision. So damned much to care for. But when I think of all the pleasure it gave Jack, I guess it was the right thing.

On this day, back at The Orange Woods, I sat in the oversize plush chair I often shared with my youngest grandbabies, Cash and Chesapeake when they were small, surrounded on all sides by the floor-to-ceiling windows Jack insisted we have to maximize the sweeping views of extraordinary sunsets. Their impermanence mesmerized us, each one so unique and powerful. Our personal panorama, over and over.

"How many people are so fortunate?" we said over and over as we experienced a stupendous sunrise, sunset, twilight, or full moon. "We've got to share this with others."

We did often, but oh how he relished his solitude. Me, not so much now.

CZ

It was Halloween night, my second without Jack. Spooky and sorrowful. I sat alone at 215 in my corner office overlooking Maple Canyon, my San Diego home darkened to avoid trick-or-treaters. Couldn't stand confronting the ghostly images and isolation on this night at The Orange Woods, either. At least there were signs of life in houses around me here—I had a sense of being a small part of something, whatever that might be.

I couldn't see the moon in the vast sky, but I sensed it.

Cash and Chesapeake were trick-or-treating at this very moment dressed as something Harry Potter–related. Carly was out with her boyfriend. Calvin was beyond stressed over his application for early decision to Amherst. It boggled my mind that my other granddaughters were scattered everywhere: Maddie in Manhattan, Bayley in Spokane, and Sophie in North Carolina. *Wasn't it yesterday they were performing plays in costumes from the dress-up trunk?*

I was still depressed about my house and property in Pauma Valley. Should I take it off the market for a while? I hated this. I was filled with dread as the holidays unfurled before me.

Hesitantly, I called Alice—not only because she was observing the one-year anniversary of her mom's passing but also because I fiercely needed her to ground me. In the excruciating time since Jack had been gone, she had been even more of a rock than ever before.

"Alice," I told her, "I miss your mom so much. She was such a rock star, much like you."

"God, me, too. But I can't begin to imagine what you are going through. When I even consider losing Steve, my heart aches even more for you. I miss Jack with all my heart."

During our conversation about loss, of her mom and my Jack, with gentleness she reminded me of the new moon tonight.

"Woodsie, once or twice a month, the moon disappears from our view; the illuminated side of the moon faces away from us. It's still there; we just can't observe it. It's the New Moon—it's about new beginnings, a time to set intentions for things you long to create, develop, cultivate, make manifest. You need to do this, WD."

I resisted, rolling my eyes, but tried my best to "get into it." I smiled at her familiar "WD." Alice had nicknames for everybody. In the beginning, she called me Woodsie; quickly, she went to Woodsie Doodle, which she soon shortened to WD. Sometimes she used all three in a single conversation.

After we talked, I went upstairs and out on the balcony off my bedroom to confirm. Sure enough, to the south an airplane was gliding in for a landing at Lindberg Field above the tree line in front of the brilliantly lit San Diego skyline, to the east a bus was traveling north across the First Street Bridge, and to the west were the remains of a glorious end-of-day sunset. But no moon.

Back at my computer, I Googled "new moon."

"The new moon has an inward feel, a void or empty quality, and therefore can be frightening to those not comfortable with uncertainty. Can you learn to trust the dark? It's the moment when the old passes away and the new is not yet here."

I gasped. Weird, the new moon. The absence of the moon shook me as the reality of my absent husband loomed large. The moon would be there tomorrow night. He wouldn't. I felt alone, displaced, and strange.

Back downstairs, after indulging in a spoonful of peanut butter, I arranged the marigolds in a vase, placed them on the dining room table, and lit a candle near where I planned to write. It was amazing how Alice could get me into this "la-la land."

In bed later, however, I tossed and turned through the unsettling Halloween night.

The next morning, I dragged myself out of bed long before sunrise and headed for the kitchen. Waiting for my cup of coffee to brew, I found myself studying the tin diorama from San Miguel de Allende hanging on the wall just above the coffee maker.

Four connected frames, decorated with vivid colors and filled with tiny Calaveras figures, make up *La Historia de un Amor.* In it, miniature white skeletons, created in clay and meticulously hand painted, portray the passages of love and romance any ordinary couple might experience together. Jack and I loved this little *nicho* box from Mexico, sometimes used as a portable shrine to an important figure or loved one. They originated as an adaptation of the Roman Catholic *retablo*, which is a painting of a patron saint on wood or tin.

In the first scene, a skeleton couple stands locked in a passionate embrace amid vibrant colored hearts and flowers. The second scene, white and lacy, is a wedding—the bride in long white dress with a veil and bouquet, the groom in tuxedo and top hat. There's a chicken at their feet. In the third scene, the couple, now a bit older, stands next to a baby carriage under a blue sky full of clouds. A baby skeleton sleeps in the carriage.

As I mused, the familiar, flavorful aroma of coffee invited me to pour. Taking my first sip, I started to turn away—but was drawn back to the final scene. I focused.

The sky is grey and dark dotted with broken hearts. There is a grave with a cross on it. Dressed in black, her head covered with a hood, a grieving widow skeleton kneels in front of her husband's gravesite.

I realized I'd gone through the stages portrayed there in my kitchen and they had been magical—except this last one. I felt a welling up inside. I breathed deeply and took another sip of coffee.

CR

Later in the day, November 1, I realized it was *Dia de los Muertos*. Uncomfortable, sometimes paralyzing emotions caused my heart to race and my knees to buckle off and on throughout the day. The holidays were coming and I felt filled with dread. Jack's birthday was three weeks away. This year the Day of the Dead touched me with profound power. I didn't even acknowledge last year's event, so raw, so painful. But one year later, *Día de los Muertos* seemed different.

Enchanted by its mysticism and devotion to ancestors and those no longer with us, I found a bit of clarity for my life and loss. I wondered if I could be healing?

CR

Vibrant Day of the Dead images danced in my mind throughout the long day. The way the Mexican culture honors its dead on *Día de los Muertos,* a Latin American custom which combines indigenous Aztec ritual with the Catholicism brought to the region by Spanish Conquistadors, has always intrigued me. It is an explosion of color combined with filial piety. Our Halloween and this most treasured of Mexican holidays share some similar practices—ghoulish consumption of sugar and sweets and decorating with skeletons, for example. Jack loved them both.

To celebrate and commemorate *Día de los Muertos,* Mexican families and friends create colorful altars in their homes, gardens, and private spaces, upon which they place food, drink, photographs, and mementos of the deceased.

Most often, the marigold is prominent in the display.

Why marigolds? Like so many flowers, they represent the fragility of life. But it is also believed the spirits of the dead visit during the celebration, and the marigolds, with their recognizable scent and vivid burst of orange and yellow hues, serve to guide those spirits home.

That afternoon, driving back to Pauma Valley and The Orange Woods from San Diego, I spotted an old, beat-up, green pickup truck on the left as I left Escondido heading north. An unassuming man and woman stood side by side near the bed of the truck, which was filled with giant, glorious marigolds. I sped by the genial-looking twosome, but quickly found myself making a U-turn and heading for the flowers.

"*Buenas tardes, señora,*" said the diminutive woman, who was dressed in a simple cotton dress and colorful embroidered shawl. The three of us communicated with a bit of difficulty. In the end, the congenial middle-aged Hispanic couple sold me a huge bouquet of marigolds for "*sólo ocho dólares, mi amiga.*"

Ten days later, the vibrant orange flowers would still flourish. The soft, full, rounded blossoms burst forth, filled with petals of monochromatic oranges and yellows, reminiscent of aromatic spices in Indian cooking—nutmeg, saffron, chilis, paprika, and turmeric.

I recalled some years before, on the first day of November, driving by the Panteón Jardín Cemetery in Tijuana. The expanse of marigold bouquets, which stretched as far as I could see, stunned me—brilliant golden blossoms placed with love on hundreds, maybe thousands, of modest headstones and grave markers by those who grieved.

ന

I began collecting *Día de los Muertos* sculptures and images on our first getaway to Oaxaca, Mexico, Jack's and my favorite romantic destination. Shortly after our return in September, I entered the docent training program at the San Diego Museum of Art.

At the museum, an exhibit of the work of renowned Mexican artist Jose Posada—in particular his most influential work, the satirical and politically acute *Calaveras*—consumed me. Their title derived from the Spanish word for skulls, these *Calaveras* were illustrations featuring the skeletons with human-looking features that would one day become closely associated with the Day of the Dead.

The most famous *Calavera* is the animated La Catrina, an elegantly attired female skeleton figure sporting an extravagantly colorful plumed hat, lavish gown, cape or stole, and fancy jewels. She enthralled me.

Mexico's grande dame of death originated in Posada's early work. Aptly named, Catrina is from a Spanish word meaning overly elegant. The Catrinas regularly denied their Mayan heritage and thought of themselves only as upper-class European.

Over the years since Posada first introduced her in 1910 in a zinc etching, Catrina has been featured in books and cartoons, on posters, as sculptures and statues, and in the works of some of Mexico's greatest artists.

I have several Catrinas from Oaxaca, dressed far more fashionable than me in my cocktail party finest. My favorite wears a lush black plumed hat with a multicolored bouquet of flowers atop it, a floor-length, vibrant red-orange dress, and a sparkly, periwinkle blue feather boa around her neck. Standing ten inches high, in her left hand she holds her parasol; in her right hand, an oversize cigar—lit.

Hard not to appreciate the humor in this art form, turning something as grim as a skeleton, a bag of bones, into something whimsical, nostalgic, sentimental, or political. I even have a miniature black-and-white dog bag of bones. The pooch skeleton wears a yellow straw sombrero and, like my Catrina, smokes a cigar. I gifted the whimsical little mutt to my delighted husband soon after I realized he was going to be a serious cigar smoker.

The skeletons work, exercise, marry, dance, kiss, frolic, and do all the things we normal humans do. I have collected and enshrined them.

At some point, it became obvious to my family and friends I gravitated to skeletons. Jamie found a skeleton necklace for me one year for my birthday; it comes out of the jewelry box every October.

I found it quite adorable when four-year-old Carly, standing tippy-toed on her chubby little legs, her nose on the lower shelf of our large library wall in the dining room, contemplated my bountiful collection of skeletons. She surveyed the figures thoughtfully, turned to her mother, and whispered, thinking I wouldn't hear, "Neeny sure likes skeletons, huh, Mommy?"

I do.

One of the simplest and least expensive works of art in our collection is also a skeleton, a dazzling white mask from Jakarta, Indonesia. Brent, after working for a law firm there, came home loaded at Christmastime with gifts of face masks for each of us. A lime green lion head for Bo; a flame-red cat face for Jamie (a devoted big brother, Brent remembered her obsession with Andrew Lloyd Webber's *Cats*); a bronze tigress with pointed ears for me; and for Jack, a full-faced, chalk-white skeleton mask. A riotous photo opportunity occurred.

Each mask had been covered with hundreds of sparkling sequins, each one hand applied by an anonymous craftsman in a faraway village. Jack's bright white face with black cavernous eye sockets and wide snaggle-toothed grin beamed with hundreds of iridescent, spangled sequins. He treasured it. Over the years, the rest of the masks ended up in little children's dress-up chests, but each year at the end of the Halloween and Day of the Dead season, Jack carefully rehung his on its hook.

Some years later, when Bo and Jennifer were no longer living in California, they completed Jack's Halloween costume and created family lore. Strolling the square in downtown Prescott, savoring ice cream cones from Frozen Franny's, Bo abruptly stopped his family in front of the window of the Western store on the corner. "Jen, look! Look at that black shirt with skeletons. I've got to get it for Dad for his birthday!"

Several weeks later, Bo presented Jack with a very expensive Western shirt made by Scully, a manufacturer of high-end, contemporary Western wear based in Ventura County, where we had spent many rich and rewarding years before our Orange Woods days. Jet-black with dual white skeletons over each front pocket, the shirt was a work of art—crossed bones on the cuffs and a trailing red rose design embroidered on the front.

Not only did Jack love the shirt, the company's history, which dates back to 1906, fascinated him. In the beginning a leather glove making concern, the company expanded and eventually helped outfit Admiral Richard Byrd's first Antarctic expedition in 1928.

Jack's costume was done! The crowning pieces: Brent's skeleton mask, which cost less than a dollar, and Bo's skeleton shirt, which set him back close to two hundred dollars.

For the next ten years, Jack's official Halloween costume, which many times morphed into a Day of the Dead costume, delighted everybody. His complete ensemble—black snakeskin cowboy boots, black jeans, the black skeleton shirt, and a black Stetson, all of which stood in stark contrast to the white skeleton mask. Every year on Halloween, the cowboy skeleton emerged, spectacularly spooky-looking and quite sexy.

I joined in one year. Prompted by Carly, now a teenager, and her YouTube makeup lessons, I learned, step by step, how to become Catrina. Flowers on a floppy hat, my face covered solidly in white and painted with colorful flowers, curlicues, and hearts (very hard to do looking backward in the mirror), and a long black gown did the trick. The cowboy skeleton and I nabbed the Best Costume prize that year.

Jack's white skeleton mask dangles solo on its hook in the corner of my bedroom today. The artist who created the fabled work somewhere across the world remains unknown.

This year, alone in my home, I created my own *Día de los Muertos* candlelit altar. A private one—me and him and the marigolds I'd bought by the side of the road, his scrawny skeleton dog with the cigar, the Stetson, a Catrina, the white mask, a tablespoon of crunchy peanut butter, and a picture of the young man I'd fallen madly in love with so many Halloweens ago.

Chapter 58

Moonlight

Gradually, I began to reenter the world.

How is it my grieving widow dress has morphed into my party dress? I wondered as I pulled it from the back of my closet.

On an eerie November night, I went to the Downtown Library Gala with Marty and Gail. She convinced me to go, and I wore THE dress. Before this, it had hung untouched in my closet for eighteen months. It had dust on the top edges where it draped lifelessly over the wire hanger.

I wasn't sure what had made me bring it into circulation after all this time. Perhaps it was because I chose not to spend money on a new outfit I would seldom wear in my current semi-monastic life. Plus, it bothered me I had spent a fair amount on the dress for Jack's memorial service and hadn't gotten my money's worth. (Or had I?)

The dress really had nothing to do with Jack. He never saw it. He didn't have the opportunity to tell me, "You look great, babe," or "Wow! You look like a million bucks, M," which is how he always reacted to a new outfit of mine. My forever fan.

It was black. Of course it was black. Black is for tuxedos and East Coast wardrobes; the even numbers on the roulette wheel and curly-headed little girls' patent leather Mary Janes; Goya's dark era paintings, bewitching witches at Halloween, and licorice jelly beans.

Black is also for the widow.

In the past, mourning clothing in black was purported to give the bereaved survivor some latitude. A figure in black projected the need for space, compassion, and time to "not move on yet." Today, however, black may be worn to the service or "celebration of life," and then the expectation is to resume life as if the world has not just shattered to pieces.

Sometimes I think it would be better if black were reserved for an extended period of mourning, as in years past. A woman wearing black told the world of her loss and signaled to others her need for compassion and sympathy. Today, a woman is a hapless mess without a reliable "little black dress" (or two or three) ready to go anyplace. Just add fancy shoes and fabulous jewelry—or not—as desired.

But somehow, tonight, when I slid the sheer, filmy, bias-cut slip and dress on over my head, a transformation happened. This dress of mine, a simple design of two pieces, broke nicely over my relentlessly developing Buddha-like belly and eternally flat chest. It also broke my life in two: with Jack and without Jack. It was sleeveless, leaving my shoulder bare—reminding me that there was no longer one to cry on.

Its semi-transparency somehow represented what life was to me now, in the present. In the past, with Jack, it had been so markedly different. He'd protected me from minutiae and shielded me from anything he thought might disturb or scare me. With immeasurable love, he wrapped me in a strong suit of armor. That was no longer the case.

I needed to be strong—a sentiment that stood in sharp contrast to the delicateness of the dress and slip ensemble. So flimsy it blew gently in the wind, almost without provocation. I felt like I did, too, sometimes.

I couldn't peer through my special floaty dress. It looked like a thick bank of fog at night, extremely difficult to navigate. It conjured up a misty, socked-in evening. Appropriate, since I must have been in a fog when I bought it. I didn't remember buying it. Where, how much, why, and how? I had stayed in a fog for a long, long time. It was better now, but often I felt I'd suffered a concussion—a life-altering, mind-blowing, trauma to my head . . . and heart.

Weariness consumed me. It was very late and once again the little black dress hung on a hanger across my darkened bedroom, looking like a shadow. Still as night. There was a sliver of a pale moon shining beyond in the midnight sky. A boring gala, but the dress had worked.

As I contemplated it tonight, in my sleepiness, it looked quite lifeless hanging there. Kind of like me. I was struck by the asymmetrical hemline in shadow, which I guess I hadn't noticed when I bought it. Now I did. It was quite fashionable, I supposed. Higher on one side, lower on the other, cutting an angle from right to left at the knee. Trendy, perhaps, but also askew . . . asymmetrical . . . one-sided . . . unbalanced . . . off kilter. The same as me.

My little black dress would soon go out of fashion. What will happen to me? I brooded over and over.

⊂⧸

By myself a week later, I reveled in yet another extraordinary sunset sky. I had returned for an overnight at The Orange Woods—the near-empty, ghostlike Orange Woods. When Jack was alive and we experienced these indescribable offerings in our universe, we talked about wanting to share it with people—friends and family. I felt selfish for a short while, knowing I was the only one having this inspiring experience with nature and whoever God is. So peaceful, quiet, and serene. How could I have this all to myself? I covered my face with my hands, feeling the dampness of tears on my cheeks.

It might have been as still as I had ever known it to be. From my perch on the sunset deck, everything settled in somberness. Not a leaf moving or a speck of dust in the air. How could it be so quiet? I thought to myself, It's quiet because it's time for me to be alone with Jack.

Softly and slowly, I questioned aloud, "Honey, how many times have I sat in this very spot and mourned the loss of you? Begged you to hear my plea?" I crossed my arms across my stomach in a protective huddle. In an emotion-choked whisper I continued, "Missing you with all my heart. You loved times like this so much. Just you and me and the mesmerizing grandeur of our world, unfolding privately before us. It made us feel so special, like we were chosen in some way."

I struggled to lock the scene before me in my mind—something to remember when The Orange Woods was no longer mine. On my left, the dark silhouettes of neighboring avocado groves covered the hills, gently cascading down into the valley, which offered rows of citrus trees, pastures, an occasional farm structure, and twinkling lights. Beyond, our special deep purple mountain, dead center across from where I sat on our sunset deck. The mountains and hills behind it diminished in intensity ending with a pale, gray-purple ridge on the distant horizon.

What to say about this panorama above me? Subtle sparks of fire flickered in it, accenting the mauve and rose and peach mélange at the base of the sky. Pink, powdery puffs scattered across the grey-blue of the November sky.

As the sun disappeared, I leaned my head back to take in the vastness overhead. Glancing backward over my left shoulder, another of Mother Nature's offerings appeared. Although I had read about it coming, the super moon—rising in the east just as the sun set in the west—surprised me. My skin tingled at the sight, a flush of goose bumps surfaced. I wanted so much to share this special moon with Jack. Moon watching was one of our favorite pastimes.

I learned later in the evening that this moon was particularly super because it was the closest full moon to earth since 1948. The moon wouldn't be as close and bright for another eighteen years. The thought of that span of time without Jack momentarily unsteadied me; a tremor jolted my body. I grabbed the edges of the table, centered myself, and once again sat still. I folded my hands back in my lap and breathed in the quietness. What confounded me most this night was the silence. End-of-the-world silence.

Chapter 59

Cigar Band

As the second round of holidays without Jack approached, I steeled myself.

One evening in early December, again back at The Orange Woods, I sat alone outside the winery, craving to be near the things he loved. I glanced over at the ashtray Bo had given him for his birthday one year. They'd shared a cigar moment that day in this very spot.

Ashes were pressed into the center of the tray. I looked down at my wedding ring and my other ring, the gold one he'd given me his last Christmas. As the sun cast a rosy glow the soft hue of babies' lips on the mountains to the east, in my mind I ventured back . . .

ॐ

He only had to ask once.

"Of course, I'll marry you," I replied in shock. It didn't matter the stage was the IHOP restaurant on the Katy Freeway in Houston, Texas, or that I had my two little boys in tow and was pretty much covered in maple syrup for this, the most romantic moment of my life.

In a Methodist church in the big city, on March 13, 1965, we married.

Later in our married life, he repeated the same question over and over: "Will you marry me?"

Jack began to smoke cigars regularly thirty-five years into our marriage—after his award-winning career in radio ended and he became a serious winemaker. Outside the winery, across from the main house—an idyllic sitting space with unparalleled views of Palomar Mountain and its foothills covered with mountain lilacs—we had created a special place right outside the winery where we could linger after our winemaking work was over for the day.

The sitting area overlooked the bocce ball court; I lined the path with half-buried, upside-down wine bottles to define the area. In this quiet place, a lush grove of Valencia oranges and his vineyard of cabernet grapes surrounded us. Jack did most of his thinking there.

At The Orange Woods, Jack's new routine evolved: golf in the morning, a short siesta after lunch, followed by a few hours in the winery. At the end of his day, he would come to me and announce, "Time for a cigar."

Preparing to smoke his cigar became a sacred ritual. With a bit of pomp, he first smelled the cigar, much like he did a fine wine. Next, he gently rolled it between his fingers; clipped the end with his guillotine cutter, taking great care not to cut it too far down; spun it gingerly as he lit the flame; and puffed a few times, until the end of the cigar glowed. At this point, he put the cigar into his mouth and began to smoke—never inhaling. His artful routine.

It was so beautiful the way the clouds of smoke mirrored the white blossoms on the trees beyond—or, in winter, the light snowfall on the mountains. Most often I waited until he had completed his ceremony before joining him for a glass of his prized Cabernet, conversation, and the setting sun.

He was a one-cigar man—smoked one a day. And he only smoked one brand: AVO, one of the most prestigious on the market. Along with the creamy, nutty taste and its evocative earthy aroma (I did smoke a bit of one with him once; he was very persuasive), its Dominican Republic history fascinated him. Creator and jazz pianist Avo Uvezian was a composer who penned, among other songs, Frank Sinatra's "Strangers in the Night." The idea of a secondary and more fascinating later-life career like Avo's appealed to Jack.

I found myself captivated by the artistry of the band design on his cigars. Its sleek, modern design featured a nod to tradition. The elegant Avo band is one of the most recognizable among connoisseurs, with its unique color schemes and stylized logo with interlocking letters.

Each time I arrived at our romantic rendezvous spot, a glass of wine would be waiting for me. Jack's favored denim jeans and beat-up boots were often covered with splashes of red wine. As soon as I sat down, he would pick up the cigar band he had no doubt worked with great care to remove in one piece without tearing, and, with his killer smile, would ask, "Will you marry me?" He would take hold of my hand and slip the paper band on my finger. It melted my heart every single time.

We spent a great deal of time at the cigar spot in our last year together planning our fiftieth wedding celebration road trip, our favorite topic of discussion at this time. But our best-laid plans blew up the day before Valentine's.

Strokes are puzzling. Looking back, there were so many signs, and yet there was nothing that alarmed anybody—me, his kids, his golf buddies. But down deep, a part of me thinks he must have realized something.

Sometime in November 2014, a short while before his induction into the Radio Hall of Fame, and Thanksgiving, Jack became very secretive. He made unexplained errand trips, shut down his computer screen the moment I came near, and seemed mysteriously energized. Because I had received more than five decades of unceasing and awesome devotion from this man, I never went to the dark side about this. I assumed he was planning a Christmas gift.

He was. A few days before Christmas, at cigar time, like a little kid, he declared, "I'm going to give you your anniversary gift early"—and on Christmas Eve, before we drifted off to sleep, he softly whispered, "I'm gonna give you your anniversary gift tomorrow, for Christmas. Hope that's okay." I curled into his arms.

Christmas morning, I awoke to the smell of coffee. As I walked down the long hall, the warmth of a fire aglow in our fireplace embraced me. James Taylor's "The Christmas Song" played softly. Jack sat by our brightly lit tree. Under the tree, a very small package wrapped in gold and silver.

As I opened the leather box, a bright little light inside shone on my gift: an eighteen-carat gold cigar band ring with my initials, M and W, interlocked, artistically designed by him to celebrate our fifty years together. My husband was too excited to wait until our anniversary in March. By the time the day came, he lay in a coma; four days later, he was gone.

The Cigar Band remained the last gift of art we shared together. I could not open the box for months. It was a very long time before I could wear the ring.

Chapter 60

End of a Dream

My heroes have always been cowboys. The latest one came along at the right time.

Selling The Orange Woods, which I desperately needed to do for both emotional and financial reasons, wrenched on as a long and problematic process.

Weeks before his stroke in February 2015, Jack and I had put our cherished place on the market with a realtor friend. During the time he lay sick and dying, nobody looked at our property. Once I put it back on the market, a fatal illness in the realtor's family stopped action again. When I looked up, it was the holidays, when nobody buys houses, and a full year had passed.

For the most part of that painful year, I lived at both The Orange Woods and my new home in San Diego. During my gradual relocation, I said to my friends, "We all have too darn much stuff. Both The Orange Woods and 215 are fully furnished, bathrooms and kitchens stocked, with a full wardrobe in closets in both houses—complete with shoes."

During this time, I read Marie Kondo's *The Life-Changing Magic of Tidying Up* and pared both places down to "just things that give me joy." I actually did take every single thing out of the kitchen cabinets and pile everything in the middle of the floor for the selection process. My grandmother's rolling pin did not make the cut. The process proved both excruciating and exhilarating.

In the meantime, I continued to pay the grove and vineyard workers, the enormous water bill, and the maintenance man, all the while enduring relentless headaches and unending worry over our one-time paradise in the country. Broken sprinkler heads, dry rot, filthy windows and screens, weeds, termites, and mice, plus a litany of other problems associated with an unoccupied house, loomed large. My increasing financial worries, combined with my staggering, relentless grief, left me incapable of managing the situation competently. Looking back, I realize my actions and decisions were robotic and not necessarily wise.

I went to The Orange Woods regularly and spent the night there at least twice a week; I was frightened by both the familiarity and the unfamiliarity there. I abhorred being there alone. I hardly slept. At some point, it became like visiting a cemetery, a time of continuing grief and loss. Jack was dead. The Orange Woods was dying. Everywhere I looked, I found Jack. Steamer, too, sometimes. The burdens were overwhelming. I began to hate being there; it was too hard and too damn sad.

Two years after Jack and I had originally decided to sell, I knew I needed to make a decision.

CB

Jamie and Bud didn't push, but they did strongly suggest I meet with Larry, their friend and realtor.

I was nervous when they first brought Larry to The Orange Woods. But when a confident Larry—a big guy, beyond friendly, a strong, charismatic cowboy with cool leather boots and an expensive belt with an engraved silver belt buckle holding up stone-washed jeans—walked through my door a floating sensation overcame me. I had a feeling my burdens were about to be lifted. My eyes darted hopefully to Jamie.

After Bud showed him around, we gathered at the dining room table.

"When I looked at your listing, I have to be honest, I thought, no way—the price is way too high," Larry said with great candor. "But I'm blown away. It's right on. This place is extraordinary, with dozens of opportunities and options. I assure you I can sell this place."

Oh my god, he appreciated The Orange Woods and sensed its magic. I appreciated this cowboy.

Unfortunately, the timing was still bad. The 2016 presidential election was approaching, and our country languished in radical upheaval. Nobody could predict what the heck Trump and Hillary were going to do—or, more importantly, what lay in store for our country. Houses weren't selling. My worry and depression accelerated.

ભ

On January 20, 2017, the nation inaugurated Donald Trump as the forty-fifth and most controversial president in our nation's history. Within ten days, Larry, the cowboy realtor, brought me two verbal offers and one written cash offer with a twenty-eight-day close, which I accepted.

In the initial negotiation, the buyers made a lowball offer. Cognizant of the length of time the property had been on the market, I expected that. In addition to being low, however, the offer required me to remove all two-hundred-and-fifty of our Valencia orange trees. Without a moment's hesitation, I refused. They came back with another offer of a slightly higher price, this time excluding all the winery equipment Jack had researched, funded, and installed with such care and commitment. I learned quickly these buyers were not the ones I'd hoped for—not people who would continue the Orange Woods dream. I became irrational, angry and frustrated, but Larry calmed me down with news he had a buyer for the equipment in the winery, a buyer who recognized Jack's reputation for quality and care.

The bottom line number fell short of my hopes and expectations, but Brent had shown me concrete reasons to "take the money and run," so I accepted.

Was it end-of-the-election-cycle paralysis or just a function of timing? Hard to say, but I knew what I had to do. Immediately, I withdrew from the rest of my life's activities and responsibilities and committed myself to the sale of this property I had effectively been trying to sell for two years. I had imagined our buyer would be young and energetic, with some money and vision, like Jack and me when we began. I'd dreamed of a buyer who would embrace the place how we always had. Unfortunately for my realtor and new friend, Larry, and for me, the transaction played out as a nightmare.

I'm not sure what the potential buyers really wanted with our house and all the land—perhaps the unparalleled view and a potential party house. But it hurt as they nickeled and dimed and dismissed what had been so precious to me and Jack.

A tough deal ensued—an exercise in self-control. In the end, sanity and patience prevailed and contracts were signed March 1, six weeks short of the twenty-year anniversary of our original purchase of the property.

The heartbreak of it all, in my mind, was I'd just sold a magical place to people who didn't appreciate the magic. It was devastating on so many levels.

But human nature is resilient, and I rebounded from my worry, hurt, and heartache when I deposited the escrow check. Outside Charles Schwab on a glistening Southern California morning, I looked heavenward with my deposit receipt in hand and said with a sly grin to Jack, "Hey honey, all the damn orange juice they can drink for close to seven figures."

༌

Slowly and methodically, I stripped our paradise. To break from the pain of the process, I walked the labyrinth religiously. When Mom died, the labyrinth had become my solace; round and round I'd walked. Now, with Jack gone, I found myself circling round and round in meditation once again.

I began to dismantle . . .

As I wrapped *Country Road,* my painting of Steamer walking with Jack, in bubble wrap for transport, I wept. A jar of peanut butter on the kitchen counter caught my eye and, remembering Steamer's antics and unabashed devotion to us both, I smiled. We always put almost-empty jars of peanut butter on the floor, not the trashcan. Steamer would stick his long nose and his even longer tongue into the jar and lick out every remaining morsel of peanut butter. I was grateful I'd painted this picture of them.

Next, I went to the bedroom and took the three Tommaso Vei paintings out from under our bed, where I had put them just after Jack died. Looking at the ample, happy figures dancing, walking together, and harvesting their grapes—lovers swept away by music, dance, and summer's heat—upset me. Quickly, I folded them into a quilt and put them in the car.

These, and other works of art but one, would find a new home in San Diego with me. *Country Road,* the image of Jack and Steamer walking away from me, would hang in my bedroom, though it was sometimes painful to look at.

Tommaso Vei's *Tales of Life* would end up in my living room, where they would continue to represent the tales of our life—unbelievable years together.

CB

From the moment Jack died, the MARILYN LOVES JACK sign haunted me. I left it in place in the winery but tried not to look. I couldn't bring myself to disconnect it. In a cruel way, the thought conjured up the torment of turning off Jack's life support, the most difficult and tortured decision of my life. Yet I could not take the neon sign to my new home—too painful, too heartbreaking. I let the light shine until I couldn't take it any longer.

Two days before my final move, the dumpster arrived. Overnight, I thought and prayed and anguished some more. At sunrise the next day, my final day at The Orange Woods, I walked to the winery. I paused at Steamer's picture by the entrance—ran my fingers over the image of his long, lean body. I had forgotten to pack it.

I removed it from the wall to take to the car. An image of the three of us, Jack and me and our dog, flashed through my mind. It had been our Christmas card one year: Jack and me on a bench, basking in Southern California's reliable sunshine; a regal Steamer at our feet, posing in his red holiday collar.

I walked into the cold winery, disconnected the transformer, and took the sign down from the wall. The glow vanished slowly. I walked with deliberation and forethought out the door to the open, empty dumpster. I stood for a moment, enveloped in the morning's chill, took a very deep breath, slowly raised the sign high over my head, squeezed my eyes shut and dropped it. A startling explosion of glass shattered the early-morning silence.

CB

Late that night, my last night of life at The Orange Woods, I did my best to relax in the unfamiliarity of my new life. I ached for the blissful dream of a life, our life, at The Orange Woods. I lay alone in my dark bedroom, unable to sleep. Deep down in my gut, I acknowledged this was the end. He was gone from me now. So, it was time for me to be gone, too.

Chapter 61

Turning Points

I lived in San Diego now. Relocating there marked a major shift, a turning point in my life. There had been other changes:

- I'd always been tall and geeky. I was still tall, but maybe a little less geeky.
- I'd raced through college in three and a half years, married, taken a dream job at a TV station. Gotten pregnant. Become a housewife, divorced four years later, and, within seven months, married Jack. Our marriage had lasted fifty years and three days.
- First had become a mother of two phenomenal and phenomenally active little boys, then had been blessed with a sweetheart little girl.
- Was raised a Texan; became a Californian.
- A big city girl, I morphed into a farmer.
- For a time, was an artist; now, had no inspiration left.
- Was vegetarian for twenty-two years; was not currently but was thinking that could change.
- I'd long hated beets. Now I was addicted. (That probably wouldn't change.)
- I'd grown up in a two-story house; lived in one-story homes for the next forty years; and was now living in a two-story again.
- I was closer to my daughter than ever before. We were spending quality time together now—both excruciatingly sad times and silly times.
- I'd lived in seven different houses growing up; I'd lived in twenty-two houses after leaving my parents' home. I'd stayed put at The Orange Woods, our twenty-third home, for eighteen glorious years, followed by two dreadful and sorrowful years. Now I'd moved again.

- I'd always lived urban—Dallas, Houston, Indianapolis, Cleveland, New York, Denver, Washington DC, and the LA area—until we moved to Pauma Valley, population 989. Now I was urban once more.
- I'd been a part of a whole. No longer. I was wandering solo once again.
- I'd been trained in journalism and had written off and on over the years. Now, I was writing with a purpose.

ॐ

It astounds me that the two decades of my life at The Orange Woods were filled with such unimaginable loss—my father, my brother and only sibling, my son's baby girl, my sweetheart of a dog, my mother, and my beloved husband of fifty years and three days—and yet the euphoric memories prevail.

It also bewilders me I find it easier to write about loss and grief than all the sheer joy. I think it should be the other way around. However, as time passes, I have realized confronting the pain is necessary. When I switch the toggle, the sadness spews with overwhelming force and I am consumed with a desperate need to exorcise unending heartache.

In contrast, when I go to my happy place, the incredible time and place in my life when it sparkled, everything is young and beautiful. There is moonlight and laughter and people who love, but I can't capture it. I am unable to do it justice. I can't find the proper language to convey the immenseness of blessings and happiness that filled my life before. Words such as melancholy, heartbreak, loneliness, uncertainty, fear, and devastation come easier. Is this a process? Am I doing what so many others have done?

In the two-plus years since my Orange Woods dream shattered unmercifully, blown to bits, I find writing about loss has provided grief therapy for me over and over. Is it enough? Will I get this all out of my system? I've stopped hanging out with people who haven't experienced loss. They don't want to hear it. So, I spend time with my widow and widower friends.

To me, the happy times were consistent, the losses devastating.

ॐ

October 20, 2017

Marilyn:
Penny finally lost the battle she has been dealing with for so long this morning. Thank you so much for caring so much for her well-being. You were a great source of comfort for her.
Gary

This sorrowful message set off an unrelenting stream of penetrating jabs to my heart and mind two and a half years after losing Jack. The magnitude of Gary's heartbreak pierced my consciousness. That he would have to go through what I continued to experience saddened me beyond comprehension. How could I help him? Was it even my place to offer solace? Would my experience be valuable? Was I an authority?

By sharing Gary's grief, I came to understand relating to another's immeasurable loss is a valuable source of healing.

I spent the day with Jamie; we tend to cling closer to one another as the holidays approach. She comforted me over the loss of my close friend. We enjoyed the newly released movie *Murder on the Orient Express,* a collection of Oscar-worthy performances whose real star turned out to be Agatha Christie and her extraordinary writing. As the credits began at the end of the film, Michelle Pfeiffer sang in her signature soft, warm, and sexy voice—a voice I've loved since *The Fabulous Baker Boys,* in which she provocatively croons "My Funny Valentine."

"Wait, honey, let's hear this song to the end," I whispered to Jamie.

She agreed we were listening to something beautiful and sat with me until it was over.

I know myself well enough to understand music is a massive trigger for my emotions. As Walt Whitman wrote in *Specimen Days,* "its soul-rousing power allows me to wander out of myself."

At home, I immediately purchased "Never Forget" from the movie's soundtrack. The lyrics ripped my heart apart. The haunting pleas to "come home and stay" made me weep for Gary.

When Michelle Pfeiffer seductively sang about "holding me in your arms so sweet," I freaked. Jack's smiling face lit up in my head. With a ferocity that shocked me, I bolted upright from my chair, knocked my speaker off the desk, and left the room. Within moments, I returned. Couldn't help myself. Back to the music.

I listened to the song over and over for the next few days. The more I listened, the sadder I became. Stop it, Marilyn, I admonished myself.

I have always loved music, the piano most of all, even though my parents forced classical piano lessons on me for years. In the movie, "Never Forget" is played on the piano—subtle and meaningful, romantic yet tense. Were the impassioned lyrics written just for me? Michelle Pfeiffer's singing—intimate and sensitive, tinged with bitterness and regret, aroused a tsunami of emotions that gushed from my being. Regularly, I forced myself to stop listening. Over and over, I turned the music back on. Eventually, I turned it off and went to bed.

Facebook jarred me early the next morning with "thought you would enjoy your post from three years ago." I stared at an image—a shot from one of our family's happiest and proudest moments, the weekend of Jack's induction into the National Radio Hall of Fame. The photo—which featured the red velvet cupcakes with a microphone and RHOF "Class of 2014" logo on top of their crème cheese frosting, a dessert Bo and Jen had designed especially for the pre-party—startled and saddened me. I abruptly closed my laptop.

What is happening? I wondered. Why am I backsliding?

I walked to the office and took the photo book Jamie had created from that once-in-a-lifetime event off the bookshelf. There on the page—Jack in his tuxedo with the colorful silk scarf peeking out from his pocket, Jack on stage speaking to the full house at The Cicada Club in LA, Jack basking in the limelight.

I had a lump in my throat most of the morning.

Soon, my thoughts turned back to Gary. How to help him in these first weeks without Penny? This deep concern appeared to be a testament to the power of grief. The magnitude of his loss had resurrected mine. I resisted, not wanting to go back.

With my second cup of coffee in hand, I went to my computer and sent an email to my fiercely private friend. I hoped to offer some solace:

I keep flashing back to when I lost Jack and thinking about what you are going through at this point. If you want to talk or prefer to be left alone or hanker to cry or cuss or get drunk or be with family or friends—whatever you need at this time, embrace that. It's the only way to get through this heartbreak.

I left my computer and restarted my day—getting ready for Thanksgiving and all the company to come.

As I began preparations, I thought of my youngest grandchildren in Arizona. Chesapeake, my fiery little eight-year-old redhead, reminded me of Mom. She was a lithe slip of a smart little girl, feminine, graceful, and a bit coy. And Cash, at seven, was turning into a full-fledged lady's man, a charmer, especially with me. I decided to give them a call.

"Hi, you two," I said to C&C when I got them on the phone, doing my best to be cheery. "Want to see the movie *Coco* the day after Thanksgiving? It's all about skeletons and Day of the Dead."

Their collective shrieks said everything.

"Let's not invite Mom and Dad," I added.

They squealed louder.

Next, I texted my five older grandkids in their faraway locations: Maddie in Manhattan, Bayley in Spokane, Sophie in Davidson, North Carolina, Calvin at Amherst in Massachusetts and Carly in Nashville: "Please don't bother me, I'm busy preparing for Thanksgiving with my college kids. Neeny" (hugging face emoji, heart emoji, blonde-haired girl waving emoji).

I was trying so hard to fend off the oncoming sense of gloom with humor.

Little by little, memories flowed out of the boxes of Thanksgiving decorations and dishes. So many memorable Thanksgivings together. Our first in Carmel, Indiana, when I was very pregnant with Jamie; even though we were poor, we bought a new dining room table and chairs on an installment plan. We still had no furniture in the living room, however. Jack's family came and we celebrated both his mom and dad's November birthdays, along with their son's, my Scorpio.

In 1967, my loving parents babysat our three little ones and prepared our Thanksgiving feast while Jack and I went to the Dallas Cowboys–St. Louis Rams football game. Jack, an original fan from the beginning of the Cowboys franchise, rabidly supported hometown boy Dandy Don Meredith, as he led the charge—and racked up the win. Me? I was just ecstatic to be out without my little band of brothers and their baby sister.

The long Thanksgiving weekends provided much-anticipated excitement and joy over the years when our kids were in college and came home for the holidays. It was now instant replay time, as the grandchildren were doing the same.

Jamie and Bud gave us the greatest of all our Thanksgivings in 1994 with the birth of Bayley, their first child. She weighed six pounds less than our turkey.

Of course, Jack and I didn't eat turkey that year, though we cooked one. A few years before Bayley (and Maddie) were born, he and I stopped eating meat. It lasted for twenty-two years. For him, it was a cholesterol matter; for me, no meat was easy, and so was following his lead. (Giving up chocolate or cheese, not so easy.) I did crave turkey every Thanksgiving, and regularly succumbed to a drumstick. Jack never did.

Visiting his family in Leiter's Ford, Indiana, in November of 2012—his last visit—Jack and I escaped for a drive in the country. Rounding a curve, I spotted a lone billboard advertising Crown Royal Maple. On a rich black background, in gold letters, the message: MEET THE NEWEST MEMBER OF THE ROYAL FAMILY.

"Jack—look at that billboard," I said. "It's Crown Royal MAPLE. Oh, we passed it, never mind . . ."

Jack relished maple. "Your hair is the color of sunshine and maple," he often said. He poured heavy-handed servings of Vermont maple syrup on his pancakes. His mom's favorite candy was Brach's Maple Nut Goodies, which hung on a hook in the candy aisle at Wiseway Grocery Store where she worked. They were often stale, but we ate them anyway. And Jack never refused a shot of fine whiskey, especially when the weather began to cool, like today. So, what could be better than a combination of the two?

He turned the car around, drove back to the billboard, and, with all the spontaneity I adored about him, said, "Let's get some!"

We drove in search of it for over an hour through the rural countryside sprinkled with red barns, white churches, and silos. Occasionally, in a local village, hay bales, pumpkins of all sizes, and bundles of corn stalks stood with scarecrows in straw hats and coveralls, decorating a farm house or fence post.

At one point, we stopped for gas and Jack inquired about a local bar in the area. Following directions, we found it a few minutes later on the outskirts of town—set back from the road with a large neon sign, Happy Hollow Bar.

Jack smiled at me, pulled into the empty gravel lot, and parked. In we went, leaving the multicolored autumn leaves and chill outside.

The flames in the large stone fireplace welcomed us, as did the scruffy bartender, who wore a Chicago Bears sweatshirt. He appeared eager for company and conversation.

"Crown Royal?" he repeated. "Maple? No kidding. Your timing is amazing. The vendor came in this morning with the new product, just in time for the holidays. You'll be the first to try it."

I struggled with the bittersweet memory of that autumn afternoon—still so palpable for me I could almost taste the whiskey even now. I walked to the cabinet and found Jack's bottle of Crown Royal Maple, half full.

Many times, the family and friends had spent Thanksgiving together at The Orange Woods. Twice at Thanksgiving, we'd had family portraits taken—once with dogs and once without, chronicles of additions and losses. Sweet, sad, sorrowful, and savory memories.

In my mind, the refrain of the song "Never Forget" lingered, about holding each other close before winter came. How many Novembers had he held me?

As the afternoon edged toward evening, I began to tense up, moving in slow motion. This latest downslide had come on me with a sudden and staggering force. I missed Jack. I missed Penny. My heart ached with the enormity of world war for Gary.

I felt the build all day. The breath of dark November saturated the air around me. I became uncharacteristically sluggish in the late afternoon. I had promised to be at yet another year's Library Gala at seven o'clock, and I detested the thought of going. My hair, makeup, party dress (not last year's black one), and Mom's glittering jewelry looked presentable. It was rare for everything to work like that. Could have been the facial the previous week. But what did it matter how I looked?

It was dark November. The time change made for ominous and early nighttime. Dark November. Next week it would be Jack's birthday. November 20. We always celebrated our birthdays together. In all those years, never apart. Huge celebrations, friends together, family gatherings—or intimate, just-the-two-of-us birthdays. His last one landed between the Radio Hall of Fame event and Thanksgiving, so we celebrated modestly: dinner with Jamie and Bud, Laurie and Brent, and Carly and Calvin at Jack's favorite steak restaurant. When he and I arrived at the table, all six sat wearing huge plastic glasses with giant fake noses and black moustaches. He enjoyed a Manhattan and his children's foolishness.

Cʒ

I pulled myself together and set out for the library. I couldn't make myself turn off "Never Forget" as I drove. The dogged unraveling of one moment in our time together continued to cascade into another and another and another. The music was an unrelenting catalyst. I controlled the tears, but the moment I entered the grand domed space and saw hundreds of men and women together, laughing, talking, hugging, kissing, I felt riveted in place, sensing a breakdown coming. Excruciating to be alone when it's together time.

I panicked, needing to find Gail to tell her I couldn't stay. I stepped onto a landing and frantically searched the room for my friend, a dedicated volunteer for the event. By the time I spotted her in the crowd, so beautiful in her dark blue sequined cocktail dress, my need to flee consumed me.

Gail hurried through the celebratory masses toward me. She flashed her news anchor smile, which quickly turned into a face of grave concern as she came close.

"I'm sorry, Gail. I've got to leave," I blurted out. Tears ran down my cheeks; mascara, too.

"What's wrong, honey?" she asked, as she hugged me and ushered me outside. Stopping, she faced me with concern. "Your hands are freezing and you're shaking. What's wrong, Marilyn. Tell me?"

I shook my head, unable to speak.

"Marilyn, please tell me what's—"

"I can't stay," I eventually wailed.

Cʒ

Driving home, thinking about the past thirty-six hours and the recollections, both mournful and merry, that had played out in my mind, battering my brain and hurting my heart, I understood why I couldn't explain myself to even my close friend.

"Never Forget" promised my days of sorrow would vanish tomorrow— and I could count on my love to be there. But he wouldn't be.

Chapter 62
Afterglow

I know when it happened: Christmas 1970. The boys were in school. Brent, an industrious third grader; Bo, almost six, and well aware of his unique talents at entertaining, especially in the classroom. Four-year-old Jamie, forever her daddy's buddy pal, jumped up and down, anxious to accompany him on a secret gift shopping expedition for Mom.

Together, she and Jack selected two of the most luxurious and extremely expensive robes for me: one a full-length silken peignoir with an all-over rose pattern in pale yellow, the other a sheer, short kimono in rich jewel tones.

At that point in my life, each morning, like a short order cook, I prepared big breakfasts of waffles, pancakes, scrambled eggs, and oatmeal for three hungry schoolchildren before piling them into the station wagon for neighborhood carpooling. Syrup had no place on these pricey dressing gowns. Nighttime didn't work, either—after homework, baths, and books, I collapsed into bed. Money was tight. I desperately needed a new vacuum cleaner and a four-slice toaster. I tried my best to hide my dismay at such an extravagant present.

Right away, Jack sensed my disappointment. "The gift didn't work, did it, babe?" he asked later as we sat snuggled together on the couch in front of the fire drinking holiday eggnog.

I felt beyond awful I had rejected his thoughtful, romantic intentions. Why couldn't I fake it better?

The scene repeated itself more often than I care to admit. At some point, however, he began to give me the precious gifts of his words.

Making a living with words requires an innate ability to think, write, and deliver on your feet. Jack did it in spades. A student of the English language, never at a loss for words, his vocabulary unparalleled, he excelled at eliciting emotion and humor. He collected words with hard K sounds—Buick, debunk, berserk, carbuncle. "They always get a laugh in a punch line," he told me. "Remember Johnny Carson's Carnac the Magnificent?"

Jack could shuck and jive street talk but was equally comfortable presenting business plans to corporate investors. Words were his currency throughout his life.

One of his real strengths was the parody song; he amazed those around him with his quick wit and talent as an unbelievable rhymer of words—never the expected, and always lightning fast.

At some point, early in The Orange Woods days, perhaps discouraged by previous gift-giving failures, he turned to his words.

Once, a silly song for Bayley's third birthday:

> I put her on my back and we take a little walk.
> She likes it when we stroll and talk that baby talk.
> I put her in the car to take her for a ride.
> She loves to cruise around with her Neeny by her side.
> We call her Bay-Ley, Bay-Ley all the time
> Blee Doo, Blee Doo, Blee Doo

He wrote serious love letters:

> How many days in forever? How long is eternity?
> How many ways have I shown you, how much you mean to me?
> Day after day we're together, year after year, you and me
> Loving those moments, I hold you, hoping they always will be.
> Time slips by, how quickly it goes, as our sunsets turn to seasons
> Through it all our love still grows for oh so many reasons.
> It's still a thrill when you touch me, when I hear you call my name
> Loving the way that you need me, knowing our needs are the same.
> How long will I be beside you, beside you wherever you'll be
> How many days in forever, how long is eternity?

Somehow, this lighthearted one, "Living in the Afterglow," written in 2011, became an anthem for us:

Cuddling at night
Living with my baby
Makes everything right
Just lookin' at the sunsets
Watchin' the season flow
Lovin' on each other
She's my perfect lover
We're living in the afterglow.

Wine is my harvest
My baby is an artist
I'm watching this lady grow
Spending all the hours
Working on her flowers
Out where the oranges grow
Loving on each other
She's my perfect lover
I'm living in the afterglow.

I'll love the girl forever
We'll always be together
I do my best to let her know
We love on each other
She's my perfect lover
We're living in the afterglow.

I adored this simple song, which portrayed our ecstatic, ordinary, true-to-life manner. The word "afterglow" captivated me. I looked up the definition and appreciated it even more:

"Afterglow: A pleasant effect or feeling that lingers after something is done, experienced, or achieved."

Countless times we turned to one another and commented, "We are living in the afterglow!" An afterglow enveloped us after sex and during sunsets, but also when the orange trees first blossomed; when Steamer performed his lone trick, the high-five; when the paper-thin, white leaves of the Matilija poppy appeared in the canyon below; when we walked together in a row of our perfectly pruned grapes; or simply when we woke to yet another privileged day of life.

The warmth and radiance of the afterglow was extinguished when Jack died. I thought forever.

CB

Late afternoon on a warm day in June before The Orange Woods finally sold the next winter, I steeled myself to read his verse again. Although I had committed it to memory long ago, I had managed to block it out of my consciousness—too painful.

At 215, alone at twilight, I sat outside under the expansive branches of the jacaranda tree, which floated its lavender poufs above my head. I read and reread it without crying. In that moment, I realized my afterglow would continue. Luxe, calme, et volupté.

Chapter 63

Mi Hombre Pequeño

My final and complete relocation from the Orange Woods to 215 filled me with uncertainty and apprehension. Was moving the right thing? My worry abated for a brief time as I recalled a recurring banter between Jack and me.

"If anything ever happens to you, I'm out of here, back to San Diego," I would declare playfully.

"Yeah, with some hot young dude." His comeback, always.

Still, my last days at our home were lengthy and filled with angst, self-pity, sadness, and a burgeoning lack of conviction. Jack had been gone over two years. Jamie had embraced my decision, steadily exhibiting excitement about my move. The house in San Diego waited for me. Still I waffled.

Remembering the packing process conjures up more of those same feelings even now. But with unending upheaval in my life, other memories—precious, fond remembrances—surfaced and steadied me.

I stood in the dining room, pushing myself through the process of change. My hand trembled as I lifted my prized sculpture, *Mi Hombre Pequeño,* from the shelf. I tightened my hold on the figure and sat down at the long walnut table, reflecting on the imaginative artist, Josefina Aguilar, who had created it. My interest in folk art had originated in Oaxaca, Mexico with our introduction to her artistry there.

ೞ

"Look over in the far corner. She should be sitting on the ground," said Alejandro, our guide, who had just navigated us to this rural village outside Oaxaca.

"*Hola,*" said the woman sitting in the corner as we approached.

Her smooth, bronzed skin with swashes of red clay dirt swiped across it highlighted her sparkling white smile. She sat cross-legged on the bare ground on a flattened, dusty green cushion in the corner of the courtyard of her family's modest compound.

The Aguilar families, all clay artists, reside in the village of Ocotlán de Morelos outside of colonial Oaxaca in three sequential residences, little more than shelters. Josefina, the second of four sisters, beamed with a shy grin when Jack appeared. She motioned us closer.

Before turning her attention to us, she took a moment to mist the large lump of clay she worked on to keep it malleable. She then gestured to low wooden chairs nearby and indicated we should sit. She giggled a bit when Jack said, *"Eres muy hermosa, Josefina."*

My husband, the international charmer, in action.

Over her intricately embroidered and vibrantly colorful Huichol blouse, Josefina wore her uniform: a handcrafted apron covered with ruddy earthen handprints. It saddened me to observe how devoid of creature comforts her home appeared to be. And yet the Aguilar clan seemed to be happy. This backwoods homestead in a rustic village radiated with comfort, joy, and lack of stress.

Later, as I wandered around the complex surveying works of art in progress, finished pieces being prepared for shipment around the world, and happy children playing nearby, I contemplated the schedules and deadlines and stress of our busy lives. Great admiration for this woman and her simple lifestyle filled me.

Josefina Aguilar creates her masterpieces, which reside in museums in New York, San Francisco, Chicago, and throughout the world, out of rich terra cotta mud, the earth of her village. She first gained international acclaim in 1975 when Nelson Rockefeller began collecting her pieces while visiting Oaxaca. A highly regarded master, she is a serious and dedicated artist, deeply involved in her work as a ceramist in her mother's tradition and devoted to preserving the family heritage. She is touted as "not to miss" in Oaxaca.

Her imaginative clay figures, *muñecas,* which depict people and rituals in everyday village life as well as religious and folkloric scenes, are highly collectible. Mermaids, crosses, women of the night, the Last Supper, weddings, funerals, and zócalo scenes are amongst her specialties.

Our hero worship of Josefina began in The Orange Woods early years after we purchased our first piece, a colorful market woman. Actually, we bought three market ladies that warm November day in Oaxaca, because we couldn't make a decision.

Josefina's works are playful, quaint and simple, and yet so intricate. Our three market women each stood eight inches high and had long black braids, white rebozos, and long, colorful skirts. One had a wide-mouthed polka-dot monster on her head with a pair of two-headed snakes on top. A winged creature with an open mouth and eyes that bulged was perched atop the head of the second. She held a brightly colored fish in one hand; in the other, a smiling coyote. The third, festooned in bright turquoise, stood with a watermelon slice in one hand and a bouquet of large white flowers in the other. On her head was the Virgin of Guadalupe, surrounded by cacti. The headdresses were easily one-third as high as the women, who showed no sign of stress from their loads. Josefina's female figurines mirrored her own image; they were self-portraits. Thick raven hair, beautiful, expressive faces, and indigenous dress full of vibrant color.

Cઢ

We returned to Josefina's open-air studio three times over the years to visit her. She was always silent and calm as she created. We continued to purchase her Frida Kahlo, Catrina, calaveras, and Day of the Dead creations.

On our second visit—a trip to our beloved Oaxaca for our fortieth wedding anniversary—a sparkle of joy lit up Josefina's face when she saw Jack. Behind the large mound of terra cotta clay, her natural resource, she quickly dried her hands on her apron, creating two more reddish smears on the front, and smiled at my husband. He had thoroughly charmed her our first time there six years before, and it seemed she, like so many others, had found him unforgettable.

Josefina, older now, smiled demurely but did not get up from her spot in the corner, so Jack sat down beside her on her faded mat, removed the straw hat he had just purchased in the market for seventeen pesos, and put his arm around her. "*Que arte estás creando hoy, señora?*"

Josefina held up a raw clay figure for Jack's inspection. He leaned toward her and, in a protective manner, put both his hands around the piece and her hands that held it.

"I want it!" he said with great enthusiasm.

She understood.

A week later, a package with Josefina's completed artwork, decorated, painted, and fired, arrived at our hotel. The ample Josefina-like female figure, fifteen inches high, wore a delightful smile, a chunky, beaded necklace, a white blouse decorated with colorful fruits, and a long, bright red skirt, her bare feet peeking out from beneath. In her left hand, she held a bunch of ripe bananas. In her right, like Madonna holding her child, she held a skeptical-looking miniature mustachioed hombre, dressed in a pink shirt and turquoise pants. She pressed the little guy lovingly to her breast. He looked warily up at her.

"Could be us," Jack joked as he held the colorful duo in front of me. We christened our piece *Mi Pequeño Hombre*.

☙

Jack and I returned one last time two years before I lost him. Upon our arrival, we were devastated to learn Josefina, the talented artisan, had gone blind.

Josefina's hair had greyed at the temples and she needed help getting up and down from her chair at the table. She no longer worked on the ground. But despite her disability, she continued to create her folk art.

Jack caressed Josefina and she nodded her head slowly. He had learned some Spanish and she understood a bit of English.

"How do you keep doing your wonderful art?" he whispered.

With remarkable calm, she told us, "My hands know what do."

Prints of those hands covered her apron.

☙

Can I possibly sculpt or recast a new me out of this saddened lump of human being? I wondered as I returned to my packing.

I took great care wrapping *Mi Pequeño Hombre* in bubble wrap. As I put it in a crate, my mind drifted again. *Will I still have my precious memories if I leave this place? Will moving from The Orange Woods diminish our history? God, please, am I doing the right thing?*

With force, I shook my head in an attempt to dissolve my lack of faith.

The late-morning sunshine invited me. I brewed a cup of coffee and went to the red swing outside. I glided back and forth, sipping and swinging in silence, staring at the mural. *Will the new owners welcome its vibrancy or will they paint over it? The labyrinth—will they take care of it? The orange trees?*

A bunny darted across my garden as I took the last sip of my coffee.

Back into the house. Just as I started to return to packing, a jolt of what sounded like Mariachi horns blared in my brain. An aha *momento,* if you will.

I sat and let it flow.

No wonder I love Mexico, I thought. It was something I'd never articulated until this very moment.

I love Mexico because of Jack.

℘

The first trip I ever took there was with Jack—a thrilling, spur-of-the-moment getaway the morning after our simple wedding.

The last trip I took with the guy of my dreams—fifty years later, also to Mexico—celebrated the end of a mega year for us, 2014, and the beginning of 2015.

I swallowed hard as my mind harkened back.

At his offhand suggestion, we jumped up from brunch in our luxurious hotel suite in Houston on March 14, 1965, and grabbed the next flight to Mexico City for a three-day weekend honeymoon. No planning. No hesitations. We were young and foolish and fiercely adventuresome. We craved excitement.

We celebrated our anniversary fifty years later in Zihuantanejo, one of Mexico's lesser-known destinations. It is located on the Pacific Coast about one hundred and fifty miles northwest of Acapulco, a romantic getaway where, in our forties, Jack and I had somewhat shocking sex on the open-air balcony on the tenth floor of our hotel.

These bookend excursions to the country I love so much provided a laundry list of fascinating contrasts.

We were madly amorous newlyweds on a budget on that first lust-driven getaway. We were accompanied on the last by three children, their spouses, and seven grandchildren. Besides our fiftieth, the luxurious trip celebrated multiple milestones: a kindergarten graduation; Bud and Bo's fiftieth birthdays; Maddie and Bayley's twenty-first birthdays; Carly and Calvin's high school graduations; and Jack's induction into the National Radio Hall of Fame.

On our honeymoon, we found our way to a bullfight. Again and again, I cried, "Honey, I can't stand to look," over the riotous screams of *olé!* that filled Plaza de Toros. The seductive matadors, dressed in ornately gilded *trajes de luz* (suits of light), tantalized the bulls. Over and over, I buried my head in Jack's chest to avoid looking. Over and over, I peeked.

In Zihuantanejo, our family scuba-dived and marveled at brilliant fish specimens in the sparkling turquoise waters on bright shores where wrongly convicted prisoner Andy Dufresne dreamed of escape in *The Shawshank Redemption,* which we had viewed in anticipation of our trip. The town, with its laid-back style and cobbled streets, population around 100,000, felt small compared to Mexico City, which continually jockeys with Tokyo, New York, Beijing, and Istanbul for world's largest city honors.

Neither Jack nor I drank when we honeymooned. We made up for it fifty years later at the open-air tequila bar overlooking the infinity pool and the bay beyond in Zihuantanejo as we sipped Casa Dragones, possibly the best tequila in the world. There, too, we relaxed in the opulence of the compound—plush furniture, woven rugs, expensive art and antiques, scrumptious meals, and the unending service of the gracious staff. In Mexico City, we had hurriedly embraced museums, cultural sights, and the Floating Gardens of Xochimilco.

In between these two most memorable forays to Mexico, there were countless others.

On his maiden voyage as a private pilot (which scared the hell out of me), Jack and our friend Gary flew us to remote Guaymas, where I first tasted shrimp fresh out of the sea—large as my fist and wrapped in crisp bacon. We slept in cabanas under the starry sky. No hotels in undeveloped Guaymas on the Sea of Cortez in the 1970s.

As our children grew into adventuresome teenagers, we made repeated trips to the beaches on the Pacific Ocean south of Rosarito in Mexico—Punta Banda. Jack and his camping buddies traveled perilously in small boats to gather fresh lobster for our dinners there. We sang songs and told stories around the warmth of the campfire. Would my grandchildren ever experience such simple pleasures?

Sex in sleeping bags on the beach in the sand in Rosarito after the kids were sound asleep rivaled the balcony in Acapulco.

"Honey, the kids will hear us," I protested.

"Be quiet then," he murmured.

cs

We visited the Spanish colonial gem of Mexico, San Miguel de Allende, several times. It was a paradisiacal April day on our first visit when we first heard the soulful crooning of Pedro Infante. Jack and I were dining al fresco on the balcony of a lively restaurant overlooking leafy El Jardín, the main square. Brightly colored *papel picado*, lattice-like designs of paper, and piñatas lined the scalloped edges of the balcony's awning.

So much loomed new and exciting on our first trip to San Miguel, a magnetic destination for both artists and expatriates. Here we first tasted chiles en nogada, a stuffed poblano with walnut sauce and pomegranate. (Extremely difficult to prepare, I would later discover; the recipe is three pages long.)

When the waiter, a jolly, portly, middle-aged fellow, approached, we asked who the singer was. He smoothed one end of his moustache before he held up a finger. "*Sólo un minuto, por favor.*" He handed us the menus, disappeared and returned in moments from the back of the restaurant with a magazine. He pointed with great pride to the handsome figure on the front and said, "*El cantante mas popular de México!*"

On the cover: the handsome Pedro Infante, Mexico's most beloved singer and screen idol, whose plaintive singing filled our evening air.

We were saddened to learn Infante had died tragically in a plane crash in 1957 at the height of his popularity, just like Richie Valens, the Mexican-American singer who popularized *La Bamba*. Valens perished alongside The Big Bopper and Buddy Holly; in Lubbock, Texas, where I went to college, Holly was a bespectacled hometown hero who was idolized for his rockabilly, rhythm and blues, and country and western music with its upbeat tempo and jittery vocals.

Infante's "Cien Años," one of Mexico's most recognized bolero songs ever, became one of our standards.

cs

The poignant lyrics of "Cien Años" were upsetting for me to listen to now—they cut to my core. And yet, the dream of one hundred years together was still a beautiful one. I could almost hear the song as I sat alone amid a few boxes in the emptiness of The Orange Woods.

In an effort to steer clear of too much pain and grief, I edged myself back to the present, walked to the kitchen, and made myself a second cup of coffee—decaf this time.

Coffee in hand, I walked back to the bookshelf and took down my last Mexican folk art purchase, *Tree of Life*, also by Josefina Aguilar. Jack and I had bought it together in Zihuantanejo. I smiled at Eve in pink and Adam in white, throwing their hands up in despair as the Virgin of Guadalupe blessed them. Carefully, I wrapped the fragile tableau and put it in the packing crate.

Momentarily, another wallop of potent doubt battered my brain. I'd lost Jack and my parents and Steamer. Was losing The Orange Woods the right thing to do? Should I stay here by myself, alone with nothing but the memories?

Fighting off my worries temporarily, I went to the powder room and one by one carried my *Damas de la Noche* to the dining room table for wrapping. The three iconic female figures in my collection were also Aguilar family treasures from Mexico.

An image of the oldest Aguilar sister—Guillermina, a warm, spirited, and pious woman—appeared in my mind. For five dollars each, we'd purchased these *Damas de la Noche* (Ladies of the Night) from her as she beamed. I had cherished these figures more and more each day since, realizing the strength of the familial bond of the Aguilar sisters and their families, crafting their art together in their tiny village.

Back at The Orange Woods, I'd loved what they'd come to mean to my clan. Most of my Oaxacan pieces there were on display together, but somehow the three *Damas de la Noche*, with their long legs and ample posteriors, scantily dressed in various lingerie ensembles—garter belts, skimpy brassieres, stockings, and thong underwear (long before Hanky Panky made it cool), had found themselves on a glass shelf in a niche in the guest powder room. I put them there at just about the time my five older grandchildren each became able to go to the potty by themselves, and they were at nose-level as the kids peed.

One day shortly after the "install," I went into the bathroom and discovered the *Damas de la Noche* mooning me. One or more of the three little girls—I suspected the ringleader, Maddie—had turned the three around, presenting the biggest naked (almost, anyway) rear ends ever. What is it about little kids that makes them flirt with naughtiness?

From the beginning, therefore, they have lovingly been called the "Big Butt Ladies," and throughout our twenty years at The Orange Woods, whenever a grandchild used the bathroom, I always found the figures rotated to stand butt side out.

I think the Aguilar sisters would have been pleased.

Many years after the first rotation of the Big Butt Ladies, Calvin created the "epic sprawling family message," a group text where we could communicate to the family as a whole. In searching for authenticity, I posed the question to the family, "Does anybody recall who first turned the Big Butt Ladies around?"

Instantly, Maddie, living and studying in Manhattan, confessed. Carly, a freshman in college in Nashville, attempted to take credit and Bayley, now a graduate student in Spokane, replied curtly to her younger sister, "You weren't even walking then. Me and Maddie did it."

The Big Butt Ladies and I moved together. Today, they are in my new home on a special bookshelf in the living room. And yes, they still get rotated by those same granddaughters, all beautiful young women today.

cs

Another magical Mexico time, Jack bought me a ceramic sculpture of a pineapple from the library/bookstore in Oaxaca.

I spotted it one evening as we strolled by the window after dinner of tacos Castillo.

"Honey, we need that pineapple," I nagged, pointing at the piece on a pedestal.

From Alice, my spiritual guru, I knew the pineapple symbolized those intangible assets we appreciate in a home: warmth, welcome, friendship, and hospitality. A pineapple to welcome my friends to The Orange Woods would be perfect.

This particular pineapple, a creation of earthenware pottery, twenty inches high by fourteen inches wide, resembled a mini potbellied stove. Earthenware pottery such as this was first made in Mexico around 4,500 years ago.

I tugged on Jack's arm, imploring him to "take a look." On overload from my souvenir shopping, he reluctantly acquiesced.

We learned the piece, rich ebony black with a green glaze, had been created by an important contemporary artist, Hilario Alejos Madrigal, from the state of Michoacán. Madrigal happened to be a good friend of the bookstore's owners, a young heiress and her handsome husband.

Looking at the pineapple up close, Jack commented, "It reminds me of a barrel cactus."

"Right," the elegant young woman explained, "this is a biznaga, inspired by the cactus of the same name, and is a cross between the plant and a pineapple."

Over a cup of Mexican coffee—a rich blend of cinnamon, spices, and coffee beans—Jack, now thoroughly convinced himself, persuaded the young people to sell us the pineapple from their private collection. They were suckers for his "retirement paradise in the country" stories, and they summoned several artist friends to join us as we visited with them. A wonderful exchange of ideas and philosophies followed, which made the pineapple something of a beacon of cultural cohesiveness in our home. Many times over the years, when we told this story, more stories of cross-cultural relationships evolved. Can it be that simple?

Our spontaneous purchase arrived at our hotel early the next morning.

Upon its arrival, a mixture of happiness and concern overtook us both. How the heck to get this treasure, extremely fragile and bulky, about the size of a hiker's fully packed backpack, back to San Diego? We were to leave the next morning.

From the moment I met him, Jack could handle anything thrown at him without a moment's hesitation. This amazing ability melted my heart regularly.

When we boarded the Mexicana flight the next day, I sat in 8C; Jack in 8E; the pineapple in 8D.

Yes, he bought a seat for our pineapple.

ॐ

One more trip for the pineapple coming up. I wished my strong sense of adventure, which was now missing from my life, would return. Without Jack, moving frightened me.

In the garage, I found a large box. Before putting the pineapple in it, I took the pillow I'd made from Jack's silk ties and shirts from the chair and put it in the box as a cushion. I touched the square made from the wine bottle shirt Jan had given Jack to commemorate his new winemaking venture. He'd worn it constantly. One skeleton from the shirt Bo had given Jack was on the pillow cover too. The rest had been incorporated into a memory quilt made by Jamie and her friend Pam.

The pineapple and the pillow cushioned one another for the journey.

☙

A photo collage of Chesapeake and Cash on a shelf nearby caught my attention. A spark of joy flickered in my heart as I thought about watching *Coco* with the two of them the previous November.

The family had gathered for a sumptuous Thanksgiving feast, our second without Jack, the day before. That afternoon, after pushing the control buttons up and down and back and forth, C&C settled comfortably into the sumptuous lounge chairs of the theater, candy and popcorn in hand. My stomach bulged from turkey and extensive fixings the day before.

When Benjamin Bratt, voicing Ernesto the Mexican matinee singing idol, warbled "Remember Me," Cash and Chesapeake and I shared collective tears as we remembered. Chesapeake, my grown-up nine-year-old granddaughter, reached for my hand, patted it gently, and rested her little red head on my shoulder. Cash, as devoted and loyal as Steamer, leaned over his popcorn and whispered, "Papa would have liked this movie, huh Neeny?"

These two youngest of my grandchildren had grown up at The Orange Woods. It would be especially hard for them when I was gone from there. Was it right for them to lose their grandfather *and* The Orange Woods? Was I overthinking this?

I would receive the most endearing response to my questions the summer after I sold The Orange Woods. My little Cash—the platinum-headed charmer with the red glasses—momentarily broke my heart.

I was sitting next to him one evening at dinner when the subject of The Orange Woods came up, as it often did in family gatherings. Lighthearted and guarded conversation followed as we tiptoed around the vulnerable middle. At some point, I sat back in my chair and withdrew a bit from the bittersweet remembrances.

In an instant, I felt a soft pat on my arm.

Cash, on my left, leaned toward me and said in a whisper, "Don't worry, Neeny, when I get big, I'm going to buy back The Orange Woods for us."

Melt.

ೞ

So many Mexico memories. It hurts to look back. By taking these artistic reminders with me to San Diego, I hoped to preserve the many good times in my mind. Art has the power to do that.

Our last journey to Mexico overflowed with good times as we said good-bye to 2014 and welcomed 2015 as a family in Zihuantanejo. It would only be in looking back, not only at the photographs but also at my wistful painting of Jack standing alone at the edge of the water looking far off into the distance, that would make me realize something ominous was going on in his brain on that last trip—determining for us, before I was ready, this trip would be our last.

Afterword

The End of The Orange Woods Years

I no longer live at The Orange Woods. I live at 215 in San Diego in a lovely home very close to Balboa Park. Occasionally, my popcorn brain resurfaces. Sometimes, when I sit alone, most often as the day ends and families and lovers and friends reunite in the warmth of their homes, I reminisce and I am overcome with sadness.

The magnitude of sorrow and loss through The Orange Woods years tortured me; it was overwhelming at times, like the dark, brooding melancholy of a Caravaggio painting—a darkness that sometimes pervades the noonday sun of my life today.

Memories can be heartbreaking to relive. But more often there are moments when I contemplate The Orange Woods and I am overcome with emotion and warmth—the warmth of a bathtub filled to the brim with lavender-scented bubbles. I am grateful.

A spirituality resonates through me as sublimely as it did years ago at a candlelit Choral Evensong. Even now, as I think back and recall that evening at Cambridge University in England where my older son studied, a shiver runs down my neck and across my shoulder. A beautiful mixture of euphoria and reverence filled me then as I sat between Jack and Brent in a vaulted ceiling chapel of the hallowed Kings College.

When I picture life at The Orange Woods, there is light—like the brilliance and joy of Henri Matisse's paintings. Or the idyllic atmosphere of Renoir's friends in *Luncheon of the Boating Party,* sharing food, wine, and conversation. The whole painting seems to sway with the summer heat. Like the paintings of these well-known artists, my recurring memories of The Orange Woods are scenes of leisure, relaxation, and beauty. The light is dappled; there is a sfumato-like softness to the scene; the edges are blurred; and it glows, reddened from the sun or illuminated in the moonlight. A grand canvas of sensuality and contentment fills my mind. What more can I ask for? I have my memories.

My time at The Orange Woods lasted over seven thousand days—three weeks short of two decades. During that time, my parents, my brother, and my dog died. My children hit the mid-century mark. Five of my grandchildren graduated from high school and went on to college. Two more grandchildren entered my world. Currently, they study Mandarin in elementary school.

Time has comforted me. I have been without Jack almost three years. When memories begin to fade, I find looking at our art and listening to our music reminds me. My journaling, an exercise in contemplation, a ritual of speaking, and a form of praying, revives precious details I have forgotten. I am grateful for those that remain strong and clear in my head and my heart.

I will never forget the romantic, inspirational voyage I took to Paris with Jack all those years ago when The Orange Woods was new. As we left France and flew west into the setting sun, I dreamt about *Luxe, Calme et Volupté*—both Matisse's painting and Baudelaire's poem. The phrase translates as easily as it sounds to luxury, calm, and voluptuousness. I fantasized about our refuge halfway around the world and longed passionately to create our own luxe, calme et volupté on our lush land in Southern California. It became Jack's dream, too. As we added each layer over the years, we did exactly that, even calling it our canvas.

He and I existed in the tranquility and grandeur of nature, along with the hummingbirds, the bees, and the roadrunners, for almost two dreamlike decades—serene stillness, except for the low-pitched rumble of Steamer's infrequent bellow; an occasional symphonic chorus of coyotes; our cherished music; and the laughter of friends and family.

To the east of our paradise, the soaring summits of Palomar Mountain protected us. Boucher Mountain to the north, our secluded backyard. Not unusual for snow to dust the upper third of the mountains in colder times of the year, looking much like our "orange blossom" snowfall each spring. I cannot count the times we shared a glass of wine on our sunset deck or strolled hand in hand amid the vines, encircled by the mountains, the hills, and the extraordinary brilliance of the setting sun.

We lazed in the lasting glow of our sunsets, but equally stunning was the mesmerizing full moon each month. Full moon nights—our romantic date nights. We especially loved the Pink Moon of April. Little did I comprehend the deeper meaning the blush of that moon would take on when I lost Jack. Until that time, we savored each full moon's enchanting radiance together, always together.

With unbridled eagerness, Jack and I embraced each new layer as we painted our canvas. Certainly, the work was backbreaking at times and we had surgical scars to prove it, but the rewards were bountiful.

Looking back, bouquets of orange blossoms, grapevines, and lavender swirl overhead in my daydreams. Children and dogs play happily. There is harmonious music in my mind—blues and country, anthems and hymns, arias and songs of romance. In my mind, I remember sunrises over the mountains in the east and the sun setting reliably and spectacularly in the west. I can taste the warmth of the wines and the simple pleasure of peanut butter. Gleaming furniture, quiet nights, warming radiant fires, fragile flowers, leather bound books, and the changing seasons take their turns pirouetting gracefully through my mind. All the memories speak to my soul. Great loss. Greater love. A life lived artfully.

Away from The Orange Woods, I have spent a great deal of time appreciating Matisse and the painting that informed and inspired our lives there. I find it fascinating to think this young French artist, thirty-five years old in 1904 when he painted his masterpiece, experimented, innovated, and challenged himself out of his traditional training into something new. With intense, saturated colors and a variety of new brushworks and paint applications, he became the greatest colorist of the twentieth century and one of the most influential artists of our time.

Matisse embraced change. I find myself at a point in my life where I am forced to cradle change. A melancholy part of me resists. But more and more, I find myself inspired by new people and new places and the challenges of life without my husband. I surprised myself recently when I joined a drawing salon, an intimate group of five like-minded souls.

With Jack, our lives echoed Matisse's thoughts when he wrote, "What I dream of is an art of balance, of purity and serenity, devoid of troubling or depressing subject matter—a soothing, calming influence on the mind, rather like a good armchair which provides relaxation from physical fatigue."

Is there a way my life alone can mirror these thoughts? Today, as I sit on my patio in the late afternoon sunshine, a familiar scent drifts my way.

At the edge of the terrace, the orange tree my son planted shimmers with white blossoms. The fragrance is one I can never forget. A fragile blossom falls to the ground slowly, like a swirl of soft vanilla ice cream.

My home is filled with our silk road of treasures. Often, I imagine and reflect on Henri Matisse as he masterfully applied his genius to painting or Charles Baudelaire as he carefully selected words for his poetry. Taking inspiration from these great French masters, Jack and I spent precious time together creating a spiritual place of order and beauty where desires were met—a world of luxury, tranquility and pleasure—luxe, calme et volupté. That world fell asleep in a warm glow of night. And what I am realizing more and more is rather than a place or an experience or a love affair, the Orange Woods is a state of mind—my state of mind. I have my memories.

Luxe, calme et volupté. Quiet and voluptuous luxury.

Recipes from The Orange Woods

Peanut Butter Fudge Cake

Group A

 1 cup butter
 ¼ cup cocoa
 1 cup water
 ½ cup buttermilk
 2 eggs, well beaten

Group B

 2 cups sugar
 2 cups flour
 1 tsp. soda

Additional ingredients

 1 tsp. vanilla
 1 box powdered sugar
 1½ cup creamy peanut butter
 1 tsp. additional vanilla
 ½ cup butter
 1½ T. peanut oil
 ¼ cup cocoa
 6 T. buttermilk

In pan, combine A on low heat until it bubbles. In bowl, mix B and stir hot into dry ingredients. Beat until smooth. Stir in vanilla. Spread into greased and floured 13" × 9" × 2" pan. Bake at 350° for 25 minutes. Cool in pan.

In bowl, mix peanut butter and oil until smooth. Spread over cake.

In pan, heat ½ cup butter, cocoa and buttermilk. Add powdered sugar, vanilla. Beat until smooth. Spread on cooled cake.

Cecile's Cookies

Cecile Wilcox was my father's private secretary for twenty-two years. Her cookies were the family's favorite treat, both in my childhood in Dallas and then with my children and my grandchildren at The Orange Woods.

½ c. butter
1 8 oz. cream cheese
1 tsp. vanilla

Cream these three ingredients. Add one package yellow cake mix, ⅓ at a time. Mix in raisins, coconut, and/or nuts. Drop onto greased cookie sheets. Bake 325° for 15 minutes.

Gazpacho de Blanco

I first tasted this white and not-so-healthy gazpacho at The Zodiac Room at Neiman Marcus in Dallas shortly after the restaurant opened in 1953. In my memory, it was not nearly as yummy as the piping hot popovers.

3 medium sized cucumbers, peeled
3 c. chicken or vegetable broth
1 clove garlic, minced
3 T. white vinegar
1 T. salt
2 c. sour cream

Tomatoes, chopped

Scallions, sliced
Parsley, chopped
Almonds, dry-roasted
Avocados, peeled and chopped
Cilantro

Blend cucumbers, broth and garlic in blender or food processor. Add vinegar, salt and sour cream. Refrigerate 24 hours. Serve in chilled bowls and garnish with tomatoes, scallions, parsley, almonds, avocados, and/ or cilantro. May be made 2–3 days in advance.

Serves 8.

Popovers

Helen Corbitt, the Grand Dame of Texas Cookery, published her first cookbook in 1957. After eight years of persuasion by Neiman Marcus' Stanley Marcus, Helen became the director of Neiman Marcus' food services. This recipe is one of her most famous bread recipes. With just five ingredients, this recipe is simple and a sure crowd pleaser!

1 cup sifted all-purpose flour
1/2 teaspoon salt
2 eggs
7/8 cup milk
1 tablespoon melted butter

Mix the flour and salt. Beat eggs until light, add milk and butter and add slowly to the flour. Stir until well blended. Beat 2 minutes with rotary beater if by hand, or 1 minute with an electric beater. Heavily butter muffin tins or custard cups and put in the oven to get hot. Fill the cups one-third. Bake 20 minutes at 450°, then reduce heat to 350° and bake 15 minutes more. Don't peek!

We always served hot with marmalade, orange of course.

Lavender Eye Pillows

I found these directions online at YogaJournal.com. When we finished ours, Carly sewed a "made in Pauma Valley" label at the end of each pillow. The label was made in China!

For each pillow

½ yard of fabric that has been washed, dried, and ironed. We used satin; linen works beautifully, too. (You will have extra fabric.)

For the filling:

  ½ cup dried beans or flax seeds.
  ½ cup dried rice, lentils, or buckwheat.
  ½ cup dried lavender or chamomile.

Mix together three or all of the above items. You'll need 1½ cups total.

Make the Pillow

Step 1: Cut the fabric
Using a ruler and pencil, mark two 4½-by-10-inch rectangles on the wrong (nonprinted) side of the fabric. With a pair of scissors, cut along the marks to create the two panels needed for the pillow.

Step 2: Sew the seams
Place the two panels' right (printed) sides together, with the raw edges aligned. Stitch a ½-inch seam around the raw edges, backstitching (sewing first in reverse, then forward over the same stitches) at each end. Leave one of the 4-inch sides open, so you can later add the filling. Stitch a ⅜-inch reinforcement seam around the raw edges, leaving the same 4-inch opening. This reinforcement will ensure that the mixture doesn't leak out of the pillow after you've filled it.

With your scissors, cut two ¼-inch notches in each seam allowance (the area between the stitching and the raw, cut edge of the fabric), one on either side of each of the four corners, making sure not to clip the stitching. Turn the eye pillow right side out for the next step.

Step 3: Fill the pillow
Spoon 1½ cups of filling into the pillow's open seam.

Step 4: Close the final seam
Fold each side of the remaining 4-inch seam ½ inch toward the inside of the pillow, and pin the opening closed. Either by hand or with a sewing machine, stitch a seam across the folded edges to close the 4-inch opening, then try out the pillow: lie down, put it over your eyes, and treat yourself to 5 minutes of deep relaxation.

Lavender Wands

Harvest your bunches of lavender early in the morning before the bees begin to buzz. Select straight stems and cut them long.

Provence, which we grew at The Orange Woods, give long sturdy stems to work with, making it very easy to make the wand. (Can use Grasso or English varieties also.)

For one lavender wand, select an uneven number of stems, any odd number greater than thirteen.

1. Tie the stems together with a thin silk or grosgrain ribbon just right beneath the blossoms. Leave one end of the ribbon short. You can hide it inside the lavender wand.

2. The next part is a little tricky at the beginning. Hold your little bouquet upside down and bend the stems over. This only works if your lavender is freshly cut. To prevent the stems from breaking, just make a little dent with your fingernail where you want them to bend.

3. Start to weave your ribbon through the stems. Pull it tight from time to time and push it up to cover up the lavender blooms inside. The weaving will take a little time, so it's a perfect craft for patient little girls on lazy afternoons.

4. If you have covered up all the lavender blooms, tie the ribbon securely and wrap it around the stems in a spiral fashion till the end. Secure the ribbon again and tie it into a nice little bow. That's it!

Mom's Favorite Baked Beans

    6 cans baked beans
    ½ lb. salt pork
    ½ c. dark molasses
    ¾ c. brown sugar
    S&P
    1 bottle chili sauce

Cut salt pork into small pieces and brown in skillet. In large bowl, combine beans, salt pork, molasses, brown sugar, seasonings and chili sauce. Mix thoroughly and bake 300° for 2½ hours.

The Orange Blossom Martini
Created for The Orange Woods by Faye Campbell

Engaging All Senses

Pour a tasty, well aged Gin in a chilled shaker (*For the less sensitive, Vodka is okay*).

Add a small amount of Dry Vermouth, if you must.

Shake until you think it is enough then shake again. Ice crystals will form.

Remove long stemmed Martini Glasses from the freezer

Float the Orange Blossom on the edge of glass

Pour the icy liquid from the shaker into the chilled glasses

Lift the glass to your lips . . . **NOW, WAIT FOR IT!**

There is a moment in time when all the elements merge and all your senses engage.

The Gin has come alive with the sassy little ice crystals and hits your lips with its icy sting.

The scent of the Blossom wiggles up your nose and it engages with the Gin in your mouth so that at that very moment, the Martini tastes like the Orange Blossom! The eyes take in the beauty of the miracle before you and say, "Let's go again"!

Valencia Vin D'Orange

On one of our trips to Europe, we became intrigued with the lore of Vin D'Orange, a popular aperitif there, especially in France. We loved learning we could combine our love of winemaking with the fruit of our Valencia Orange grove. We combined our Orange Woods Chardonnay with our oranges, lemons from a friend's grove, sugar, vanilla beans, and some stronger spirits!

The label for the Pauma Valley version of Vin D'Orange featured my art, three oranges from our grove. We loved knowing long after the oranges were gone, the vibrant sunflower-yellow orange lingers, not on the trees, but in the bottle.

2 (750 ml) bottles white wine
1 cup vodka
4 oranges, with the peel, scrubbed and chopped into 1-inch pieces
1 lemon, preferably organic, quartered
1 cup sugar
1 cinnamon stick
1 vanilla bean

In a large glass jar, mix together the sugar, white wine, and vodka until the sugar dissolves. Add the orange and lemon quarters. Scrape the seeds from the vanilla bean and add them to the jar, then drop in the pod. Cover, and let stand undisturbed for 1 month in a cool, dark place.

After one month, remove and discard the fruit; remove the vanilla pod. Pour the mixture through a mesh strainer lined with a double thickness of cheesecloth or a coffee filter, then funnel the vin d'orange into clean bottles. Cork tightly and refrigerate.

Serving

Serve over ice in small glasses with a twist of orange or lemon zest.

Storage

Vin d'orange will keep for at least 6 months in the refrigerator.

Scrumpdidilicious Jalepeno Corn

This all-time decadent Texas favorite was introduced to us by my mom's housekeeper, Erma Sutton.

  1 stick butter
  1 package (8 oz.) cream cheese
  ½ cup milk
  3 cans whole kernel corn
  3–4 jalepeno peppers, seeded and diced
  2 cups shredded cheddar cheese

Melt first 3 ingredients in sauce pan. Add corn and peppers. Pour in baking dish. Sprinkle cheese on top.
  Bake 350° for 30 minutes.

Three Onion Casserole

Laurie brought this very delicious Three Onion Casserole from The Silver Palate Good Times Cookbook several times at Thanksgiving and we all lapped it up. Wonderful on Christmas Eve with Prime Rib. Perfect one-dish vegetarian meal too! This decadent casserole should definitely be a once a year treat. We all deserve it!

  3 tablespoons unsalted butter
  2 large yellow onions, thinly sliced
  2 large red onions, thinly sliced
  4 medium-sized leeks, well rinsed, dried, and thinly sliced
  salt and fresh ground pepper to taste
  1½ cups grated Havarti
  2 packages (5 oz each) Boursin with herbs, crumbled
  1½ cups grated Gruyere
  ½ cup dry white wine

Preheat oven to 350°. Butter 8-cup baking dish with 1 tbsp. butter. Make a layer in baking dish, using a third each of the yellow onions, red onions, and leeks. Sprinkle the layer lightly with salt and pepper. Top with Havarti and make one more layer of onions, leeks, seasoning each with salt and pepper. Top this layer with Boursin. Layer remaining onions and leeks and top with Gruyere. Dot the top with remaining 2 tablespoons butter. Pour wine over all. Bake for 1 hour. Cover the top with aluminum foil if it gets too brown. Serve immediately.

Yeast Rolls
Josephine Vardeman

> 2 cups warm water
> 2 packages yeast (quick method)
> ¼ cup sugar
> 4 tablespoons oil
> 1 teaspoon salt
> 4 cups flour

Dissolve yeast, then add other ingredients. Add flour gradually until you have a thick dough. Pour out on floured bread surface and knead. Put dough in a large bowl in a warm place and let it double in size. Knead again. Make into rolls and let rise again. Grease pan and tops of rolls. Bake at 450° until tops are golden brown.

Acknowledgements

When I finally completed the manuscript for this book, I entered the editing and polishing stages. As I read and re-read passages I knew I had written, it was like another writer had entered my body and knew the password to my laptop. Over and over I remarked to myself "I can't believe I wrote this" or "Where on earth did that come from, Marilyn?"

It was only in reflection that I understood that the writer really was another person, a soul suffering from extreme grief. A woman in shock and trauma. A person so very sad.

As French-born novelist and short story writer, who gained international fame with her journals, Anais Nin, wrote, "We write to taste life twice, in the moment and in retrospection."

I continue to savor my extraordinary existence at The Orange Woods and am down-on-my-knees grateful for this beautiful chapter of my life.

This book could never have been written in another time of my life. It had to be completed while I was in the trenches. In that deep and sorrowful trench. Over the almost three years from start to finish a small battalion of people, some without ever realizing, helped create the magic of The Orange Woods and made my book possible. I am eternally grateful.

In random, adoring order . . .

David Miles, who shouldered far more than his share of our training sessions workload at The San Diego Museum of Art so I could do this side job. But more than that, David was the man in my life from the moment I lost Jack. Without his support, nodding head of approval, unparalleled intelligence and optimistic outlook, I would have crashed.

Deidre O'Flaherty, who walked the widow's walk ahead of me; Kathee Christensen and Margaret Priske, who walked along with me, and Mary Kay Boehm, behind me, who let me share my grief in example.

Renato Salazar, who enthusiastically created our Drawing Salon at the time when I needed that kind of intimacy most. I treasure collections of like-minded individuals and this became one of my most important throughout the time after losing my husband and is even more so today.

The docent community of The San Diego Museum of Art and especially Ruth Broudy. There is great solace in art and I found immeasurable comfort from my friends there who love art.

Judy Reeves, the shining star who led and inspired me from that first moment in her Personal Narrative writing class at UCSD.

My Read & Critique group, Rose Lochmann, Connie Henry, David Reed, Carrie Danielson, Janice Alper and Barbara Huntington, the endearing assemblage of writers who surrounded me through endless iterations which began with tears and continues today with love, laughter and friendship.

My beginning writing pals at Texas Tech University in Lubbock, Texas, Carolyn Jenkins Barta and Donna Christopher Ingham, who long ago beat me to the publishing gate.

Linda Olson, whose memoir, *Gone: A Memoir of Love, Body and Taking Back My Life,* will appear shortly after mine and whose story has inspired me in untold ways I never imagined.

Janice and Frank Finks, my forever Texas connection.

Alice and Steve Southerland, Faye Campbell, Sue Chadwick and Ralph Chadwick, Nancy Rick and Teri Raley, my Ventura circle of brothers and sisters. The move to The Orange Woods broke all our hearts, which only strengthened the forty-year bonds.

Darlene Shiley, who throughout her close friendship with Jack, made him laugh, especially over "Shiley Coffee," and continually bestowed her resources, especially at the end.

Sue Turnbull, Jan and Bruce Longenecker, Linda Pickering, Laura and Gerry Lewis, and Gary Graham, who shared The Orange Woods glory days with us and continue to make me laugh and feel safe.

Lynda McKinnon, who tenderly coaxed me back to the bridge table, my first step out of seclusion.

Jack's best band of brothers—Paul Menard (and Patti), Tim Curtin (and Lana), Gary Adcock, Denver McCune, Tom Anthony (and Jodi), Roy Anderson (and Dorothy), Jim Carroll, and Bob Bullock (and Suzy).

Laurie Kariya, my young farmer friend and Jack's devoted Twilight Golf partner, who introduced me to Dr. Dayna Arnstein. At my most anxiety-filled moment, the doc was there. My appointments with her over the first year of loss lowered my blood pressure and shepherded me back into life.

Jeanine (and Norm) Wallace, who first baked the Peanut Butter Fudge cake for us and has been my "city fox" friend for over forty years.

Brooke Warner and Krissa Lagos of She Writes Press and Jennifer Redmond, for their invaluable advice, editing and direction as I wrote.

Marni Freedman, who coaxed me on finding the "emotional center" in the very beginning.

Felicia Campbell—everybody needs a thirty-something social media whiz in their writing world. Felicia was mine and her patience and creativity introduced me to techie things I never knew existed.

MB Hanrahan, whose startling and spectacular art added beautiful spice to our lives in the country. Anne Mudge and Michael Stutz, whose artistic creations were my first companions in my new home in San Diego.

Larry McKenzie, the cowboy realtor whose dogged determination allowed me to find a new life in that city.

Gail and Marty Levin—Gail is my walking buddy who constantly provided insight and Kleenex as a surprising stand-in for my husband. She is my closest confidante. In my depths, she counseled,

"Please keep writing and please keep sharing. When I've gone through a crisis, I've likened my writing to 'cutting my arm and bleeding on the page'. But somehow I always felt a little stronger for it."

Karen Gowen, a strong and courageous woman who volunteered as managing editor for my book a year after losing her own husband. While I hope that sharing our grief helped her along the path to healing, I can only imagine the overwhelming sorrow she experienced as she read and re-read this book. For me, working hand in hand with Karen has given me a new and powerful friendship, the greatest gift.

Finally, I winced when I first read "The minute a writer is born, a family is ruined." I pray not one member of my family is harmed in any way by my writing. And I ask forgiveness for the ways my memories differ from theirs.

My family. My stepdaughter, Jackie, her daughter and husband, Shanna and Tim; Jack's sister Barbara and his nieces and nephews and their families, all in Indiana; my adopted son, Larry Z and his wife, Lynda, and most importantly, the real stars of this book and of my life, Jamie and Bud, Jennifer and Bo, Laurie and Brent, Maddie, Bayley, Sophie, Calvin, Carly, Chesapeake and Cash.

And lastly, to Jack, an extraordinary human being who taught me, loved me and inspired me. I am blessed.

Book Club Discussion Questions

For the person(s) who chose the book: why did you select it?

What are your thoughts on the cover? Do you think it represents the book well?

How do the opening and closing lines/paragraphs set (or don't) the mood for the book?

Which format did you read? Use (print, eBook, audio) How did that experience impact the story?

Several significant threads run through this memoir. What are they?

What were the major strengths and weaknesses of the book?

What emotional reactions did it promote (what mood does the author set)?

Is the author's background reflected in the book? How was her life affected by her husband's background?

How was the author's life changed by meeting and marrying Jack Woods?

Does the author change significantly? If so, what events trigger those changes?

Is this a love story? If so, other than the author and her husband, what is this a love story about?

How are the time and place in which the book was written reflected in the text?

Did the setting enhance or detract from the story?

What is the relationship between the past and present of the writer's life? Does the structure of the book depend on moving between her past and present?

What is the author's style? Does she present herself as a victim?

Does she approach her own story with a sense of irony, sympathy, distance, humor or something else altogether?

How much does she change over the course of the memoir?

What do you think happens after the book ends?

Are true-life stories potentially more powerful than fictional ones? Why or why not?

Was your life affected in any noticeable way by reading this book? How?

About the Author

Marilyn Woods is an artist, teacher, and educator. She holds degrees in journalism and psychology. Marilyn began her career as a broadcast journalist. After earning her BA in Journalism from Texas Technological University, she and her husband became pioneers in radio syndication, which led them to live in major cities around the country, including Los Angeles, New York, Washington, DC, and Dallas. Her life changed when the pair gave up big city life to purchase a small farm in Pauma Valley, California, population 989.

There, she and her husband planted a Provence lavender field, built a bocce ball court and a labyrinth of white stones, installed a vineyard, built a boutique winery, and learned to be vintners and farmers. At the same time, Marilyn also became a docent at The San Diego Museum of Art through their rigorous two-year training program. Her life changed again with the unforeseen loss of her husband, which prompted Marilyn to return to city life to live alone for the very first time. This led her to a new chapter in her life, in which she focuses on art and writing in her wise and street-smart, contemporary and emotional voice.

Her love of California, nature, family, art and a big black dog named Steamer populate her humorous, sometimes heart-wrenching, portraits of an extraordinary life.

CPSIA information can be obtained
at www.ICGtesting.com
Printed in the USA
LVHW032106120720
660468LV00002B/152